West Kennet Long Barrow

Landscape, Shamans
and the Cosmos

Peter Knight

Best wishes,
Peter K
Avebury
2012

Stone Seeker Publishing
Wiltshire UK
Honouring ancient wisdom and the Earth

Published Spring Equinox 2011
by Stone Seeker Publishing,
Wiltshire, England, UK
Website: www.stoneseeker.net
Email: stoneseeker@waitrose.com

ISBN: 978-0-9560342-1-2

Also by Peter Knight

Ancient Stones of Dorset - 1996
Sacred Dorset - On the Path of the Dragon - 1998
Dorset Pilgrimages - A Millennium Handbook (with Mike Power) - 2000
Earth Mysteries - An Illustrated Encyclopaedia of Britain - CD-ROM - 2004
Thirteen Moons – Conversations with the Goddess - 2007 (& 2010 ed.)
The Wessex Astrum – Sacred Geometry in a Mystical Landscape (with Toni
    Perrott) - 2008

Website: www.stoneseeker.net
Also on MySpace and FaceBook

Cover images:
Front cover – background: virtual impression of equinox sunrise; right centre: skull
from WKLB; centre left: shaped flint from WKLB; bottom left: megaliths in morning
sunshine; bottom right: Beaker pot B8 from WKLB.
Back cover – top left: equinox sunrise entering west chamber; top right: Gemini and
Orion alignment, looking west; bottom left: aerial shot of WKLB
(© English Heritage); bottom centre: artefacts found inside WKLB;
bottom right: antler found in NE chamber.

Cover design & other images © Peter Knight, except where stated.

Printed and bound by CPI Antony Rowe, Chippenham, Wiltshire on FSC paper.

MIX
Paper from
responsible sources
FSC® C013604

Dedication:

To my Ancestors and Mother Earth

Contents

Abbreviations

WKLB – West Kennet Long Barrow
ft – feet; m – metres; km – kilometres
hz – hertz; khz – kilohertz
BC – before the birth of Christ (i.e. prehistoric)
AD – the Christian/historical period
op. cit. – opus citatum (same as previous reference above)

Author's Note: Kennett or Kennet?

On most Ordnance Survey maps, as well as some local road signs, the spelling of *Kennett* is used, with two t's, whereas, in **all** the archaeological books and papers I have come across (plus most general books), it is spelt *Kennet*. I have adopted the latter here, in line with current convention.

Chapter 1.
Introduction

'In the Avebury area we have the perfect fusion of
landscape and monuments.'
(Paul Devereux, 2011)

This book is the result of a labour of love. Over many years, I have developed a love and respect for West Kennet Long Barrow, as well as a special 'connection'. I care for the monument on a weekly basis (by clearing 'ritual litter', and removing wax from stones), and I also scattered the ashes of my departed father at the site, which forged a deep emotional bond. I offer this book so others may find the wonders that have been revealed to me, and that this Neolithic shrine may receive the respect it deserves.

The long barrow is one of the most precious, magnificent and, nowadays, most frequented of Wiltshire's ancient monuments. Archaeologist Aubrey Burl described the site as, '… the finest megalithic tomb in England and Wales…' (Burl 2002, p. 21). Its modern excavator, Stuart Piggott, proclaimed the barrow as, '… one of the most famous megalithic tombs in the British Isles'.

Barrow comes from the Old English *beorg,* meaning *mound.* Kennet may have derived from *Cunetio*, whilst it is *Chenete* in the Domesday Book. By 1227, it had become *Kenate*, and *Westkenete* was recorded in 1288.

There are 180 megalithic chambered tombs listed in Southern England (Joussaume 1988, p. 59) and West Kennet Long Barrow (WKLB) is officially listed as Avebury 22, Ancient Monument no. 21708, and is included in the Avebury World Heritage Site. It is the best preserved of all long barrows, and almost the longest, comprising hundreds of tons of chalk and earth within a 100m long mound, plus a passage and five atmospheric chambers at the east end, which are guarded by large sarsen stones. The whole monument was designed to impress from the outside, and to transform once within.

WKLB is situated 16 miles north of Stonehenge, midst an ancient and sacred landscape just south of Avebury. The village that gives the barrow its name is to the NE of the monument, in the valley of the River Kennet, which flows between WKLB and Silbury Hill. Traffic thunders by on the busy A4, echoing the route taken by the Romans as they marched between London (Londinium) and Bath (Aqua Sulis). And yet, a 10-minute walk south from the road, up the ridge, transports us back 5,600 years to the Neolithic, the New Stone Age. Standing on the huge, elongated mound of the barrow, one can barely hear the traffic below; the silence is broken only by birdsong, the occasional tractor, and perhaps the voices of people milling around in the chambers below our feet. Our spirit is elevated by the views, which extend for miles in every direction. It is a landscape peppered with sacred sites, such as Silbury Hill, East Kennet long barrow, The Sanctuary, and the mounds on Overton Hill. To the south,

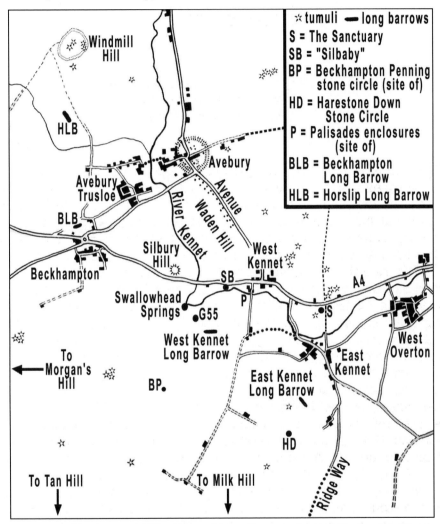

The sacred landscape of West Kennet Long Barrow, showing the key localities.
The area shown is about 4½ miles N-S, and 3½ miles E-W.

Milk Hill and Tan Hill, Wiltshire's two highest summits, raise the skyline; to the north the River Kennet snakes across the valley floor like a primordial serpent. One gets the feeling that everything is connected, that everything we see is in fact, 'not *on* the land, but held *within* it' (Knight 2007, p. 161), part of something far greater than the individual elements; there is a distinct sense of sacredness. It was the landscape, after all, that first gave Mankind the notion of 'sacred space'.

This spiritual view of the land is a concept held by aboriginal people today, and one of my aims is to present sound evidence that our Neolithic ancestors were closely connected to *their* landscape, in ways we are only now rediscovering through Paganism, Druidism, Native American spirituality, Taoism, and even by way of environmental and 'green' issues.

A subject that really interests me is *cognitive archaeology,* the study of what may have been going on within the minds of our ancestors; to this end, a new breed of archaeologists, armed with fresh ideas and new technologies, are re-appraising the archaeological record. I will be dipping into their work regarding WKLB, for it seems that archaeologists and 'earth mysteries' researchers draw ever closer to each other as they find themselves on common ground.

I will present evidence, based on the efforts of other authors, archaeologists and my own research, that the builders and users of West Kennet Long Barrow (WKLB) had a profound knowledge of astronomy, sacred geometry, earth energies, as well as acoustics and sacred sound. They had a shamanic-based cosmology, a belief system whereby the departed ancestors survived physical death, and could in fact be contacted. They were, '… human beings who were far more gifted and cultured than we have been led to believe' (J Foster Forbes, *The Unchronicled Past).*

I believe that WKLB was never just a place for the dead, and I will present evidence that the monument was **always** more than a tomb. It was multi-faceted and multi-functional, used on different occasions for a wide variety of ceremonies and rituals. These included burial, cremation, shamanic contact with the ancestors, deity veneration, astronomical observation, initiation, rites of passage, and perhaps more. To say WKLB was just a tomb is like saying a church was built purely for weddings! What about services, funerals, christenings, baptisms, Sunday school, and the other activities that are centred on a village church? Indeed a church, especially in days gone by, was the very hub of a village, a focus, a meeting place, a central component of a community. I would suggest that this is exactly what WKLB was to a group of Neolithic farmers over 5,000 years ago.

On a personal level, I first visited WKLB in 1991, when my spiritual path was in its genesis. I had been interested in archaeology since childhood, but I was now visiting ancient sites with 'new eyes', seeking to *experience* them, rather than just marvel at their construction. I now had questions; had sacred sites been ruined beyond any practical purpose, or could I still have profound experiences at such places today. I soon found that I could indeed *interact* with these places, as I learnt how to sense, feel, dowse, drum, chant, pray, meditate, dream, and much more.

This relationship with ancient sites has persisted, indeed developed, to this day, and has given me precious insights into how Neolithic people, thousands of years ago, related to their sacred places, their landscape, the heavens above them, and their ancestors. I was indeed shown how to, '… see in the dark the people who have gone and who left no word or sound behind them' (Burl 2002, p. 4).

Today WKLB inspires artists, musicians, singers, dowsers, and poets alike. Many are affected by the dark chambers, the connections it gives them with the past, and the sheer *power of place*, the feeling and knowing that we are privileged and blessed to spend time at a place that is truly sacred, in every sense of the word. Here, people have experiences they cannot understand, see lights and other phenomena they cannot explain, and feel an ethereal quality that may repeatedly draw them back. WKLB is still 'open for business', and we would do well to seek out the mysteries it holds, mysteries that can still be coaxed out of the darkness if the intentions of the seeker are honourable and pure. The barrow, in fact, '... reflects back the meaning and significance we are seeking from it' (Trubshaw 2005). I would add to this that our attitudes

Aerial view of West Kennet Long Barrow from the east. The huge megaliths can be seen at the east end, with the long, westward pointing mound behind. The barrow sits on a high ridge, in magnificent isolation, midst a sacred landscape.
(Image: English Heritage, used with permission.)

and beliefs also *determine our experiences*. I think this has always been the case at WKLB. Shamans and initiates thousands of years ago had a myriad of different experiences, depending on the mindset of the individual. Nothing has changed.

In this age of global warming, pollution, famine, natural disasters, and worldwide uncertainty, I believe the time is right to reconnect with the Earth in a spiritual way, as Mankind did thousands of years ago. This may help us relate to those cultures of long ago; for these were people **who only took what they needed,** and who may have much to teach us today: 'It is our cultural problem that we regard societies without writing as being primitive' (Wyatt 2010, p. 133). To look back in time may well help mankind survive the future. The time has surely come to look to places like WKLB, to gratefully accept what we are offered, on both a personal level, and for all Mankind.

Chapter 2.
Mounds of Mystery

'Folklore tales almost always contain some germ
of prehistoric fact, mixed with much accumulated imaginings.'
(Alfred Watkins, *The Old Straight Track*)

Prehistoric mounds have long captured our imagination. These mysterious masses of earth and stone have variously been the abode of fairies, goblins, dragons, giants, and all manner of Otherworldy creatures. Lights, sounds, spectral apparitions, crop formations, and UFO's have all been experienced in the vicinity of barrows, be they Neolithic, Bronze Age, Viking or Saxon. For example, the *Mabinogion,* the ancient Welsh sacred manuscript, habitually refers to burial mounds being the abode of spirits, fairies, and strange races.

A record of 1629 tells how Buckbarrow in Dorset was haunted by a goblin, whilst two barrows on Bottlebush Down were visited by a 'crowd of little people', seen by a Victorian curate (Knight 1998, p. 31). Buried Treasure and other magical objects are said to be concealed inside several barrows across the UK, and fairies have periodically been seen also, such as at the Carn Gluze barrow in Cornwall.

Old English chapbook showing fairies dancing next to a mound. Note the door in the mound, the green man in tree, and 'magic mushroom'.

Genesis 6:4 states, 'There were giants in the earth in those days'. Certainly many barrows bear the name *Giants Grave*, such as at Combe St Nicholas, Somerset, and Melcombe Bingham, Dorset (Knight 1998, p. 198). I have recently visited several Neolithic chambered sites in Sardinia, many of which bore the name *Giant's Tomb.* The sheer size of such mounds may have been the origin of such legends, or else that the entombed ancestors were 'giants of men'!

Barrows may also be associated with the Devil, such as the Devil's Den, near Avebury, the Devil's Armchair (Corscombe, Dorset), and the Hellstone, also in Dorset (Knight 1996, p. 17). Stone 98 at Avebury is known as the Devil's Chair. Many other sites were regarded as the Devil's handiwork, which resulted in their destruction, often encouraged by an intolerant Church.

Medieval tales of barrows being the resting place of either Gawain or King Arthur, or indeed dragons, may have ancient origins, remnants of prior ancestor worship and shamanic practices thousands of years ago. Folklore concerning heroes venturing down into the Underworld may owe much to the prehistoric use of barrows; initiations, rites of passage, meeting the ancestors, all echo classical heroic myths of journeying to meet the Gods. From his pioneering work on Irish Neolithic sites, Martin Brennan concluded that, '… It is clear that from the earliest mythology surrounding the mounds that they were never considered to be graves but, on the contrary, were regarded as abodes of living gods conceived and borne there' (Brennan 1994, p. 13).

Tales of the occupation of burial mounds by witches or 'hags' are widespread, as are stories of various female deities residing in hills and caves - the Underworld itself. The Grey Mare and Her Colts, a Dorset chambered long barrow, may have been named after the Goddess Epona/Rhiannon, who is associated with horses (Knight 1996, p. 18). These and similar tales may be memories of the perceived 'supernatural' powers of shaman women, the

17th Century drawing reflecting the belief that chambered barrows were built by an alliance of men and giants.

priestesses and magical practitioners of prehistory, who would venture into the dark voids of caves, temples and barrow chambers to contact the ancestors. Conversely, shamanic practices long ago may have birthed the archetypal concept that spirits and deities resided deep within the earth.

From the Viking *Beowulf* chronicles comes the verse: 'Draca sceal on hlaew, frod, fraetrum wlanc' *(The dragon shall be in the tumulus, old, rich in treasures)*. In previous publications, I have shown how barrows across the UK have dragon folklore. The beast is said to guard hidden treasure in a barrow called Wormelow Tump, in Herefordshire. On Exmoor, dragons lived in a group of Bronze Age tumuli at Challacombe. The long barrow at Walmsgate, Lincs, is reputed to contain the body of a dragon (Knight 1998, p. 195). La Hogue Bie, a Neolithic mound in Jersey, is said to be the grave of a dragon-slayer.

In Dorset I have listed several barrows associated with hidden treasure or golden objects, such as at Badbury Rings, Cowleaze, Bere Regis and Thickthorn. But what is 'treasure' really referring to? Is it in fact a memory of the sanctity of the place, or ancestral wisdom, or perhaps even of earth energies experienced long ago? (Knight 1998, p. 196-197).

Regarding WKLB, the mound is visited by a white spectral figure (some say a Druid or priest), at sunrise on mid-summer's Day, accompanied by a red-eared white hound. In *Ghosts of Dorset,* Robert Matthews tells us more: 'Tall and dressed in a white cloak, this old man stands to face the sunrise. At his side is a large, powerful dog with a white shaggy coat and reddish ears. Silently, this strange pair watch the Sun come up over the Marlborough Downs; then they turn and enter the tomb… this man and his dog must qualify as among the oldest ghosts in Britain'. Another version of this tale tells us that the dog is in fact black, although it remains a mid-summer apparition.

Tales of spectral white hounds with red ears are widespread. They may be distant memories of some ritual activity at the mound or even someone buried

A 'Witch's Mound' in Holland, in a 17th Century illustration by Johan Picardt.

within in ancient times. It invites comparison with myths concerning the Hounds of Annwn, who are red-eared, and the legends of the Beltaine Wild Hunt, tales of initiation and journeying to the Underworld. On some Romano-British artefacts, the Earth Goddess Epona is shown with dogs, and the God Nodens is sometimes depicted as a dog. In Greek mythology, a faithful dog, Sirius, often accompanied the giant Orion, who in some texts is the son of Mother Earth. In other myths, the star Sirius, also known as the Dog Star, is connected with underworld initiation. Interestingly, I have found some astronomical alignments between Sirius and WKLB, as we will see later.

In 1776, Colonel Drax spoke of local folklore concerning an underground tunnel linking Silbury Hill and WKLB. Other than referring to a physical tunnel, which seems unlikely, this may be a corrupted memory of Otherworldly realms under the earth, such as portals through which shamans ventured. Such tunnel tales could also be referring to the flow of underground earth energies, which are sometimes seen as 'serpent flows', linking these stories to snakes residing beneath the ground; to prehistoric people, the *surface* of the land was only one of a multitude of aspects of the Earth Goddess.

All these myths show the close association between people living on the illuminated surface of the land, and Underworld realms inhabited by strange beings and the ancestors. Michael Dames affirms that, 'West Kennet Long Barrow was not a dead end' (Dames 2010, p. 99). It was part of a never-ending discourse between the living and Otherworldly realms.

From what is known today of non-literate, aboriginal cultures, it may be safe to assume that Neolithic people had a rich and imaginative oral tradition. At the October 2010 'Stars and Stones Forum', near Bury St Edmunds, one of the speakers, Robin Herne, discussed the relationship between the local landscape and the people living there, and the importance of oral tradition, of story-telling, to pass down the myths of the land: 'Otherworldly beings are usually tied to a geographical place... If we know the stories of the place we live in, we have a link with that land, a bond... and we have an incentive to protect it'.

Thousands of years ago, the long mounds were already regarded as mysterious places, magical interfaces between the world of the living and other realms. And it was the shaman who bridged these worlds. Today, we may witness and experience things that spark our imagination, just as may have happened to others long ago, experiences that birthed many of our myths.

Chapter 3.
Neolithic People
and the Long Barrows

'Surely many noble bones and ashes have been
contented with such hilly tombs, which may, if
earthquakes spare them, out last all other monuments'.
(Sir Thomas Browne, 1658)

The story of West Kennet Long Barrow (WKLB) is the story of ordinary people, like you and me, who lived, ate, slept, played, farmed, hunted, birthed offspring, and eventually died here, over 5,000 years ago. They were people who had the same concerns as we do today, about their children, where the next meal was coming from, whether their unborn would be delivered safely, and how secure was their homestead. Yet the early Neolithic was a time when great changes were afoot. The very fabric of life was shifting, and with it people's spiritual beliefs, and how they related to their landscape. More than ever before, they forged new ties to a landscape they increasingly depended upon - farming had arrived.

Long before the time of long barrows, Palaeolithic hunters roamed the cold, often frozen Wiltshire Downs; just yards down the slope from WKLB a flint hand axe was found, which was tens of thousands of years older (Burl 2002, p. 84). In common with at least five other local Neolithic sites, WKLB yielded evidence of pre-barrow activity, either during the Mesolithic or the very early Neolithic; sherds of plain pottery were found in the old soil, buried beneath the construction of the long barrow (Piggott 1962). This implies that this particular locality probably had great spiritual significance long before any mound was constructed.

The Mesolithic Age was transitional, a time between the last Ice Age and the postglacial, between nomadic hunting/foraging and farming. And ritual was already present; remains such as antler headdresses suggest shamanism was being practiced, probably in the form of sympathetic magic to attract prey to the hunter. Local settlements dating to 8000 BC suggest that hunter-gatherers would inhabit particular localities when the seasons and foraging dictated.

Mesolithic remains at Cherhill, west of WKLB, show that groups temporarily stayed in one place, at a sort of 'base camp' for hunting sorties.

At around 8000-6500 BC, Britain was cut off from the European mainland, which brought about both genetic and spiritual implications. With the incoming of the Early Neolithic (4200-3000 BC), farming arrived in Southern England, bringing with it a widespread clearance of vast forests of oak and elm. The chalk downlands, with their light, mineral-rich soils, were easy to cultivate with simple tools, such as antlers, and also provided abundant flints for fashioning implements for hunting, agriculture, and the hearth. The change from hunter-gatherer to farmer was one of the most crucial transformations that Mankind has ever undertaken; it has altered, quite literally, the face of the planet.

It is not coincidence that this period marks the appearance of great megalithic circles, henges, and communal field monuments. New evidence suggests that the change from nomadic hunter-gatherer to farmer was not simply due to incoming waves of more aggressive monument builders, crossing over from the continent, bringing with them new technologies. The change was more gradual, yet no less successful: 'The hunter-gatherers dropped their spears and picked up ploughs. Unfortunately, we are still no closer to understanding why' (Russell 2002, p. 168). Perhaps we have been looking at monuments from the wrong angle. I suspect that chambered long barrows were not a side-effect of agriculture at all, but were a necessary element of a need to control and dictate the landscape: 'The monuments that define the Earliest Neolithic are clearly part of this desire to dominate and domesticate' (Russell 2002, p. 173). People were organising themselves, in what was a triumph of will power, to build monuments on a scale never seen before. 'A new sensory experience of place and landscape and new modes of dwelling led directly to new ways of thinking and new sets of cosmological ideas explaining the place of people in the world' (Tilley 2007, p. 330).

The clearance of woodland for agriculture and monument building is a primary feature of the Neolithic. But this change from a hunter-gatherer to a farming culture was not even rigid chronologically. There is evidence that some early Neolithic enclosures, like Windmill Hill, were only used seasonally. This implies, as I have said, that a percentage of the population were still semi-nomadic. It has been suggested that the hunter-gatherers were roaming the landscape in search of game and that the farmers were stationary. In fact, it was not hunter-gatherers who colonised new land in the Neolithic, for they would not venture beyond their regular hunting grounds for fear of starvation. It was in fact the farmers who were the colonialists, venturing into new areas out of necessity; they had herds to feed, and had larger families, whose offspring would ultimately need their own land.

Farming is all about accumulation, and is less dependant on the availability of wild herds and game. Perhaps once some clans adopted farming, neighbouring ones may have followed. Yet they did so not out of a desire to make life less difficult, for farming was hard: 'Hunters did not become farmers because it was an easier way of life; if that were the only motivation, then we would all still catch our breakfast in the woods' (Williams 2010, p. 89).

It has been argued that it was in fact **women** who brought about the Neolithic agricultural revolution, through their knowledge of edible, medicinal and psychoactive plants. It was a time, after all, when God was feminine!

In Southern England, nomadic hunting gave way to farming around 4400 BC or thereabouts (North 1996, p. 2). These early Neolithic farmers came, arguably, from Brittany and/or Ireland, and would have surely appreciated the abundance of large sarsen stones littering the landscape, similar to the granitic outcrops used in the megalithic sites from whence they had come. Ironically, these huge monuments have led to us to know more about their spiritual and funerary beliefs than their daily, more mundane, lives.

The climate was milder than now, bathed in the warmer post-glacial Atlantic Period. In Britain, there were deciduous trees growing as high as 750m (2400ft) in altitude, much higher than today. Regarding Britain, the period 7000-3700 BC has been called the 'Climate Optimum' by some climatologists. Around 3800 BC, for example, summers were 2-3°C warmer than present, whilst the winters were 2-4°C milder. During the later Neolithic, however, temperatures were to drop to just a degree or so higher than today.

As well as being a food source, wild creatures such as wolves, aurochs (wild oxen), boar, badgers, and vipers, held dangers for the clans. Amidst all these hazards, people constructed belief systems to help them get by, and to this end also sought magical assistance. A spiritual connection between themselves, the land, and the ancestors was a key element. To Neolithic people, '… there was no distinction between the natural and the supernatural world… the dead were not excluded from this vision of the world' (Burl 2002, p. 90). It was not a time when shamans simply visited some abstract 'race of the dead'; it was a time when the 'dead' wandered the earth.

By 3600 BC, most fertile stretches of local land had been cleared for farming, and there were Neolithic settlements at Windmill Hill, Waden Hill, Overton Hill, Cherhill, and Hemp Knoll (Beckhampton). This ushered in a sudden rise in the number of huge megalithic structures. Our ancient ancestors were able to move blocks of stone weighing many tons, and align monuments with incredible precision, often astronomically, and, as far as we can tell, without the use of either the wheel or slaves.

Not long after people occupied Windmill Hill, around 3700-3600 BC, they built the spectacular chambered tomb that is West Kennet Long Barrow, which was sited so as to be visible from where they lived and farmed. It has recently been convincingly argued that the siting of WKLB may have been influenced astronomically (Mann 2011), which we will look at in more detail later. The Mesolithic hunter-gatherers would have already been very familiar with, and knowledgeable of, the movements of the stars and it makes sense that they would have continued to follow stellar movements even after agriculture had arrived. However, their spiritual cosmology would have progressively evolved, because of major lifestyle changes brought about by the adoption of farming: '… their religion and symbolic repertoire adapted to suit the new means of making a living… the belief system was appropriately transformed' (Lewis-Williams & Pearce 2005, p. 20-21).

Marion Dowd has demonstrated that caves were not just used for shelter in the Neolithic, and that their primary role, as well as excarnation and inhumation, may have been remembrance of the dead: 'There was a strong symbolic or ritual sense shared in Neolithic Ireland between passage graves and those certain kinds of cave that they resembled' (Dowd 2008, p. 305). I believe we can also apply this to Southern England; in areas where chalk geology dictates there cannot be any natural caves, people were building chambered long barrows as substitutes.

British Neolithic long barrows were built between 4700 BC and 3000 BC, the vast majority between 3650-3000 BC. They are generally divided into two groups - earthen long barrows, and structures with megalithic chambers. Both types usually have ditches alongside, from which the mound material was quarried. Around 300 of the earthen variety are known in Scotland and England, many of which are still visible today as large rectangular banks, some over 100m in length; at 104m, East Kennet long barrow is the longest in the UK. Archaeologist Mile Russell has put on record that, 'The great majority of earth and timber long mounds across Southern Britain are curiously empty... ' (Russell 2002, p. 14). In other words, they were **not primarily tombs**. These monuments were used by the clans as, '... cult centres for the protection of the living' (Burl 2002, p. 104). We shall return to the issue of *non-funerary* activities later.

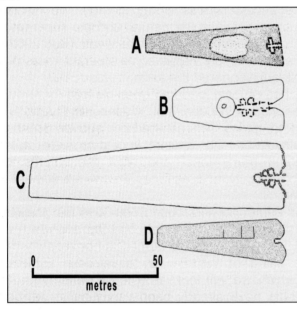

Comparisons of design and size of some Cotswold-Severn Group chambered long barrows. Note the great length of WKLB, and the relatively small percentage taken up by the chambers.

A – Wayland's Smithy.
B – Notgrove, Gloucs.
C – West Kennet.
D - Randwick, Gloucs.

Barrows are to the same scale, but not to the same orientation.

As already stated, there are 180 megalithic chambered mounds in the south of England. Stone chambers are usually accessed by passages, the majority having entrances opening towards sunrise. WKLB belongs to the Cotswold-Severn group, whose main features are trapezoidal stone cairns or earthen mounds. These mounds are often long and narrow, tapering at the opposite end from the chambers. Some of these were preceded by wooden structures, so-called 'houses of the dead'. The Cotswold-Severn group is mainly confined to the area between Bristol and Oxford, although some occur outside that immediate area. Good examples of the group are Wayland's Smithy, Belas Knap, Stoney Littleton, Notgrove, and WKLB itself. Chambers vary in size and orientation, and most seem to have contained human bones. Significantly, their design allowed *repeated access* from the outside after completion. Large stones often restrict entry today, suggesting that these were blocking stones, set up as they went out of use.

Although archaeologists now generally draw a clear distinction between the uses of earthen and chambered long barrows, there are nevertheless some associations between the two types; they can be of a similar age, they can also be close to each other geographically and, as I have recently found, there may exist sightlines and astronomical alignments between chambered and non-chambered mounds.

In the Avebury area there are about 30 known long barrow sites, of which 17 are thought to have been chambered; more may have been lost to agriculture and ignorance. These mounds occur in valley bottoms, hilltops, hill slopes, and even in woodland clearings, and all are built primarily of local sarsen stone. They are sometimes on sites used in earlier times, and it has been suggested that one of their functions was as territorial markers,

WKLB itself was built on grassland, from which woodland had probably already been cleared. It has been proposed that its builders may have sheltered at the G55 site, where a Neolithic refuge was found in 1964 (p. 39-41). These people kept sheep, pigs, cattle and goats, as well as domesticated dogs. They grew a form of wheat called emmer, as well as barley and cultivated flax, during summers that appear to have been drier than today. Child mortality was high, probably due to drinking faeces-polluted water and using inadequately cleaned and unglazed pottery, a problem rife for thousands of years to follow.

At this time, trade was already well established, bringing fine stone axes from the Lake District, Cornwall and North Wales, and shellfish from the shores of the Severn Estuary and the Bristol Channel. The people who brought them no doubt bartered with the locals of West Kennet. To facilitate these long-distance journeys, ridgeway trails were forged, many of which still survive today across the chalk downs of Southern England.

It has recently been argued by some that the introduction of farming was not necessarily a good thing for communities, or for Mankind as a whole. Lucy Wyatt incisively observes that, 'There is no smooth transition between hunter-gathering and farming... to become a farmer is to become something completely different... farming entirely alters one's relationship with the natural environment' (Wyatt 2010, p. 46). Furthermore, people may have previously led healthier lives: 'Hunter-gathering is in many respects a healthier lifestyle, and it was with the introduction of farming that we started to experience disease and tooth decay' (op. cit. p. 48).

Farming led to a change in Man's spiritual relationship with the land. Joshua Pollard and Andrew Reynolds nicely sum up concepts, quite alien to us today, of how Neolithic people regarded the landscape they inhabited: '... Drawing upon both archaeological evidence and ethnographic analogy, we can begin to create a picture of a landscape not only invested with myths, meanings and histories, but one perceived as a potent and animate realm inhabited by spirits and diverse non-human agents' (Pollard & Reynolds, 2002, p. 29). This is a praiseworthy admission by two forward-thinking archaeologists. To put it another way, Neolithic people inhabited a *living landscape*, with its constant cycles, a living book, so to speak, on which tribal myths were, '… captured by the very outlines of the landscape' (Lévy-Bruhl 1983). And for thousands of years this 'myth giver' has been epitomised and expressed the world over as the Earth Mother/Goddess.

So, in the early Neolithic, people began to erect massive stones and huge earthen mounds, structures that needed much manpower and considerable social co-operation and co-ordination. 'We are well aware that in order to shift

Huge sarsen stones still litter the landscape to the east of Avebury. Many display shapes that may have been seen as inhabitant spirits.
(Image: Sue Wallace.)

blocks of considerable weight, a large number of people had to be brought together, several villages teaming up, impelled by a single purpose, but for whom, or what?' (Joussaume 1988, p. 298). A good question.

The answer, I suspect, was the need to connect spiritually, not just physically, with the immediate land they occupied and farmed. They were also perhaps 'staking a claim' on their land, like early colonists and gold prospectors. It has indeed been argued by some archaeologists that the establishment of a formal burial site, such as WKLB, not only legitimised a family/clan's claim over an area of land, but also *its resources*. However, population density was still very low in the early Neolithic, easily able to support those living in the Avebury area. The main purpose for such monuments may well have been to give clans spiritual and emotional roots - a sense of place, a sense of belonging: 'The mounds may have represented a more intimate territory, that of home and a sense of eternal belonging' (Williams 2010, p. 109). It may be that several families banded together to help construct these sites, just as the Amish societies in America join forces to construct a new house or barn for one of the families of their community.

Archaeologist Francis Pryor makes the point about tombs being more than just places for the dead - they bonded people: '... tombs are to do with the dead and the afterlife - but they're also to do with the social bonds that hold extended families together. I find that funerals are almost the only occasions when I get to meet my more distant cousins. Such things, surely, would have been equally important to people in the Neolithic' (Pryor 2003).

Chambered mounds were not places of habitation, just as parishioners today do not live in their church, but rather nearby; the dead inhabited their own world. When a body loses its organs and fleshy parts, it also loses individual identity, proven by the fact that many bones in WKLB were moved around and mingled with others; many skulls and larger bones were removed altogether, confirmation, perhaps, that the people knew the ancestors had already moved on to another realm. Bones were being circulated around the local landscape, showing how the ancestors could **actively intervene** in the affairs of the living. Perhaps the observation of how plants die, yet are 'reborn' through their seeds, may have birthed the belief in an 'after life'; death was seen as a vital part of rebirth and life.

Analysis of human bones from West Kennet Long Barrow has shown a mixed plant/animal protein diet, with very little dietary variation between the skeletons of the different chambers: 'This would suggest that those interred belonged to a single family group' (Pollard & Reynolds 2002, p. 45). It is perhaps safe to visualise an extended clan, occupying the Kennet Valley and the land as far south as Milk Hill and Tan Hill. This comprised several farmsteads, who would periodically come together for burials, rites of passage, seasonal feasting, times when they would exchange news, barter goods, gossip, discuss farming techniques and, of course, orally retell their myths. Astro-archaeologist John North points out that, 'The intelligence and intensity of feeling that is evident from so many of their remains, together with what is known of other non-literate cultures, makes it virtually certain that they [Neolithic people] had a rich and imaginative oral tradition' (North 1996, p. 5).

And one of the places at which to hold all the above may have been WKLB. According to archaeologist Prof A Whittle, the monuments of the Avebury area are designed to encompass and celebrate, '... the mythic, ritual, or sacred dimensions of Neolithic life' (Whittle 1997, p. 151).

It would also appear that the very materials used in these impressive monuments, namely the sarsen stones, were a key element, and not just in terms of providing building material. Sarsens are a very hard sandstone, which litter fields locally, especially to the east of Avebury and WKLB. In the 17th Century, antiquarian John Aubrey romantically described the sarsen fields: 'One might fancy to have been the scene where giants fought with huge stones against the gods'. Sarsen stones have distinct surface features, and many may have developed identities, perhaps even bestowed with names, way back in the Neolithic, just as we have given names to stones since. Perhaps even when lying prone on the landscape, sarsens were imbued with spirit, and some may have been perceived as oracle stones; their later incorporation into megalithic sites may have been meaningful, beyond that of mere construction.

The stones themselves were *spiritual and mythic components of the landscape* and, as a consequence, of the chambered barrows into which they were subsequently incorporated, such as WKLB. 'The significance of sarsen may have accrued with time as stones became firmly embedded in stories and myths of the landscape' (Pollard & Reynolds 2002, p. 73). Many sarsens were to become moot stones, meeting places, or markers for travellers.

The sarsen chambers of WKLB are impressive and, '… more elaborate than those normally associated with Cotswold-Severn tombs' (Pollard & Reynolds 2002, p. 65). The Cotswold–Severn long barrows are characterised by a passage that was not closed off to the outside world, thus allowing periodic access, probably to commune with the ancestors. Aubrey Burl points out that in the rest of Wessex there were over 130 long barrows, of which only four had stone chambers, whereas in the Avebury/Marlborough Downs area nearly 60% were chambered (Burl 2002, p. 96).

There is also a noticeable split between long barrows east of Avebury and those west of it. To the east, most were merely earthen, whereas to the west the majority were chambered. This geographical division between megalithic and non-megalithic was not based on the local availability of sarsen stones either: 'Decisions of whether or not to build stone chambers need not have been geologically determined… but could well relate to the intended function of these barrows' (Pollard & Reynolds 2002, p. 63).

It's sheer size leaves little doubt that WKLB was designed to dominate its immediate landscape. In effect, the barrow was *a component of the landscape*. We will now look into this aspect further.

Chapter 4.
The Sacred Landscape
and Placement

'A legend is captured in the very outlines of the landscape…
living books in which the myths are inscribed.'
(Lucien Lévy-Bruhl, *Primitive Mythology*)

West Kennet Long Barrow (WKLB) stands as a dominant feature on a ridge south of Avebury. There is a marked intervisibility between the monument and several sites in the local landscape, and this may have been one of the aims of its builders. Going back 5,600 yrs, the monument would have stood out even more prominently than it does today, its mound of white chalk rubble reflecting the light of both the Sun and the Moon. With its massive size and length, combined with immense sarsen stones, this structure was designed to make an impression, to have an effect not only on participants within, but also on observers from a distance. Referring to the Avebury landscape and its monuments, Aaron Watson observed that, 'The visual appearance of this place is also of central importance, especially where architecture is set against the wider landscape in ways that cannot easily be understood when viewed in two dimensions' (Watson 2001, p. 302).

As I have stated before, I regard WKLB to be not **on** the landscape, but **held within it**. It may, therefore, have been part of the very fabric of the myths of the land; it was not just a receptacle for ancestral bones, but for ancestral memory too and, indeed, the memory of the Land. For although the monument marked a significant place on the landscape, the land in itself was mythologized; the monument had deeper meaning because the people regarded themselves as being **held within the land,** like WKLB.

The monument provided a central focus for a community that was scattered around in small farmsteads. It provided continuity and a tangible connection, the glue that held a clan together and connected it to the ancestors, the seasons, the stars, and the land itself. Over a long period of time this prominent landscape feature continued to declare a communities' right to the land, '… a sort of 'we were here first' sign' (Russell 2002, p. 63). John North reiterates this: '… for there is no more conspicuous object of inheritance in need of defence than land' (North 1996, p. 13). The Avebury area may not have been able to support more than a population of around 500, and any newcomers may have been met by people who were ready to defend what they saw as their 'clan-soil' (Burl 2002, p. 106).

The 18th Century drawings of William Stukeley show many of the Avebury monuments that were intervisible in his day. He left us the earliest views of WKLB set midst the greater landscape, and its relationship to other sites. Stukeley walked and observed the landscape - he connected with it. Paul Devereux went through a process of connecting in the 1980's, as he tried to unravel the meaning of the Avebury landscape: 'We have a Neolithic landscape preserved here - we must be able to read it' (Devereux 2010). Through a combination of brilliant observation and intuition, seeing the land with 'new eyes', he found some exquisite relationships between some of the sites (Devereux 1992, p. 137-150). He concluded that his experiences had taught him to, '… respect the subtlety of placement of the monuments with the natural topography… I came to understand that the monuments and their natural environment were indivisible: they were one… I was at last prepared *to be shown* whatever Silbury or the Avebury complex in general wanted to reveal. Zen in the art of archaeology' (Devereux 1992, p. 139).

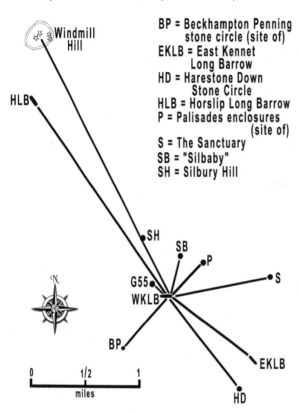

BP = Beckhampton Penning stone circle (site of)
EKLB = East Kennet Long Barrow
HD = Harestone Down Stone Circle
HLB = Horslip Long Barrow
P = Palisades enclosures (site of)
S = The Sanctuary
SB = "Silbaby"
SH = Silbury Hill

Map of the sightlines between WKLB and some of the other sites in the area.

Michael Dames sees an intricate physical and spiritual relationship between the monuments and landscape, as they follow the seasons of the turning year of the Goddess, who is personified and manifest in the very fabric of the land: 'The Avebury religion sprang from natural physical realities, and crystallized into architectural forms' (Dames 1977, p. 11).

My many visits to WKLB have confirmed to me that several Neolithic and Bronze Age sites are intervisible with the barrow, and have been so since they were built. In 2010, my partner Sue and I set about walking the landscape, in the footsteps of Stukeley and Devereux, to see from where WKLB was visible, and from where it was not, as well as to look outward over the landscape from the barrow. I was struck many times by the precise positioning of sacred sites, and how intervisibility and alignment was sometimes determined by a matter of metres; their builders saw the landscape not merely as a backdrop, but as an integral component. Aaron Watson concurs: 'Places can become especially potent if these ideas are reinforced by the natural form of the landscape' (Watson 2001, p. 304).

Placement of monuments was often determined, at least in part, by astronomical alignments. The Sun, Moon and the stars had been observed since much earlier times and key events, such as the solstices and lunar standstills, could now be permanently recorded through careful *positioning of monuments in relation to each other.* Clearly, the people saw themselves as much a part of the heavens as they did the land. I will cover this more fully later, such is the wealth of new astronomical discoveries.

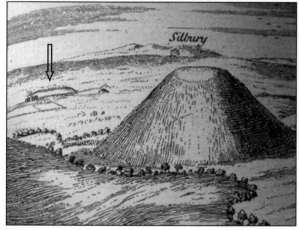

William Stukeley's 18th Century view of WKLB (arrowed) from the top of St James' Church, Avebury.

I frequently see people arrive at WKLB, stand high on the mound, and gaze at the beautiful landscape that unfolds before them. All visitors pick out Silbury Hill, which rises magnificently out of the valley to the north. Many see the barrows on Overton Hill, and perhaps even spot the site of The Sanctuary, next to the A4, especially if they have been there. My aim here is three-fold. Firstly, I want to give a guide of what to see from WKLB, to explain the landscape that these pilgrims are admiring. Secondly, I wish to show how WKLB appears from around the landscape. This could surprise many, who may not be aware of how intervisible it is from other sacred sites. Thirdly, I want people to walk the landscape again, not just to look at our images. This surely is the bottom line: to walk again in the footsteps of our ancestors, to connect once more with the landscape - my landscape, your landscape, the landscape of our ancestors.

West Kennet Long Barrow sits on the apex of a ridge at roughly the 175m (575ft) contour, and anyone who walks up there on a hot summer day will find that it can be quite a trek! But my visits soon showed that the ridge is in fact either at a similar height, or in some cases *lower*, than the surrounding hills. More to the point, it is lower than some other local sacred sites, from where one may be looking *down* to WKLB. The monument is in fact circled by an extended 'bowl' of natural topography, which is very subtle and easily missed. WKLB is the early monumental hub of a more extensive landscape, much the same way that Silbury Hill was in the later Neolithic (Devereux 1992, p. 145). It intrigued me that several Bronze Age sites are intervisible from WKLB, in directions that mark key astronomical alignments. This suggests intentionality,

25

demonstrating how, many centuries after the closure of the barrow, people still saw the monument as a key part of their ceremonial landscape. People had to have been standing at WKLB in the Bronze Age for the alignments to be realised. They knew that the ancestors interred inside were *their* ancestors too.

Looking to WKLB

Beckhampton Penning

The first site is the former locality of the Beckhampton Penning Stones (grid ref: 098671), SW of WKLB and about 1km (c.1100yds) south of Silbury Hill. The site formerly comprised of sarsens stones, all of which have now gone, which were variously regarded as either a stone circle or a barrow. In 1743, William Stukeley called it the *South Downs Barrow*, '… an oblong work, like a long barrow… but no tumulus'. In 1885, Alfred Charles Smith saw 22 sarsens, forming an oval 80x66m (c.88x77yds), with a N-S axis, and his plan is shown below. The site was marked *stone circle* on the 1919 OS map, and in 1957 Leslie Grinsell recorded stones lying in heaps, with just a few still in situ. Its total obliteration by farmers/landowners since that time is a sad testament to Man's ignorance, and the fact that such practices were still going on.

Michael Dames sees the former site as the 'navel' of a huge landscape Goddess figure involving many of the key sacred sites around Avebury, including WKLB (Dames 1996, p 190). He also perceives the plan of the site as having Goddess symbolism, in the form of a rectangle with an extended neck (headless), also seen on a sarsen at Stonehenge (Dames 1996, p 198).

The site features in an alignment cited by Paul Devereux and Ian Thomson; their 'SW9 – Silbury Hill Ley' goes from Marden Henge to Bincknoll Castle, via Silbury Hill, Avebury Henge, and the Beckhampton Penning stones (Devereux & Thomson 1979, p. 130-131). For more alignments see p. 171.

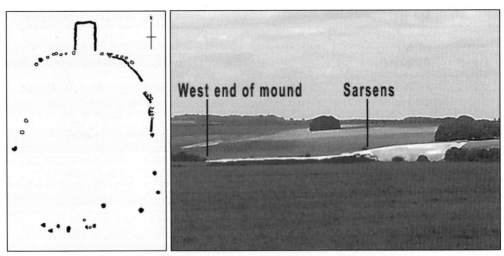

Left: A C Smith's 1885 plan of the Beckhampton Penning stones.
Right: View of WKLB from the site of Beckhampton Penning, looking NE.

Viewed from here, the whole length of WKLB is visible, but only just! The base of the mound aligns perfectly with the brow of the hill on which we stand, in an apparently intentional placement. In the image above, the mound shows up well in front of a white field beyond. Regardless of whether the lost stones were part of a Neolithic long barrow, a Bronze Age tumulus, or a stone circle, this site was chosen with great consideration in relationship to WKLB.

There is also a lunar standstill alignment between the two sites (p. 195).

Horslip Long Barrow

Moving around the outer sites clockwise (see map above), the next locality is Horslip Long Barrow, situated almost due south of Windmill Hill (at grid ref: 086705). In 1743, William Stukeley described a mound that was, '... of large bulk, length and height'. Alas, no more. This Neolithic monument is now almost completely ploughed out, although excavations in 1959 yielded a site 50m (164ft) long, dating from 4,000-3000 BC. In common with some other local earthen barrows, no burials were found, but it did have ditches along each side, like WKLB. Lines of pits at the site may have been viewing positions for an early mortuary house.

Horslip long barrow pointed towards WKLB, the axis of the mound aligned to an azimuth of 135°. John North found alignments at Horslip with the stars Deneb (in Cygnus), Betelgeuse (in Orion), and possibly the rising of Sirius, the

View of WKLB from the site of Horslip Long Barrow (zoom lens view), showing the incredible alignment of the slope of Silbury Hill with the megaliths of WKLB, which just 'touch' it.

brightest star in the sky (North 1996, p. 68-71). I have also found alignments with these stars at WKLB, as will be shown later.

According to Michael Dames, the barrow site is situated at the 'hip' point of his composite landscape Goddess (Dames 1977, p. 190 & 193).

Standing on what is left of the mound, one looks south to a landscape dominated by Silbury Hill. And first glance one might enquire, 'Where is WKLB?' But it is there, immersed in the landscape. If one looks immediately to the right of Silbury Hill, about a quarter of the way up from the base, the mound can be seen snaking left-right, the true extent of its 100m length being well appreciated from here (image above).

The placement is even more exquisite than might first be appreciated. If you trace the barrow to its eastern extremity (you may need binoculars to fully appreciate this) you will see that the megaliths at WKLB appear to just 'touch' or 'kiss' the western slope of Silbury Hill - a truly amazing sightline over two miles in length.

Paul Devereux was the first to appreciate this during his 'connecting' with the landscape: 'It seems as if the builders of the great mound respected the Horslip-West Kennet sightline with some precision… It is difficult to believe that the builders of Silbury were not deliberately responsible for this precision' (Devereux 1992, p. 149-150). In my opinion, Paul, never a truer word has been spoken.

Windmill Hill

The next site on our clockwise circumnavigation of the landscape of WKLB is Windmill Hill (grid ref. 086714). At nearly three miles long, this is the longest sightline dealt with here.

Windmill Hill was an early Neolithic causewayed enclosure, an occupational and ritual site that was first used sometime before 3700 BC. The site covers 21 acres and is 366m (1200ft) in diameter; excavations revealed large amounts of ritual deposits, such as human and animal bones, antlers, over 20,000 sherds of pottery, chalk phalli, spheres and figurines.

Disarticulated human bones, mainly long bones and skulls, were found here that might have been brought from WKLB, where these bones are under-represented (Pollard & Reynolds 2002, p. 53).

This large gathering place was multi-faceted, and was much more than a defensive earthwork or trading post. It hosted major seasonal feasts and ceremonies, involving hundreds of people. Several Bronze Age tumuli jut out of the hill today, a token of the importance of the site thousands of years ago, and proof that its use spanned a long period of time.

Michael Dames also places Windmill Hill on the 'hip' point of his proposed landscape 'Composite Goddess' (Dames 1977, p. 190).

A seven-mile long alignment has been advocated, which commences at Windmill Hill, before going on through one edge of Avebury henge. After this, it passes through other sacred sites, the line eventually terminating at Martinsell Hill Camp (Devereux & Thomson 1979, p. 134).

Our visit to Windmill Hill was not disappointing. Approaching the hill along quiet lanes and paths felt like a pilgrimage, that we really were approaching a major sacred place. At the top, the landscape opened up to us as we sat on one of the round barrows. And there, to the south, was Silbury Hill again, rising magnificently, with the prominent ledge on the east side, just below the summit. Incredibly, from the top of Windmill Hill, the western end of the mound of WKLB aligns with this ledge! Paul Devereux commented on some archaeologist's suspicions that the mound of WKLB may have been extended at a later date to ensure it touched the slopes of Silbury when viewed from Windmill Hill. Conversely, Windmill Hill aligns with the top ledge of Silbury

View of WKLB and Silbury Hill from Windmill Hill. Note how the barrow aligns with the top ledge of Silbury (arrows). The mound may have been extended to reach the slopes of the Silbury, as seen from Windmill Hill. (Zoom camera view.)

when viewed only from the western end of WKLB: 'The viewing location was a specified spot in the ceremonial landscape... It was not a map line - it was a *sight* line' (Devereux 1992, p. 141).

What amazing design and engineering skills must have been involved in the late-Neolithic to construct a huge mound like Silbury Hill that it was so intricately aligned with Horslip, WKLB, and Windmill Hill, all of which were already several centuries old.

Silbury Hill

So we come to Silbury Hill itself. This truly is one of the wonders of prehistory, the tallest mound ever constructed in Neolithic Europe. It was built in three stages between 2900 BC and 2350 BC (Pollard 2002), eventually comprising 350,000 cubic metres (12.5 million cubic ft), a feat that may have taken 3 million man-hours to complete. It is Britain's pyramid, rising to 40m (130ft) above the valley floor, erected of chalk, flint, and earth, built with a stepped profile. Some signs of these steps can be seen today, the top ledge being particularly obvious, especially on the east side; it has been suggested that this was deliberately left exposed (Devereux 1992, p. 129). Originally the whole structure would have been pure white, glistening in the landscape, reflecting the light of both the sun and the moon. My virtual reconstruction of what this may have looked like is shown on p. 58.

Europe's highest prehistoric mound was constructed, however, on one of the lowest points in the Avebury landscape. It was not like some Pharaoh's ego monument, on a hilltop or prominent plateau. I feel it was built with great humility, care being taken that the artificial hill should not rise above those that were natural; the symbolic Goddess should not rise above her actual body.

Michael Dames has placed great importance in Silbury Hill, as symbolic of the gigantic pregnant Goddess; this is sacred imagery on a monumental scale. Silbury contains no tombs, passages, or burials – the full belly of Mother Earth rises from the valley floor. It is the, 'Axis Mundi, the World Axis... Silbury can be seen as a 'centre of the world' image... a place where all essential modes of being and all imagined realities intersect and come together' (Dames 2010, p. 46-47). Dames' three books on Silbury are classic reads and are highly recommended (Dames 1976, 1996 and 2010).

Much later, the Romans built a large settlement around Silbury Hill, implying that it had spiritual significance in their day; a platform of Roman age was dug into the lower slopes of the hill. John North (1996) and Nicholas Mann (2011) have discovered astronomical alignments that involve Silbury Hill, and I have recently found others, which we will look at later.

Silbury Hill also stands on the Ana Line of the Wessex Astrum landscape hexagram, which we shall look at in more detail later (image p. 174).

It has recently been demonstrated how, at certain times of the year, the setting Sun appears to 'roll down' the slopes of Silbury, when viewed from or near the site of the Palisades Enclosures; the angle of the Sun's motion mirrors the slope (Marshall, Currie and Glastonbury 2010, p. 291-305). Marina Graham has produced a beautiful photographic sequence of the event (see her pages on www.youtube.com).

Silbury Hill from the air, taken during a flight I took over the Avebury landscape.

Silbury proudly stands at the hub of the ceremonial landscape, as if holding court over the surrounding sacred sites. A fence now discourages the public climbing Silbury Hill, depriving people of the fine 360° views from the summit. From the top is a much better and closer look of WKLB than the previous sites described thus far. The details of individual megaliths can be made out, as well

View of WKLB from the summit of Silbury Hill, half a mile to the north. Individual megaliths can be made out at the east end of the dark, elongated mound. Note how the ridge on which it stands slopes eastwards.

as people standing and sitting on the mound, giving a sense of scale of just how large the structure is (image above). Observe too, how WKLB slopes gently to the east (left) as it follows the gradient of the ridge; the chambered end is not on the summit. The view also shows something I have mentioned before; namely that WKLB, despite being on a ridge, is *lower* than the hills that surround it. It is in a shallow bowl – held within the body of the Goddess.

'Silbaby'/ Waden Mound

The next site is a more controversial one. This is a mound-like structure hidden in a copse between Silbury Hill and West Kennet village (at grid ref. 107683). In some of his 18th Century drawings, antiquarian William Stukeley illustrated a barrow-like structure being dissected by the 'Roman road', now the A4, east of Silbury Hill. This could be the 'Weeden Hill' mentioned and drawn by Stukeley, and the 'Great Bank' shown on other old maps.

This feature has been termed 'Silbaby', as it has the appearance of a smaller version of its famous neighbour, from which it is visible. The southern slopes of the feature show up well on Google Earth.

The elevation at the top, where the road cuts through, is around the 156m (511ft) contour, below which its slopes fall steeply onto the flood plain of the River Kennet, where Waden Spring rises from its base. It looks to me as if the southern end of Waden Hill may have been purposefully sloped back and the

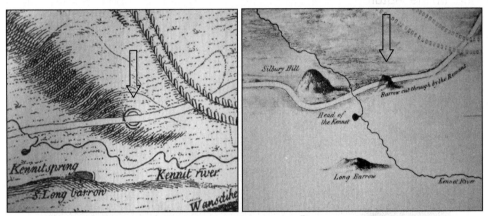

Left: The 'barrow' shown on Williiam Stukeley's 18th Century drawing. 'Silbaby' arrowed. Right: 19th Century map showing 'Silbaby' as a hill with steep slopes.

top levelled off, as if to give the appearance of an artificial mound when viewed from the Kennet valley. At the very least, people may have taken advantage of a chance topographical oddity in the landscape. Its slopes can be seen from the track up to West Kennet barrow or from the path heading east towards the village of East Kennet.

Pete Glastonbury rediscovered the mound in 2004 and has recently brought it to the attention of archaeologists. The site is next to the Palisades Enclosures (see below), a major Neolithic centre, and it is a mystery why archaeologists

'Silbaby' or Waden Mound, from the south. The slopes mirror those of Silbury Hill, nearby. Waden Spring rises at its base.

32

had ignored this prominent landscape feature for so long. Glastonbury and Marshall recently surveyed the site and found it to be elliptical, slightly elongated east-west, and that the top is 11m (36ft) above the valley floor (Marshall, Currie & Glastonbury 2010, p. 291-302). A core was bored into the mound in the autumn and more results are to follow, whilst Archaeologists have now acknowledged the site as *Waden Mound*. It may yet prove to be a prehistoric feature, although it has also been suggested that it may be a midden associated with the Roman settlement nearby.

From the summit of 'Silbaby', WKLB straddles the skyline.

Our site visit to the top of 'Silbaby' in the summer of 2010 found a flat level area, which was unfortunately overgrown with a forest of tall and very antisocial nettles and brambles! But for large trees, Silbury Hill would have been visible. From the top, WKLB is prominent on the skyline, and this is one of only a handful of sacred sites where the barrow has the sky, rather than the land, as a backdrop. The top of 'Silbaby' is only about 20m (65ft) below that of WKLB, so the mound of the latter can be seen almost down to ground level.

Goddess symbolism in a flint nodule, found by Sue Wallace at Waden Spring. Height = 15cm (6 ins.).

Our site visit also revealed two megaliths in the undergrowth on the southern slopes, both near the waters of Waden Spring. A wintertime visit may well reveal more. WKLB is visible from Waden Spring, although only the upper parts of the mound are seen, as we are now down in the valley of the River Kennet. Glastonbury found a votive axe in the pool to the east of the mound in the spring of 2005. On our site visit Sue Wallace picked up a lump of flint from the dried out riverbed that

33

resembles a plump Goddess, complete with a face (image above). Many such finds have been uncovered in the vicinity of sacred sites. Even the land gives us her image, and as such she sits on our mantelpiece – a gift from the Earth Goddess.

West Kennet Palisades
The next location is close-by, and is the site of the West Kennet Palisades Enclosures, an important late Neolithic ceremonial monument (grid ref: 108683 – although the site covers several acres). The site was first recognised in aerial photographs in the 1950's and was excavated between 1987-92 by Alasdair Whittle (Whittle 1997). Huge timber circles had been erected, and carbon dating yielded dates between 2500 – 2000 BC, very late in the period of major monument building in the Avebury area. Freestanding, unshaped trunks

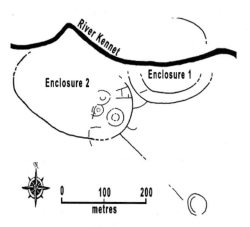

Plan of the late Neolithic Palisade Enclosures at West Kennet. (After Whittle, 1997.)

of oak, which may have totalled 40,000m in length (Pollard & Reynolds 2002, p. 114) marked out two large enclosures, a huge undertaking, as well as smaller outlying timber buildings. The site is notable because the River Kennet flows right through it, which I suspect was intentional for both symbolic and practical purposes. It has been suggested by archaeologist Parker-Pearson that wooden monuments represent the living world (for trees are alive, as are

WKLB on the skyline as seen from the site of the Palisades Enclosures. The mound seems to rise and fall out of the wheat fields like a dragon or serpent.

rivers) and that we are not dealing with ancestors, which are represented by megalithic sites. This may be an over simplification, but the Palisades certainly saw scenes of great feasting, as large amounts of waste and discarded bone and antler testify. The River Kennet seems to have been an integral part of the site: Michael Dames argues that the enclosures, '… were *intended* to embrace and incorporate the holy stream in the narrow part of the valley… the river appears to complement the enclosures' (Dames 1996, p. 220). He also sees the intervisibility of the Palisades with WKLB, Silbury Hill, and the Sanctuary as further evidence of *'The Avebury Cycle'*, through which people honoured and played out the turning cycles of the year, linking monuments, agriculture, and the ancestors.

From the Palisades site, next to the River Kennet, the mound of WKLB rises out of the skyline like a dragon or serpent, periodically bobbing up out of the wheat fields. We shall return to this view later; but then we shall be seeing it during the Neolithic night.

Just east of the enclosures site, a 2m (6½ft) long sarsen stone lies next to the path to East Kennet village (at grid ref: 112082). We cannot be sure if the stone was left here during transportation (to WKLB?), or was a standing stone in its own right, but from it the long barrow is visible on the skyline.

The Sanctuary

The next site intervisible from WKLB is The Sanctuary. This is situated on the southern spur of Overton Hill, next to the busy A4 (grid ref: 118679). A lay-by and gate enables easy access, as the rumble of the traffic and the stunning views vie for our attention. Stukeley drew stones here in the 18th Century, not long before they were destroyed. Archaeologists found the holes of six concentric circles of stones and wooden posts, indicated today by ugly concrete markers. Wooden buildings were erected around 3000 BC, followed

Looking west from The Sanctuary, as seen by William Stukeley on July 8th 1723. WKLB is arrowed.

later by a stone circle of 42 megaliths, 42m (138ft) in diameter. The site marks the termination of the West Kennet Avenue, which goes from here into the mighty henge; winding its way, serpent-like, across the landscape, it guided travellers into Avebury. The Sanctuary may have indeed been, '... a reception centre for Avebury pilgrims' (Mann 2011).

Dowsers have found that the Michael energy current of the famous St Michael Line flows up the stone avenue into The Sanctuary, where it crosses the Mary current (Miller & Broadhurst 1989). Interestingly, William Stukeley saw the site as the head of a huge landscape snake, and was very angry at its destruction. With views of WKLB, Windmill Hill, East Kennet long barrow, G55 and Silbury

WKLB from The Sanctuary, just after sunrise at the September Equinox, 2010. The individual stones can be made out, and note how foreshortened the mound appears. (Zoom view.)

Hill, this site was of profound importance in the later-Neolithic: 'Despite the present appearance, the significance of the site should not be understated...' (Pollard & Reynolds 2002, p. 106). The Sanctuary had many functions, it appears, but one may have been concerning the dead. It was, '... ideally situated as a central ossuary... around 2900 BC the dead may have been brought [to The Sanctuary] to be attended by a medicine man or witch-doctor' (Burl 2002, p. 141-2), i.e. a Neolithic shaman. Burl also comments on a summer solstice sunset alignment at the site.

Paul Devereux showed that when Silbury Hill is viewed from The Sanctuary, the distant skyline touches it between the summit and the top ledge (Devereux 1992, p. 142 & 145), a phenomenon that also occurs when Silbury is viewed from WKLB.

The best time to see WKLB from The Sanctuary is in the morning, when the Sun illuminates the blocking stones face-on, and our image above was captured at the 2010 autumn equinox sunrise. The individual stones are clearly defined, and note how foreshortened the mound appears from here, due to the fact that the axis of WKLB aligns approximately towards The Sanctuary. We shall return to the site later, detailing astronomical alignments with WKLB.

East Kennet Long Barrow

This massive long barrow (grid ref: 116668) is the next site from which to view WKLB. It is a mighty 4.2m (14ft) high, and at 104m (c.345ft) it is the longest barrow in Britain. Standing on private land, it is now covered by large trees, which make it a prominent feature in the landscape: 'East Kennet planted with trees bristles like a defensive porcupine against the horizon' (Burl 2002, p. 98). Incredibly, it has never been excavated, but I suspect it may be chambered, like WKLB, as stones can be seen jutting out of the mound.

Michael Dames places the long barrow on the 'thigh' of his landscape Goddess figure (Dames 1997, p. 190). He remarks that the axis of the mound itself is, '… aligned with the thigh'. Dames perceives the alignments of long barrows as contributing to the manifestation of the overall Goddess image. He also notes that East Kennet long barrow and WKLB are involved in a solstice alignment, something I have confirmed visually with spectacular results, and will detail later when we look at astronomy.

WKLB and Silbury Hill as seen from East Kennet Long Barrow. Note how the top of Silbury Hill coincides with the skyline. (See also image p. 188.)

From East Kennet long barrow we look, just under a mile distant, slightly *down* upon WKLB, as we have done before. It straddles the ridge of which it dominates, and the individual megaliths can be discerned. To the right rises Silbury Hill, the top of which intricately aligns with the distant skyline (see Devereux 1992, p. 142). We will return to East Kennet long barrow later, for Sue and I were to witness the midsummer sunset from here.

Please note that the barrow is accessed via private land and permission should be sought from the owners at 'Fox Twitchen', Church Lane, East Kennet.

Harestone Down Stones

The stone site on Harestone Down is our next port of call on our circumnavigation of the WKLB landscape. Harestone Circle and Cove (grid ref: 113664) was discovered by Terence Meaden in 1996 (Meaden 1999, p. 109-112), when he noted that he could find no earlier descriptions of this site. The stones lie scattered on a ridge, to the SW of East Kennet long barrow. Meaden identified a cove, which included a 10-ton megalith with two other attendant stones, which he thought to be aligned to the midwinter sunset, which is unusual for the Avebury area.

Around 25m (c.80ft) to the NE of the cove are the remains of a 10m (33ft) diameter circle, with four outer stones surrounding a pyramidal central one. A little to the SW of the stone circle is a megalith with a deep vertical groove: 'If this is Neolithic symbolic imagery, then a megalith sacred to the local Earth Goddess may have been indented' (Meaden 1999, p. 113).

The view to WKLB from the Harestone site is one of the most spectacular we witnessed on our treks around the landscape (image next page). The façade and chambers of WKLB exactly align with the axis of Silbury Hill, only when

Two stones of the Harestone megalithic site, Harestone Down. The deep groove on the left stone may have been intended as Goddess symbolism.

seen from this site. The alignment is exquisite and must surely have been intentional. The sight is awe inspiring, as we appreciate how the three sites, separated by several centuries, line up beautifully. We are close enough to see the individual stones of WKLB, dominated by the blocking stone (45), and the full extent of the 100m-long mound can be appreciated. Also note how the top of stone 45 coincides with the line of the ridge.

Note that these stones are on private land (please seek permission from the owners at 'Fox Twitchen', Church Lane, East Kennet). The stones can be accessed via a gate from a nearby public footpath. The stones are best seen when vegetation is low during the winter.

The chambers and façade of WKLB align with the axis of Silbury Hill, when viewed from the Harestone circle, seen here in late afternoon sunshine, June 2010. (Zoom view.)

Site G55

A lesser known sacred site is that of G55. It is 300m WNW of WKLB (grid ref: 102679), a little further along the same chalk ridge as the barrow, at an altitude of 179m (560ft). Aerial photos alerted archaeologists that something of interest

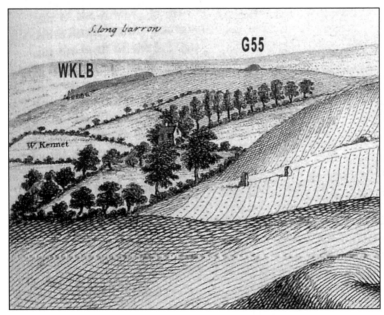

WKLB and G55, as seen by William Stukeley from barrows on Overton Hill. (Graphics inserted by the author.)

was at the spot, as well as two drawings by William Stukeley in his *Abury* (1743), in which he showed a quite impressive round barrow to the west of WKLB (see image above). Today, a barely discernable dip in the ground is all that remains of the site, which was excavated in October 1964 by the late Isobel Smith (1911-2005). Smith published the main work of Keiller's excavations of Avebury, and also excavated the Beckhampton long barrow, and one of the digs at Windmill Hill. Her excavations of G55 revealed Bronze Age pits, and three cremations dated this phase as just after 1500 BC, with a succession of Peterborough, Grooved Ware and Beaker pots. But beneath lay a surprise. Smith found a Neolithic settlement site, with the remains of domestic refuge spread over a 100x40m (109x45yds) area. Over 600 sherds of pottery were found plus over 1000 flint implements. One large pit had a cattle skull set upright next to a deer antler. Arrowheads, a horn pendant, and a small cup were also unearthed.

The site was first utilized around 4000 BC and was in use for several centuries thereafter. Isobel Smith concluded that the site may have been frequented for, '…perhaps 1000 years, and the earliest activity could have been related to the construction of the long barrow' (Smith 1965, p. 25-30). It has been suggested that Bronze Age people were drawn back to the previous Neolithic site because of its history as an ancestral place. Its close proximity to WKLB was not co-incidence, I suggest, and was part of, '… a way of life which included respect for ancestral monuments such as West Kennet Long Barrow' (Case 1995, p. 15).

Michael Dames argues that G55, '… functioned as a pre-Avebury henge for the May festival' (Dames 1996, p. 199). The site is midway between WKLB and Swallowhead Spring, both of which were entrances to the Underworld.

WKLB as seen from G55, a Neolithic and Bronze Age site nearby, which may have been occupied by the builders of the barrow. The tallest stone of WKLB can be seen to the left, with East Kennet long barrow in the background, behind the mound's tail.

At G55, we are only a few hundred metres from WKLB, and the mound stretches out before us, undulating on the apex of the ridge (image above). The top third of stone 45, the 'blocking stone', is all that can be seen of the megaliths when the grass is long, as on our visit. I find it inconceivable that people using G55 would not have held WKLB with great reverence, due to its close proximity and its dominant appearance.

WKLB as seen from tumuli on Overton Hill. These round barrows mark
solstice astronomical alignments with WKLB (see image p. 190).

Other Views of the Barrow

WKLB is visible from the prominent group of tree-covered barrows on Overton Hill (grid ref: 115686), NNW of The Sanctuary (image above). We shall see later how these mounds play a vital role in the astronomy of WKLB. From here, the midwinter solstice sunset occurs over WKLB (image p. 190).

From the south, WKLB is visible from the northern slopes of Milk Hill and Tan Hill, although it is diminutive in the landscape as we are viewing it from over two miles distant. It is *symbolically* present however, nestling in the hinterland between these two hills and Silbury Hill. Open fires at night, and rising smoke from daytime fires, would have been visible over such distances, as feasts and ceremonies were played out at the barrow.

At one time, fires and torches at WKLB would have been seen *directly* from the summit of Morgan's Hill, and vica versa, before the intrusion of plantations in recent times. Now we can just make out the top of the beeches and the two masts (image p. 56). Intervisibility could have been a determining factor, I suspect, in at least partly influencing the orientation of the axis of WKLB; astronomical observation also came into play, as we will see later.

Clearly, WKLB was at the spiritual and ancestral heart of a dramatic, sacred landscape. Julian Cope incisively comments on this: 'Kennet was a planned ceremonial landscape… it was conceived as the sacred omphalos or Navel of the Neolithic world, with all the attendant weight of responsibility which that role implies' (Cope 1998, p. 30).

River valleys, hill ridges and hog-backed hills led our distant ancestors into this exceptional landscape, people who later developed the ridgeway tracks that brought in further settlers, pilgrims, and traders. And West Kennet Long Barrow stood at the heart of it. To many Neolithic people who saw it up on the ridge, it must have seemed that it had always been present there, just as their ancestors had always been present, and, more to the point, always would be; WKLB and the ancestors *were the landscape.* As one archaeologist perfectly expressed it: 'The landscape simultaneously passes on and encodes information about the ancestral past' (Tilley 1994, p. 40).

Chapter 5.
The Long Barrow Today –
A Guided Tour

'West Kennet Long Barrow was certainly no mere grave –
it was a used ritual centre.'
(Paul Devereux.)

Now I would like to take you on a tour around West Kennet Long Barrow, as you will encounter it today, to help you familiarise the monument. Hopefully this will be an aid to your visits, and later your understanding of the work of previous researchers, and my own findings.

WKLB is best approached on foot, by walking to it across the landscape, to see it appear and disappear as one advances toward it. Most people, however, park up at one of two lay-bys on the busy A4, of which the eastern one is signposted. One can look south from here and see WKLB riding the skyline, like a sleeping dragon or serpent. The tallest of the megaliths can be seen at

megaliths   tip of mound

WKLB on the skyline, as seen from the lay-by on the A4, to the north.

the extreme left. Note also how the west end of the mound, although much lower than the east end, continues to be visible due to the fact that it sits higher up the ridge.

Passing through the gate to a path, one soon leaves behind the invasive noise of the traffic. On the left is encountered a small tree with a hole right through the base, which my 5-yr old daughter Leela thought to be a fairy door. By the

As one approaches WKLB up the path, the full extent of the 100m long mound gradually becomes visible. (Photo: Diane Gall, with permission.)

time the small bridge over the River Kennet is reached, WKLB is lost from view, although this is a good place to look back to Silbury Hill. The field between the bridge and the hill was the scene of excavations in 2010, when a large Roman settlement was confirmed.

Through another gate and passing the cloutie offering oak, we then turn right to ascend the hill up a wide and much-frequented path. WKLB is still out of sight, and remains so until one is almost at the top, at which point it surfaces like some antediluvian creature. As one approaches, more and more of the barrow

The megaliths at the east end of WKLB at sunrise on the equinox. Stone 1 is on the left, whilst stone 45 is the tallest, on the right. Behind these is the entrance.

extends westwards, until the full extent of the 100m mound, aligned approximately east-west, becomes visible. The sight is impressive, as it was meant to be: 'The barrows were shrines and temples whose sacred nature is confirmed by the great length of the mound, far longer than the restricted space of the burials, demonstrating how essential appearance was to the builders' (Burl 2002, p. 100). WKLB was designed to make an impression!

The Exterior

As one approaches the western end, the dimensions of the sarsen megaliths become apparent, particularly the centre 'blocking stone', stone 45 (see plan below). The total length of this 30-50 ton stone was measured over 3.5m (12ft) during excavations, and even today over 3.3m (11ft) rises out of its newly acquired bed of concrete. A deep crevice in the centre is thought by Terence Meaden to be symbolic of the vulva of the Goddess (see p. 131-2). I suspect that other shapes and simulacra in the stones may also have been critical factors in their selection. A façade of smaller stones extends either side of it, approximately N-S, and the entrance lintel can be seen behind. In between some of the megaliths can be seen runs of smaller stones, which people often think were brought in as part of the restorations. But they are original, brought from many miles to the west, a peculiarity we shall return to.

In the next chapter we shall look out across the landscape from WKLB, but for the time being we shall go around to the other side of stone 45, and stand behind it in the forecourt. The remains of a crescental design can be made out, defined by stones 3, 5, 6, 37 and 38. Standing in front of the entrance, we are flanked by stones 44 and 46, rising vertically and butting up against stone 45. It was previously thought that these two stones were put up as the monument was closed down, but some now disagree, astro-archaeologist John North and myself included. I believe the stones are a key element of several astronomical alignments, as we shall see in Chapter 15; they help restrict and define the light of the Sun, Moon, and bright stars coming into the passage and the inner chambers.

Looking into the dark interior of WKLB from the entrance. Venturing into the darkness is one of the shamanic elements of the site, and always has been - one enters the womb of the Earth Mother.

Into the Womb

The entrance lintel is at present 1.8m (6ft) above ground level, and beyond it are the passage and the dark recesses of the internal chambers. On a bright summer day it may not seem that daunting, as additional light now enters the interior through very intrusive and ill-conceived skylights. On a dark overcast day, at dusk, or during the night, the view changes, as one gazes into an inky blackness. This point of entry is liminal, as we pass from the light into the dark, from the known into the unknown, from sunlight and warmth into the cooler, often-damp inner sanctum. This is part of the WKLB experience – a step into the unknown, into the realms of the dark

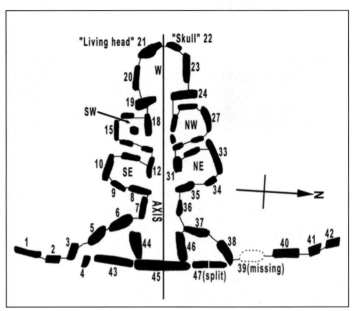

Plan of WKLB, with numbering of the standing stones by Stuart Piggott during the 1955-6 excavations. The axis and direction of north are from John North (1996). The 'Living Head' and 'Skull' are based on the work of Terence Meaden.

and the mysterious. We enter the womb of the Earth Mother, in the footsteps of our ancestors. The shamanic aspects of WKLB are dealt with later, as they are key to understanding the monument and how it was used, and how we can interact with it today.

Before us a passage, 7m (23 ft) long, beckons us into the gloom. The only original capstone of the passage that remains in situ is between stones 19 and 24, which we will see later is above an acoustic hot spot! This stone is 2.4m (8ft) above the floor and, '...we can assume the passage roofing was at approximately the same level' (Piggott 1962, p. 16).

Stone 17, now lying in the SW chamber.

Venturing into this central passage, we immediately encounter the SE and NE chambers either side, and one can walk into these with little effort. Large upright sarsens define the chambers, with gaps filled by small tiles of Jurassic limestone. The capstones of these chambers are very rough and pitted, which I suspect has to do with the acoustics. Both of these ante-rooms contained human skeletons and ritual deposits. The SE chamber is penetrated by the rays of the summer solstice sunrise (see p. 186-8). The capstone of this chamber was found lying on the mound to the south, and was returned to approximately its original position by Piggott in 1955-6. The NE chamber has a corbelled roof, which is topped by a massive sarsen, still in situ, 2.3m (7ft 6ins) above the floor. This chamber is open to the Imbolc sunrise.

Moving further down the passage we find two more side rooms, the NW and SW chambers, both of which also held burials. The SW chamber, on the left, is the smallest and lowest, and most people have to stoop to access it. The capstone is in situ but is hidden from above by the modern turf. The chamber is 1.5mx1.8m (5ftx6ft) and the ceiling is 1.7m (5ft 9ins) above the floor. On the ground sits stone 17, which at one time stood between stones 13 and 18.

Left: The west chamber, the largest in WKLB.
Above: The infilling between the sarsens by small slabs of oolite and Forest Marble, brought from several miles to the west.

Today, people often sit on it for meditation. On the passage side of stone 18 is a long, smooth area, where Neolithic people sharpened their flints.

To the right, access to the NW chamber is hampered by a stone around which one has to skirt, but beyond it one can stand up, as in the SE and NE chambers. The NW chamber capstone is in situ, supported by corbels 1.8m (6ft) above the floor.

At the end of the passage is the west chamber, the largest and highest, which is illuminated by a skylight installed by Piggott and his team in 1956; in ancient times, this would have been a dark place. It is 2.4mx2.7m (8ftx9ft) in size and is polygonal, with one surviving original capstone at west end, 2.4m (8ft) above the ground. This chamber was excavated by Thurnam in 1859, when he unearthed the remains of five adults and a child, as well as ritual objects. It seems to be that the largest chamber contained the least number of burials, suggesting that this chamber, more than the others, was not so much for the dead as it was for the living. Profound symbolism is also present here, with a profiled 'Living Head' on the left, and a 'Skull Stone' profile on the iron-rich stone to the right. The acoustics of this chamber can be striking. When we bring groups here on the full Moon, the weird acoustic properties, and the powerful energies, can be readily felt.

Originally, the whole of the roof of the west chamber was corbelled, somewhat like an igloo, creating a bell-shaped chamber. Despite the concrete and skylight, some corbelling does survive in situ. My guess is that this design could have been to accentuate the effect of being inside a womb, as well as to facilitate both the acoustical properties and the earth energies, which we shall look at in more detail later.

Inside WKLB, certain stones appear to possess facial features, which is probably not coincidental. Dark eyes return our gaze; phalluses rise from the ground, and weird figures dance in the flashlight. And one sometimes gets the feeling that someone is watching us.

The Penetrating Light

Despite the restricting 'blocking stone', it is amazing how we can see shafts of light coming in from the outside world, and even view segments of the landscape. For instance, sitting against stone 21 in the west chamber, we can still see a bit of open sky, and so too from stone 22. From the NW chamber, a chink of light and a small section of skyline can also be seen. Try it! These are at the heart of some amazing sightlines (see Chapter 15).

Sitting against the back wall of the west chamber, looking out to the blocking stone, gives us little clue as to the spectacles once witnessed from here, prior to its erection. Light from both the Sun and Moon around the equinox, and on certain other dates, would have enveloped the observers' senses. WKLB has always been about the *interaction,*

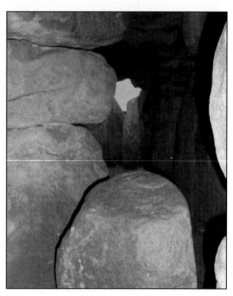

View from the NW chamber, showing how daylight and the skyline can be seen, despite being so far into the monument.

with the ancestors, the Moon, the Sun, the stars and, ultimately, with ourselves and our own inner nature; personal demons are purged, followed by a 'rebirthing' out from the womb.

So as we make our exit, we may have that feeling of renewal, of a new start, perhaps having received a 'healing' of some kind. We are soon back out in the light, perhaps a little relieved following our ordeal, but knowing that we are privileged to have been inside such a hallowed place.

The Mound

One of the qualities that make WKLB stand out from other long barrows is the enormity of the mound. As I showed earlier, its length is exceptional at 100m (c.330ft), only slightly bettered by its neighbour East Kennet Long Barrow

(104m/345ft - the longest in Britain); its height of 3m (10ft) is also not far behind the 4.2m (14ft) of East Kennet. Estimates for the length of the WKLB mound have varied by up to several metres, such are the problems evident in measuring a structure which has a very undulating surface (due to later damage by farmers and other pillagers) and a west end that tapers out. John North gives 'around 100m', and I think we shall go with that! The mound tapers

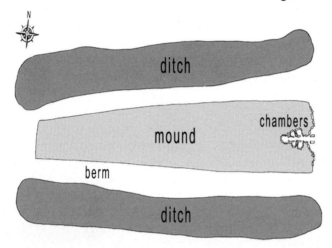

Plan of WKLB, showing the megaliths before the blocking stones were added. The small size of chambers in relation to the mound length is striking.

to the west, but its height drops little due to a rise in the ridge. The mound seems to have been extended from a more humble beginning, which Paul Devereux suggests was to create the visual sightline between WKLB, Silbury Hill, and Windmill Hill (image p. 29). The mound's axis points to Morgan's Hill, mostly obscured now by intervening trees (see image p. 56). I feel this alignment was intentional and important.

The mound was created from chalk rubble and earth quarried from two ditches, which run parallel to the mound. These were up to 3.6m (12 ft) deep and 6m (20ft) wide at the top (Piggott 1962). The ditches have become filled with sediment, but their positions are often betrayed by darker soil and an increase in vegetation. The extent of these ditches seems to vary with every plan, and

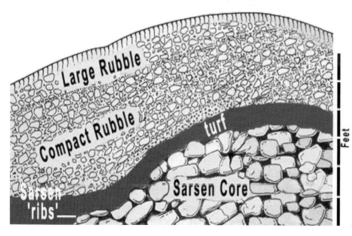

Cross section through WKLB, near the eastern end, showing the sarsen 'spines', the core of sarsen rubble, and layering above. (Redrawn after Piggott.)

even a magnetometer survey in 2001 did little to clarify matters. The aerial photo (p. 51) shows dark strips either side of the mound, marking the two ditches. A flattish berm, or low platform, 6m (20ft) wide, once separated the ditches from the mound, but nowadays this mainly survives on the south side. This feature has been little commented on in the past, but may have been a gathering platform, used for astronomical purposes.

The chambers only occupy around 8% of the total length, but the remainder of the mound does contain stones. Piggott found a spine of sarsens going down the entire length, shown above. Dowsers have suggested that this conducts earth energies along the mound into the chambers. The mound may also have been surrounded at some stage by a halo of small sarsen stones, peristaliths,

Southern profile of WKLB, seen at the west end looking east along the mound. The berm shows up best on this side. The ditch is now mostly filled.

mound

berm

ditch

although this is by no means certain. Two small sarsens laying at the base of the mound today may well be from modern field clearance.

Perhaps the size of the mound was linked to the belief that the souls of the ancestors resided within. 'The long mound as 'house tomb' would have expressed all the social, economic, religious and political interrelationships of a particular community' (Russell 2002, p. 63).

One thing is for sure; the mound was once pure white, which must have been an incredible sight, reflecting both sunlight and moonbeams. Visionary artist Monica Sjoo has commented on this: 'The outside of this elongated mound was originally covered in white chalk so that it gleamed in the moonlight… West Kennet's elongated entrance recreates a vaginal birth channel and its interior womb chambers lie beyond, within the darkness'. The stark contrast between the white exterior and the darkness of the interior may have been part of the visual power and experience of WKLB.

John North records the mound as being aligned to azimuths 267° (west) and 87° (east), just off due east-west. North proves that this was not bad planning, but of vital relevance to the astronomical alignments of WKLB (see Chapter 15). He also comments on the ditches, which he sees as possible stellar observation points in themselves (North 1996, p. 79).

Our quick look at what WKLB looks like today will be augmented later with deeper insights into the excavations, symbolism, astronomy and earth energies of the site, all elements of which help make the monument what it is. WKLB can be experienced on many levels, and I would suggest that this was the case back in the Neolithic.

Time now to stand on top of the mound and look out across a magical and timeless landscape, and unravel the views that delight our eyes.

Close-up aerial image, showing the megaliths, mound and two darker strips that betray the positions of the flanking ditches.
(Image: English Heritage, used with permission.)

Chapter 6.
A 'Womb' With A View

'...monuments were placed such that many
barrow sites were clearly visible from them...'
(Woodward 1996).

So far we have looked towards WKLB from the surrounding landscape, and we have taken our initial venture inside the 'womb tomb' as it is today. I would now like to acquaint you with the views looking across the landscape *from* the monument. People often come up to WKLB and may indeed identify Silbury Hill, and perhaps the round barrows hidden in trees on Overton Hill; but what else? Let us now locate the sacred sites and some other features that are discernible from WKLB.

The View North
Standing on top of WKLB we have a glorious view to the north, with sweeping views from the Beckhampton area right around to Waden Hill. In the valley

The view north from the east end of the mound at WKLB. Compare the
appearance of Silbury Hill with that on p. 58.

52

below snakes the River Kennet, with the A4 beyond. There can be little doubt that it is Silbury Hill that dominates this view, rising like the hump of a whale that is surfacing from the depths of the ocean.

Paul Devereux noted how WKLB aligned with both Horslip Long Barrow and Windmill Hill, and how the top ledge of Silbury aligns with the skyline from here (Devereux 1992). From Waden Hill have come some scatters of early Neolithic flints and Terence Meaden found small sarsens resembling heads, showing signs that they had been worked (Meaden 1999, p. 132). Waden may be from an Old English derivation *weoh-dun,* meaning 'holy place' or 'shrine' (Pollard & Reynolds 2002, p. 232). The name may also come from Woden or Odin, and therefore named by the Saxons. Julian Cope speculates that, prior to being a 'male' hill, it would have been regarded as feminine, and that the long, rounded ridge could even have inspired the design of long barrows (Cope 1998, p. 30). Waden Hill is also involved in a Beltaine and Lughnasad 'double sunrise' phenomena as seen from SIlbury Hill (Devereux 1992, p. 148).

The View North-east

Moving around eastwards, we see the southern end of Waden Hill, as the gentle slopes of 'Silbaby', where it meets the flood plain of the Kennet. Just to the east, is the site of the Palisades Enclosures, where huge wooden posts were erected in the Neolithic. The skyline coincides with the ancient N-S Ridgeway track, from which WKLB can be seen at several points. On Overton Hill, clumps of beeches indicate important Bronze Age round barrows, some of which mark solar and lunar events as seen from WKLB. This suggests that either Neolithic sites may have preceded these, as has been found elsewhere locally (e.g. G55), or else WKLB was being used for astronomical observations after the closure of its chambers. We shall later deal with our observations of the Sun rising out of these barrows at the summer solstice.

View to the NE from WKLB. The positions of the present major lunar standstill and the summer solstice sunrise are shown (compare with image on p.187).

53

The View East

Scanning around to the east we are greeted with a ridge that is quite close to us, Overton Hill. The site of The Sanctuary can be located where the traffic of the busy A4 disappears over the crest of the hill. The tower of West Overton church is seen just to the right, but East Kennet church and the village are obscured by trees.

At the equinoxes, the Sun rises above the left barn down in the valley in the foreground. We were fortunate enough to observe this event in 2010 (see images p. 184-5).

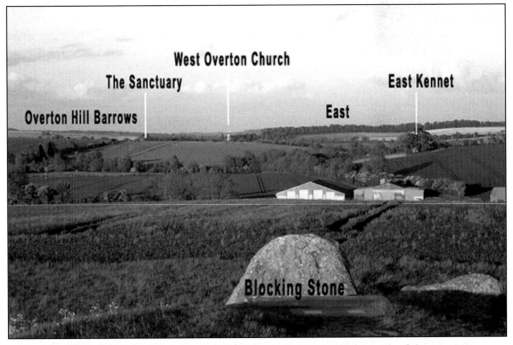

The view east from WKLB. The axis of the monument is just north of due east.
(See equinox sunrise images on p. 184-5).

The View South-east

Moving further around the landscape, we now look to the SE, where the eye is drawn to the large clump of trees just below the skyline. This is East Kennet long barrow, and the angle of the trees reflects the orientation of the mound. Seen from WKLB, this long barrow is aligned with some key astronomical events, such as the winter solstice sunrise and some Neolithic stellar phenomena (see Chapter 15).

To the right of the barrow are some open fields, and then some small, isolated groups of trees, before a slight rise is discernable; this modest hill is Harestone Down, the site of the stone circle and cove described earlier. To the right, denser woodland can be made out on the skyline, which crown the higher rises of Thorn Hill and Furze Hill.

Panoramic view to the south-east, showing the trees on East Kennet long barrow and the rise of Harestone Down, on which megaliths stand.

The View South

The views south from WKLB are some of the most beautiful and spectacular in the whole of Wiltshire. We can look across two miles of open meadows and fields, which gently undulate as the chalk creates a geographical wonder. The two highest hills in the county reveal themselves on the skyline; Milk Hill on the left (294m), and Tan Hill to the right, with its double summits (294m and 274m).

All Cannings Down and Allington Down are remarkably unspoilt, and reward the rambler with isolated walks, disturbed only by the activities of the farmer, herds of deer and circling buzzards. Ancient enclosures, long barrows, tumuli, and Iron Age dykes show this to have been a special area way back in prehistoric times.

Tree-covered East Kennet long barrow (arrowed), framed by stones 44 and 45.

The view south to Milk Hill and Tan Hill, Wiltshire's highest summits. The scenery here is both expansive and peaceful, and several ancient monuments are dotted around the landscape.

Milk Hill and Tan Hill will come into play later, when I will reveal how they mark the rising and setting of certain prominent stars during the Neolithic, some of which are no longer visible from this latitude.

The View West

Looking westwards from WKLB there are more points of interest. At around 247-249° is Beckhampton Plantation, visible as a prominent tree line. This is the site of a former long barrow, and is of interest in the fact that at around Samhain (end of October - early November) the Sun sets into the trees, suggesting an alignment between WKLB and the barrow.

Next, I found that the axis of the mound aligns with Morgan's Hill, where ancient tracks, a Roman road, and Wansdyke all converge. Earthworks and tumuli surround this holy hill, which rises to a lofty 260m (853ft). It is capped by the well-known beech clump, and two infamous masts.

Left: The present view of Morgan's Hill from WKLB, largely obscured by a plantation.
Right: Unobstructed virtual view, with its twinned-summit profile.

From WKLB today, an intervening plantation conceals all but a few of the beeches and the top half of the masts; but long ago things were different, when more of the hill was visible by looking along the mound of WKLB. More than this, we see twinned summits; similar ones can be seen from other sacred sites, where they are symbolic of the breasts of the Earth Mother, such as the Paps of Anu (Knight 1998, p. 185), the Grey Mare and Her Colts (Knight 1996, p. 33) and Mount Psiloritis, on Crete. Another local example has recently been described; when viewed from the east, Adam's Grave and Mill Barrow look like breasts, complete with 'nipples' (Wakefield 1999, p. 10).

During the Neolithic, the Sun set into the Morgan Hill summits around mid-October and in early April. This is just *prior* to Samhain in autumn, and not long *after* the spring equinox. In 2010 we observed the Sun setting into Morgan's Hill from WKLB on October 4. I now suspect, however, that the key alignments here are in fact *stellar*, as we shall see later.

Something similar to the original, unimpeded, view can be seen if one walks away from WKLB west along the ridge, and slightly down the north slope. After about 150m the twin summits of Morgan's Hill become visible – without the intervening trees. The view isn't as good as it would have been from WKLB, due to the slight intervention of a ridge, but it's not bad.

The View North-west

Looking NW now, we see tree clumps on top of Cherhill Hill protruding over a nearer 262m (860ft) hill (with its intriguingly named *Witch Plantation*). The phallus that is the Lansdowne Monument stands erect on the hill, confirming a sightline that is over 3 miles in length. In the Neolithic, this would have marked sunsets in early May, which later became Beltaine.

Finally, we come almost full circle, as we gaze at a large assemblage of trees rising out of a dip in the landscape around Beckhampton. We will return to this later, to show how we observed the Sun at summer solstice setting into this area.

The author sitting on WKLB, connecting with a landscape to which he had just returned his father's ashes.

Our 360° panoramic tour brings us back to Silbury Hill, rising magnificently to the north. My impression of how it may have originally appeared is shown below, a pure white pyramid rising out of the valley.

I hope what has gone before will encourage you to visit WKLB for some of the astronomical events. But, more than this, I urge you to go there on each and every occasion possible, in all weathers, under the light of the Sun and Moon, on balmy sunny days and on cold winter ones too. For the landscape, like the weather, never sleeps, and neither does WKLB; to simply sit on top of the ancient mound, gazing silently out over the ancient, ever-changing landscape, can be a meditation unto itself.

The pure white structure of Silbury Hill, as it may have
appeared from the east end of WKLB in the late Neolithic.

Chapter 7.
Early Research – The Antiquarians

'On the brow of the hill, south from West Kynnet, is this monument,
but without any name.'
(John Aubrey, 17th Century.)

People have long held a fascination for West Kennet Long Barrow, including the Romans, who may have left votive offerings at the monument. John Aubrey seems to have been the first to record WKLB in the 1660's, his alleged drawing being the very first. Doubt has been cast on whether this was in fact a different barrow, due to the numerous stones he drew around the mound. There is the possibility, of course, that these were removed prior to William Stukeley's visits of 1723 and 1724, as he shows no stones at all surrounding WKLB. Aubrey describes the barrow in his *Monumenta Britannica* (1663-71): 'On the brow on the hill, south of West Kynnet, is the monument, but without any name… at the end rude grey-wether stones tumbled together… and a circular trench'.

John Aubrey, the first to describe WKLB in the 17th Century.

In 1776, Colonel Drax spoke of local folklore telling of an underground tunnel said to link Silbury Hill and WKLB. We shall return to this later, and try to ascertain what this may have really been referring to.

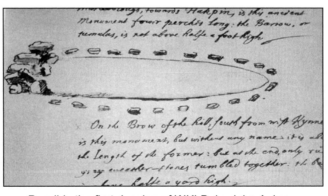

Possibly the first drawing of WKLB, by John Aubrey.
Note the stones around the mound.

William Stukeley

The author holding a rare copy of Stukeley's 1743 volume *Abury,* in Devizes Museum.

An antiquarian by the name of William Stukeley (1687-1765) now enters centre stage. He was the son of a Lincolnshire lawyer and after taking his MB degree at Cambridge, studied medicine at St Thomas' Hospital, London. In 1710, he started a practice in Lincolnshire, before returning to London in 1717, where he became a Fellow of the Royal Society. In 1718 he joined the Society of Antiquaries, where he was secretary for nine years. Stukeley was one of the first learned gentlemen to be attracted to freemasonry (he was a personal friend of Isaac Newton), and in 1721 became a Freemason himself. His papers are among the earliest sources on the new Grand Lodge. Stukeley's principal labours were his elaborate and profusely illustrated works on Avebury and Stonehenge, which appeared in 1740 and 1743, the first of a multi-volume historical series. He visited Avebury for the first time in 1719, which initiated years of field trips to sites in the area, including WKLB.

Stukeley proposed that there had been an ancient patriarchal belief system that was the, '... original religion of all mankind', and he believed that the Druids and the early Christians were the descendants of this religion. He wrote copiously on other supposed Druidic sites, becoming known as 'The Arch-Druid'. In 1729, he took holy orders, and went on to be a rector in Lincolnshire and London. (See also Mortimer 2003 and Piggott 1985.)

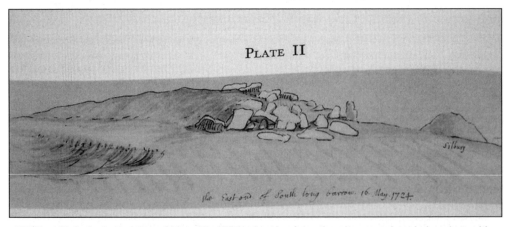

William Stukeley's drawing of May 16, 1724, showing how the site was already in ruins, with collapsed megaliths. Silbury is to the right. Note the flat berm, or platform, towards the left.

Stukeley's hand-drawn sketches and descriptions of the Avebury area have yielded invaluable information to researchers for decades. Archaeologist Stuart Piggott regarded Stukeley's records as, '... of considerable value'. His sketches frequently show barrows and stones that have now vanished, so in this respect are important elements of the archaeological record. I recently had the pleasure and privilege of holding and examining his 1743 volume on Avebury at Devizes Museum. What a pleasure! I was able to see for myself, and photograph, the famous images I had seen reproduced in so many books, plus examine others I had not been aware of.

A feature of Stukeley's drawings is that he often showed himself in the foreground, often doing the sketch! He also had a tendency to exaggerate the size of stones (perhaps it's a man thing!). Stukeley visited the barrow in 1723 and 1724, and saw it as the grand tomb of, '... an Arch-Druid', and gave it the name South Long Barrow, on account of it being south of Avebury and Silbury Hill. He states, 'It stands east and west, pointing to the dragon's head on Overton-hill [The Sanctuary]. A very operose congeries of huge stones upon the east end, and upon part of its

Detail of William Stukeley's view of WKLB from the south. I wonder which figure is Stukeley.

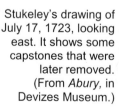

Stukeley's drawing of July 17, 1723, looking east. It shows some capstones that were later removed. (From *Abury,* in Devizes Museum.)

61

back or ridge, piled one upon another… doubtless in order to form a sufficient chamber for the remains of the person there buried – not easily to be disturbed. The whole tumulus is an excessively large mound of earth, 180 cubits [i.e. 344 feet] ridged up like a house'. Stukeley then goes on to surmise about the reincarnation beliefs of the people, which reflected his own Masonic view of the cosmos: 'People who made these mausolea had a very strong hope of resurrection of their bodies, as well as their souls, who thus provided against their being disturbed'.

Stukeley's close up views do not show any stones skirting the mound, as Aubrey observed, but in two of his more distant views some stones are shown. It is not clear if Stukeley meant these to be diagrammatic, or if he actually saw stones, but did not describe them. It could be that these 'lost' stones were

WKLB from the south, by William Stukeley. The size of the stones and the mound have been exaggerated, a characteristic piece of 'artistic license' used by Stukeley.

taken away by a certain 'Farmer Green', whom Stukeley tells us also removed stones from a neighbouring barrow around 1710. In his notes he also goes on to say that, in 1685, '… Dr Took, as they call him, has miserably defaced South Long Barrow by digging half the length of it'. It could be that 'Dr Took' was in fact a certain Dr Toope of Marlborough, who was pillaging bones from local burial sites to concoct, '… a noble medicine that relieved many of my distressed neighbours'. It seems that the infamous Dr Toope had only disturbed the top few layers at the east end, presumably put off by the compactness of the secondary filling.

Stukeley's illustrations show how capstones and the huge stone 45 were torn down and pulled to one side by farmers and other vandals, some of which were later reinstated by Piggott in 1955-6. Stukeley's drawings show, for instance, that the capstone of the SE chamber had already been dragged to the position where it was found in 1955.

Early Archaeologists

Sir Richard Colt Hoare's researches in the district were made around 1814. He speaks of WKLB as being one of the most remarkable in the area, and wondered if the mound covered the graves of some slaughtered army, but eventually concluded it was not: '... it extends in length 344 feet... it rises as usual towards the east end, where several stones appear above ground, and here, if uncovered, we should probably find the interment, and perhaps a subterraneous kistvaen' (*Ancient Wiltshire,* Vol ii, p. 96). His suspicions were later to be proved well founded.

In 1849, the barrow was visited by Dr John Merewether, Dean of Hereford. At the east end he found, '...at least thirty sarsen stones, in which might clearly be traced the chamber formed by the side uprights and large transom stones... and below, round the base of the east end, were to be seen the portion of the circle or semicircle of stones bounding it'.

Damage to the site continued into the 19th Century, as John Thurnam recorded: 'Tenants, even in the present century, have stripped it of its verdant turf, cut a wagon-road through its centre, and dug for flints and chalk rubble in its sides'. He sentimentally comments how the barrow transcends all the mutilations: 'In spite of all this, however, the great old mound with its grey, time-stained stones, has still a charm in its wild solitude, disturbed only by the tinkling of the sheep-bell and perhaps the cry of hounds'.

John Thurnam

So, over 4,000 years after the barrow was finally sealed, it fell upon John Thurnam to undertake the first archaeological dig into West Kennet long barrow, in the autumn of 1859 (the same year as Charles Darwin's masterpiece, *On the Origin of Species*). Thurnam was a medical superintendent of the asylum at Devizes, and used his patients for labour, on the premise that it would be good 'occupational therapy'! He recorded the length of the mound as being, '336 feet... and a maximum height of 8 feet'. He noted three capstones covering what we now know to be the west chamber, and a hole, '... whence the cap-stones seemed to have been removed'. At the east end of the mound he noted, '... a large flat slab, nearly twelve feet square, partly buried in

John Thurnam, the first excavator of WKLB.

the turf'. This must have been stone 45, lying where Piggott and Atkinson found it some 100 years later. He also noted the courses of oolitic limestone dry-stone walling, which filled gaps between the standing stones (see Thurnam 1860 & 1867).

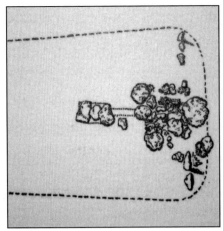

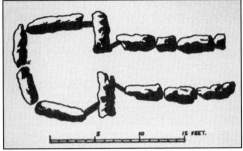

John Thurnam's plans made during his 1859 excavations, showing the west chamber. He failed to find the four other chambers.

The landowner granted permission for Thurnam to dig only on the condition that none of the stones on the surface were taken away. So he dug into the west end of the chambered area, under the three capstones he had found, entering what we now know as the west chamber.

He removed a capstone from above the west chamber, and recorded what he thought were fragments of Roman pottery whilst digging down. He describes how one of the capstones, weighing three tons, fell into the chamber during access, and which he subsequently replaced, '…with great dexterity by our men'. Compared to other digs by antiquarians of his day, this act was very carefully done by Thurnam, for it was not until two days later that the chamber was finally entered, via the passage. Thurnam was not allowed to excavate further eastwards but did note how the roof was corbelled, narrowing progressively upward.

The west chamber was almost full to the roof with chalk rubble, very

Some original sketches of the elaborately decorated pottery sherds John Thurnam found in the west chamber. (Manuscript in Devizes Museum.)

compacted and full of pottery fragments, representing 50 or more vessels, which were, '... up to two-gallon containers'. They were very elaborately carved, as shown above. Clearing this infilling, Thurnam states that, '... a few scattered bones of animals, flakes and knives of flint, and fragments of British pottery were picked up... a rude bone pin and a single bead of Kimmeridge shale'. At a depth of five feet he unearthed a, '... 3-9ins layer of blackish, sooty, and greasy-looking matter... flint flakes and implements and bones of animals were much more numerous than above'. These layers of dark, decomposed plant material contained the bones of goat, sheep, ox, roe deer antlers, and boar tusks. Piggott and Atkinson were to later find these layers in the other chambers, and they are one of the most important elements of the barrow, representing ritual deposition long after the time of the primal burials, as we will see later. Thurnam found bones representing five adults and a child, buried with little or no grave goods. He also noted the imported 'dry-stone walling' between the sarsen stones.

Thurnam shows a great attention to detail, more than most of his contemporaries, recording the positions of the skeletons, their condition, 'racial origins', and age. He was particularly interested in the skulls, no doubt due to his medical profession. We will refer to these later, as we re-appraise his findings in the light of new interpretations by today's archaeologists.

For now, his finds in the west chamber can be summarised, with some quotes from Thurnam, thus:

Skeleton 1 was found in the SE corner, a young adult about 17 years of age, with a fractured skull that, '... appeared to be the death blow'. It had large teeth, which were slightly eroded, but the wisdom teeth had not yet erupted.

Skeleton 2 was found almost in the centre of the chamber and was male, 'a large and powerful individual... with a 20ins thigh bone', aged about 50. Like the first, he found injuries to the skull, '... a fracture, probably the death wound, extended from one temple to the other'. The teeth were very eroded.

Skeleton 3 was located near the SW corner, also male, about 30-35 yrs old of medium stature, with no marks of injury to the skull, which was, '... of a beautifully regular and somewhat lengthened oval form'. The lower jaw was found about 0.3m (1ft) from the skull.

Skeleton 4 was found in the NW angle of the chamber, a 30-35 yr-old with legs flexed and an elongated skull, similar in appearance to skeleton 3, '...especially in the face'. Thurnam noted how well the skull was preserved, that it was, '... of an ivory whiteness and distinct traces of natural oil or medulla. He thought this skeleton to be of, '... the chief for whom this chamber and tumulus were erected'. This skull also lacked any signs of violence. Nearby was found a black flint, which he took to be a circular knife with a short projecting handle. This may have also had symbolic significance (see image p. 111 and front cover).

Skeleton 5 was incomplete, represented by temporal bones, the lower jaw, some vertebrae and arm bones. The estimated age was simply 'middle-aged'. It was accompanied by perforated pottery.

Skeleton 6 was represented by part of a child's skull, a 1-year-old infant, and was found against the base of the west wall, right on the axis of barrow, between stones 21 and 22 (the *Living Head* and the *Skull Stone*). It must have been regarded as a special child to be afforded such an important position. Three sharp flint flakes and some pottery accompanied the child's remains.

Thurnam found heaps of pottery, a small amount of oak, and, '... a curious ovoid sarsen stone weighing 4¾ lbs; it was tinged with a red colour from exposure to fire'. Another round nodule of flint, 'weighing about 1 lb', was also found. All in all, nearly 300 flints were collected during his dig, some of which were very fresh - there were numerous signs of on-site knapping. Were these new flints made purely for the dead? Or were they votive offerings, fashioned where they were to be left. Perhaps flints made on-site were seen to have

Thurnam's 1859 drawing of the west chamber, looking east down the passage. Some artistic license was used!

My virtual reconstruction showing John Thurnam and a workman during the 1859 excavation of the west chamber of WKLB. (Mannequins from Kent's Cavern, Devon.)

some special significance or power?

He also noted burned fragments of bone (see Piggott's discussion about this later), which may have resulted from accidental burning after defleshing.

Thurnam dug along the passage for nearly 4.6m (15ft), but failed to recognise the two side chambers, due to their infilling. He back-filled the passage and west chamber and replaced the capstone, apparently with great care.

He interpreted the infilling of the west chamber and passage as collapsed mound material, thinking this to be the reason for the disarticulation of the bones. A century later, Piggott was to find that both the infilling and scattering of the bones had been part of Neolithic ceremonies. Thurnam himself speaks of bones being 'scattered' across the floor of the west chamber, which we will see later was probably due to shamanic practices.

Above is my virtual reconstruction of John Thurman's excavation of the west chamber, showing him making notes as his workman digs away. I hope this captures some of the spirit of this early dig.

John Thurnam went in to produce an in-depth treatise on prehistoric skulls in 1865, *Crania Britannia,* due partly to his findings at WKLB.

Then, surprisingly, little work was done on WKLB for almost 100 years. William Long measured WKLB as 'about 300ft' in 1858, and in 1876 discussed WKLB as a possible ossuary. James Ferguson summarised research on WKLB up to his time in *Rude Stone Monuments* (1872). The barrow then became one of the earliest sites to be declared an Ancient Monument by Pitt-Rivers, in his role of Chief Inspector, thus sparing it from any future wanton damage. In 1927, Maud Cunnington produced some fine drawings of John Thurnam's pottery finds (Cunnington 1927), which can still be viewed in the library of Devizes Museum today.

Early Maps

WKLB also appeared on some early maps. We have already seen some, in the form of Stukeley's 3D 'maps', and a 19th century example showing 'Silbaby'.

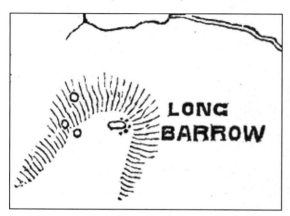

Ferguson's map of 1872 (left) shows WKLB as 'LONG BARROW'. It is interesting in that it shows three circles, possibly barrows, west of WKLB. The northernmost is well positioned to be the G55 site.

When we think of maps today we think Ordnance Survey. The lower map below is from the 1889 Wiltshire 1:10,560 map showing Sarsen Stones and trees. Thurnam described several ash and elms growing on the north side of the mound in 1859, and that, '… shade is not wanting'.

Close-up of Ferguson's 1872 map, possibly showing G55 and others to the west of WKLB.

The upper image below is from the 1900 series, to the same scale, showing the long barrow and stones (plural) but no trees.

We are now in a position to look at the main excavations at WKLB by Piggott and Atkinson in 1955-56. The scene we see at WKLB today bears little resemblance to what was visible prior to that date. The façade stones at the

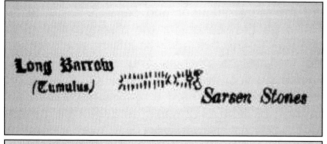

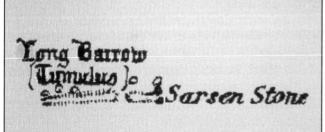

Late 19th and early 20th century maps showing WKLB. Stones are shown on both, at the east end. The circles on the lower map may be trees, which we know once stood on an overgrown mound.

east extremity were either fallen or half-buried, and the interior chambers and passage was completely inaccessible. The barrow was indeed in a sorry state, as this painting below confirms. Piggott, despite some controversy involving his 'over zealous' restoration, nevertheless enabled today's pilgrims to venture into the heart of the barrow, as shamans did thousands of years ago.

View From West Kennet Long Barrow. Atmospheric painting by the late
John Piper, showing the ruinous state of the eastern end in 1944.
(Original in colour.)

Chapter 8.
Modern Excavations and Surveys

'Too old
For ghosts, even –
Only the rain haunts here
In narrow rooms like marrow bones
Sucked clean.'
(Ann K Schwader)

The definitive excavation of West Kennet Long Barrow was carried out in 1955 and 1956 under the direction of Prof Stuart Piggott (with Prof Richard Atkinson), under the umbrella of the Dept of Prehistoric Archaeology, University of Edinburgh (see Piggott 1958 & 1962).

Stuart Ernest Piggott (1910-1996) was already well known for his work on prehistoric Wessex. In the 1930s he had worked with Alexander Keiller, who funded digs from the profits of his Dundee marmalade business. The two dug numerous sites in Wessex, including Avebury and the Kennet Avenue, and in 1939 Piggott joined the excavations of Sutton Hoo. In 1946 he was offered the Chair in archaeology at Edinburgh University, and succeeded in making it a department of international standing. He went on to excavate Wayland's

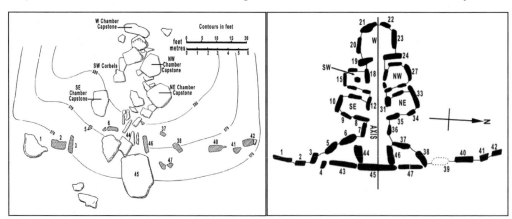

Left: The position of the stones at WKLB at the start of the 1955 excavation (after Piggott, with additions). Right: The site plan today for comparison, to about the same scale.

Smithy in 1952-3, and to produce several books and important papers. He received a CBE in 1972.

Piggott's initial examination of the site, in June 1955, revealed a mass of overgrown and partially covered stones at the east end; some fallen megaliths had been dragged away from their original positions and were strewn over the lower slopes of the mound. The façade and forecourt could barely be made out, due to deposition of later sediment and, it turned out, by *intentional* filling in the Late Neolithic. The plan above (left) shows the state of the site at the start of the excavations, with the present plan for comparison. The main blocking stone, no. 45, was lying prone and partially buried in the earth, and was measured at 3.9mx3.0m (13x10ft). The capstone of the SE chamber had been dragged away to the SW (later to be re-instated). The other capstones were in situ, as were many of the stones of the façade. Stone 46 was in situ and standing, but stone 44 was not, and was leaning at an acute angle (we

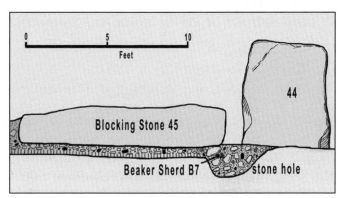

shall return to these later, as they play a vital role in astronomical sightlines). The area of the forecourt had been badly damaged by digging, probably in the 17th Century, and if a capstone ever existed between the entrance and stone 45, it had gone. The shape of the crescental forecourt could be made out, as was a stone revetment behind.

Stone 45 was found prone by Piggott and Atkinson, as shown here. A Beaker pot in the stone hole showed it was erected during the latter phase of use, in the later Neolithic. (After Piggott, with additions.)

The forecourt had been filled in the later Neolithic; Peterborough and Beaker pottery were unearthed in this area, as well as a leaf arrowhead, and a human skull at the base of stone 38. Dating of these finds led Piggott to the conclusion that stones 43-47 were erected later than the others, when access to the chambers was finally blocked (Piggott 1958, p. 237). Two cremations found near the entrance may have been connected with the closure of the site, as cremation is generally associated with the Late Neolithic and Early Bronze Age.

A trench was dug just west of the chambers which revealed that the mound contained sarsen boulders, 'a central core or axial spine', around 1.2-1.8m (4 - 6ft) high, which had smaller offshoots coming out at right angles, comprising half a dozen boulders (see image p. 49). The sarsens were naturally rounded, not cut or quarried. These were then covered by dark organic matter, a layer of turf, '...presumably cut from stripping the surface of the quarry ditches' (Piggott 1962, p. 11). Over the boulders and turf, chalk rubble was piled, fragments of which are seen weathering out of the mound today. This material was quarried from the long flanking ditches, which were 6m (20ft) wide and the top, and dug to 3.6m (12ft) below a ground level of solid chalk. In the upper layers were found Romano-British sherds and a perforated bone bodkin. Beneath the mound early Neolithic Windmill Hill Ware pottery was unearthed.

Piggott found no evidence for peristaliths around mound, or any stone holes. He suggests that any former stones may have been small and not earth-fast and so would have been easily removed for building material. He gave the length of the mound as '330ft', but amended it to '340ft' in 1973. He measured it as being wider at the east end, narrowing westwards, and that it rose to a height of about 4.2m (14ft) above the Neolithic ground level. A berm, or horizontal platform, separated the ditch from the mound (see image p. 50).

The huge size of the mound has been commented on recently: 'The biggest in Southern England at 100m long… there is a marked cut through it towards the eastern end. Although sometimes described as an old trackway, this cutting may show that there are two long barrows here set end on end… an interesting possibility' (Timothy Darvill, 'Long Barrows of the Cotwolds and Surrounding Areas').

Inside

Stuart Piggott expressed his astonishment and delight that Thurnam had missed much of the passage and all four side chambers. He found, 'a passage 23ft long leading to a polygonal western chamber, and two pairs of lateral chambers opening from it, three of these being rectangular, while one (the north-west) is polygonal' (Piggott 1958, p. 237). Like the west chamber, they were filled to the ceiling with chalk rubble, human bones, and other debris,

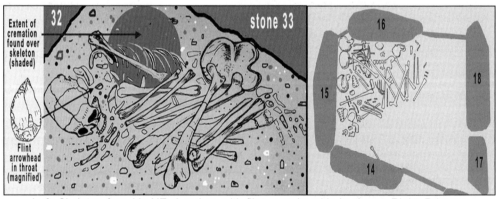

Left: Skeleton found in NE chamber, with flint arrowhead in its throat. Right: Primary skeletons in the corner of the SW chamber. (Redrawn from Piggott and Judith Dobie.)

such as large numbers of pottery sherds, stone tools and beads. The huge sarsens were joined by panels of dry-stone walling, made of oolitic limestone of Jurassic Age, probably from Calne or the Cotswolds to the west. The SW and NW chambers were blocked by two smaller sarsen stones (nos. 17 and 30). He also noted the smooth areas on some stones (such as on the passage side of no. 18), caused by the sharpening of flint axe-blades; he comments that this may be connected to the considerable number of felled timbers used as rollers for transporting sarsens across the landscape, and as beams to lever stones into position.

Bones and More Bones

Each chamber was filled almost to the roof with secondary deposits, which have led to much discussion, as we will see in the next chapter. Primary burials were found in all chambers and most of the skeletons and scattered bones lay at the rear of the chambers.

In the NE chamber three almost complete skeletons were found at floor level. One skeleton was complete up to the shoulders, but its skull lay 0.6m (2½ft) away, the remainder having been dispersed elsewhere. The complete skeleton of an elderly man found in northeast corner of the chamber was curled up, foetal-like, with a flint arrowhead embedded in his throat (image p. 72). Carbon dating revealed that this might have been the last chamber to be used for interment, explaining why he was still complete. On top of him were cremations of a male and female. Beneath him were the disarticulated bones of a female; similarly, at Hazelton North passage grave (Gloucs), a single adult male was laid over a mass of, previously deposited, disarticulated bones. A single roe deer antler was found near the entrance to the NE chamber (image p. 108).

In the SE chamber two more complete skeletons of a male and female were found, and the skeleton of a young adult may also have once been present, before the bones had been 'disassembled'. A wide scattering of bones was noted in this chamber, as Thurnam had seen in the west chamber nearly a hundred years before.

Noteworthy was a cache of long bones in the NW chamber, whilst in the SW chamber were three skulls laid in a row against the rear wall (see image p.

Cross-section of the NW chamber, prior to excavation, showing the secondary Neolithic filling above the primary burials. (Redrawn after Piggott.)

Geometric designs on a Beaker pot found in the later deposits of the NW chamber. (On display in Devizes Museum.)

72). One of these had a pronounced elongated skull (see images p. 94). The practice of positioning skulls in rows against megaliths has been observed elsewhere, such as at Hazleton North, and in French passage graves, such as at La Chaussee-Tarancourt, and at Rostock in Holland.

Julian Thomas and Alasdair Whittle suggest selection in terms of gender and age in the primary interments. The prominent type in the west chamber was adult male; in the SW and NW they were mixed adults; in the NE chamber they were mainly elders, whilst the SE chamber contained the greatest number of young adults and juveniles (Thomas & Whittle 1986, p. 133).

Top: round-bottomed Peterborough Ware pot from the NE chamber, with bird bone and fingertip impressions. Bottom: geometrical motifs on a Beaker pot, lovingly reconstructed from deliberately broken fragments. (Both on display in Devizes Museum.)

Regarding the burials, Piggott noted a shortage of skulls, and that skeletons were concentrated at the rear of the chambers. We shall look more into the interpretation of this in terms of shamanic ritual in the next chapter.

Regarding the issue of whether the deceased were related, it seems likely that they were members of an extended community. Individual families were part of a wider collective, what we might term a clan, and that, '... up to five families may have been sharing the same monument' (Burl 2002, p. 107).

Whilst many bones were, 'meticulously stacked against the walls' (Burl 2002, p. 110), elsewhere there was apparent disorder. The bones were particularly jumbled in the SE chamber, near the entrance, inviting the possibility that they were thrown into the darkness from the outside.

The primary burials were gradually covered with secondary material, yet not in a single act of closure, but rather over a long period of time.

Analysis of the skeletons revealed that the height of these people varied between 5ft 2ins to 5ft 11ins for the men, and between 4ft 10ins and 5ft 4ins for the women. Signs of arthritis were present in some skeletons, but their teeth show that they generally enjoyed good dental health.

74

Pottery

Piggott found at least 250 individual pots in the chambers and passage, most of which had been *deliberately* smashed. A striking find was an almost complete bell-beaker (no. B8), found upside down in the uppermost filling layers of the NW chamber, just below the capstone. It is almost 20cm (8ins) high (see images p. 73 & p. 109) and richly decorated with intricate diamond or lozenge markings, that Terence Meaden and Michael Dames believe are spiritually and ritualistically relevant, as we shall soon see. 'The ornament is unusual for Britain' (Piggott 1962, p. 45), but has also been found at Bincombe Down in Dorset. The geometric design is more common on the European mainland, at sites in Denmark, Germany, Sardinia, and Iberia. This find was crucial in dating the latter phases of WKLB, as Beaker pots (with their waisted profiles and elaborate decoration) generally become common in Britain around 2500 BC, whilst declining in use around 2100 BC.

Several round-bottomed pots, known as Peterborough Ware, were unearthed, and it has been suggested that these may have been associated with rituals concerning the dead, whilst more straight-sided Grooved Ware (formerly called Ryno-Clacton Ware) may have been associated with world of the living. As well as pushing fingernails and shells into wet clay, ornamentation was also fashioned by pressing in grains of emmer (wheat), barley, and apple pips; seeds are 'living', and hold the potential of new growth. Was this significant in respect to 'rebirthing' the ancestors following their physical demise?

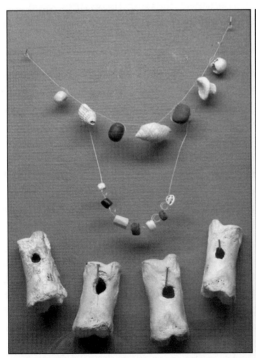

Left: Perforated beads, shells and ox toe bones from the secondary filling at WKLB. The latter may have been used to create sound! Right: Bones, flints, a perforated stone mace head, and bone pins from WKLB. (Finds on display at Devizes Museum.)

When WKLB was eventually sealed, these Beaker people made the largest offering of Peterborough Ware in the whole of Wessex: 'The ancestors were invited to occupy stone houses, dark, quiet and difficult of access, and cajoled to remain with the hospitality of gifts… ' (Whittle 1996, p. 1).

Most of the pottery was in sherds, i.e. fragments, and Piggott came to the conclusion, as had Thurnam, that the pots had been smashed *outside*, not within its confines. He also noted that although there was fire damage to a few finds, there were no signs of open fires inside the chambers or passage; the darkness could not generally be penetrated by firelight.

Thomas and Whittle also found a bias in pottery deposition in the various chambers. For instance, the largest number of sherds (totalling 291) was found in the west chamber, followed by the NE (206) and then the SE (159); the SW chamber had only 8 fragments. Even the large surface area of the passage only yielded 38 fragments (Thomas & Whittle 1986, p. 144). Regarding the secondary deposits, although human bones seem to be more or less equally distributed in all five chambers, very few animal bones were found in the west chamber, and no pots at all in the *primary layers* of the SW chamber!

The animal assemblage included roe deer, red deer, horse, badger, pig, sheep, goat, dog, jackdaw, blackbird, and possibly wolf. The shamans using the site were depositing objects with great care and thought, and I shall look more into this aspect in the next chapter. During the final phases of WKLB few animal bones were deposited, and although Piggott noted the remains of rabbit, polecat, vole, mouse and rat, he considered these to have accessed the chambers by burrowing in after the barrow had been sealed.

Other Ritual Objects

On display in Devizes Museum is a wonderful array of other objects found inside WKLB, such as perforated shells pendants, all of marine origin, plus 20 bone beads, jet and shale beads, bone pins, needles, ox bones, and antlers. A broken chalk mace-head (found in the NE chamber) had been converted into a pendant, says Piggott. Some of these pierced objects, according to Michael Poynder, may have been early dowsing pendulums. Perforated ox toe bones may have even been used as early flutes or whistles (see p. 123). Ox bones were especially abundant and were found in every level of the secondary deposits of every chamber, and in the passage. These objects, and some others, deserve special attention later, regarding their shamanic use.

The Party's Over

The chambers were filled over a long period with clean chalk rubble (it had not silted naturally) and contained runs of charcoal and pottery sherds. There have been differences of opinion regarding these deposits, as to whether they were a single act or else demonstrate extended activities, made by people seeking comfort from the ancestors in times of greater uncertainty.

The final stages of WKLB were rituals held in the crescent-shaped forecourt, possibly because the chambers were full. This arc of stones is found elsewhere, such as the Bridestones in Cheshire, and the Grey Mare and Her

Colts, in Dorset (Knight 1996, p. 114-6). The finds of the forecourt were nearly all secondary, inferring that prior to this time the area had been kept clean and free of debris. A small late Neolithic leaf arrowhead was found on the old land surface between stones 44 and 46.

The base of the huge blocking stone, no. 45, had been packed with sarsen boulders along the outer edge, '… as if instability was feared or anticipated' (Piggott 1962, p. 19). Remember that when this stone was put up it would have been one of the biggest megaliths standing in Britain. Busty Taylor has suggested to me that this stone may have originally been a capstone in front of the entrance (covering the forecourt) as the size of the forecourt mirrors its dimensions. It's food for thought. The hole taking no. 45 does seem to have been too shallow to hold such a large stone in place, as if it was not part of the original design. However, it has been suggested that this 'blocking stone' was part of the *original* structure (see Chapter 15 for a discussion on this).

Even after closure, when WKLB fell out of funerary use, it was certainly not ignored or neglected, as we shall soon see.

How Old and How Many?

So when did all this activity take place? 'It seems unavoidable that the use of the West Kennet tomb, from building to final blocking, can hardly have spanned less than a millennium' (Piggott 1962, p. 78). Of the primary burials, it has been advocated that, 'Construction occurred in 3670 – 3635 BC… the last interments of this initial use of the chambers probably occurred in 3640 - 3610 BC' (Bayliss, Whittle & Wysocki 2007, p. 85-101).

Over 30 carbon dating results have now been obtained for WKLB. These dates included human bones obtained from the four chambers excavated by Piggott. They are as follows, with *primary* human burials given first, followed by the *secondary* deposits:

NW chamber: 3783 - 3373 BC and 2875 - 2830 BC.
SW chamber: 3709 – 3363 BC and 2830 BC.
SE chamber: 3709 – 3363 BC.
NE chamber: 3646 – 3345 BC and 2750 BC.

These dates, of course, do not necessarily date the extent of the monument's use - they only date the sampled human remains. The *primary* deposits of the chambers may have occurred over a period of just 30 years, or even less. Then followed a period of more than 100 years when no human bones were left inside the barrow, which is quite a mystery; bones were then left in the chambers as the infilling began, which was a slow and ongoing process that persisted for several centuries until the chambers were full.

It will be noticed that the initial dates of the primary burials of the NE chamber are later than the others, and that they also persist after the rest; so for a while only this one chamber may have been in use for burial. It also yielded the latest dates for the secondary deposits.

Between 3000 and 3250 BC there was something of a 'Dark Age' in Southern England, with reforestation and the spread of scrub and weeds across deserted fields. Regarding the temporary cessation of use after the primary deposits, we can only speculate as to whether it was due to a worsening of the climate, an epidemic, plague, overuse of the land or crop failure, perhaps leading to some cultural conflict or loss of faith. Long barrows were no longer built after around 3100 BC, although some of the early ones were still in use. West Kennet was abandoned, some of the stone cladding collapsed, and it was not for some considerable interval that clan members returned to reinstate it (Burl 2002, p. 119). After perhaps a hundred years of neglect, WKLB was then tidied up and restored (op. cit. p. 131), and new forms of pottery became prominent. Then, over about a 500-year period, c.2800 - 2300 BC, the chambers were tightly and purposefully packed with chalk etc., directly on top of skeletons that had been on the floor since c.3700 - 3600 BC. The people doing the filling and final closure were the Beaker People, as Grooved Ware, Peterborough Ware and Beaker pottery testify.

Piggott saw the closure as a denunciation of previous ideals. He suggested a final date of closing to be around 1600 BC, which is the date on the English Heritage on-site plaque. However, it has been suggested, based on more recent re-evaluations, that, '… the final closing of the monument could be as early as 2000 BC' (Thomas & Whittle 1986. p. 150).

Whatever dates are eventually agreed upon by archaeologists (and that day may never come) WKLB was the focus of people's attention, on and off, for some 1600 years, an incredible length of time for a 'funerary' monument. Piggott even found evidence that the *site* of WKLB had been used prior to the

Model of WKLB in Devizes Museum. With several of the capstones removed, it shows the design of the chambers and passage.

construction of the monument. Similar cases have been found at other British long barrows sites, such as at South Street, Fussell's Lodge, and Haddenham, where there had been earlier timber buildings. It has been argued that such places may not always have been associated with funerary practices. These earlier timber buildings and smaller mounds, '… were not intended to act as tombs. These structures were intended to act as a form of cultural or social archive' (Russell 2002). These *temporary* timber buildings evolved into long barrows, which incorporated the *permanence* of stone.

Just how many individuals were interred in WKLB has also been the subject of some debate. A total of 40-45 is often quoted, but the problem has always been matching up the scattered bones, and the fact that some skulls and longer bones were absent (we shall deal with this in depth in the next chapter). The latest estimates for the individuals of the *primary burials* suggest the total could be as low as 36. Many more bones were later added, of course, in the secondary phases. Aubrey Burl concluded, '… the tomb may have received the bones of several hundred individuals' (Burl 2002, p. 279); most were not complete, however, perhaps being intended as 'token votive offerings'.

Piggott also paid tribute to the builders of the barrow: 'To see the monumental façade with its huge blocking stones at the entrance, and to walk into the great chambers, is an experience which brings home to one the architectural capabilities of those builders in massive stones who, before 2000BC, were already in North Wiltshire mastering the basic techniques which were to be used by their successors at Avebury and Stonehenge' (Piggott 1958, p. 242). A worthy tribute with which I fully concur; the people who raised the huge capstones and massive blocking stones (weighing up to 30-40 tons) contributed to a tradition of skills that would go on to erect the iconic monumental circles that were to follow.

The Romans

Six bronze Roman coins were found by Piggott in the topsoil in the area of the façade. They dated from the late 3rd - late 4th century AD, and Piggott considered them to be more than accidental loss, that they had been hidden for later retrieval. It has been suggested that they were votive offerings, especially in view of the ritual finds at nearby Silbury Hill (Reynolds and Pollard 2002, p. 179). The practice of votive offering was carried out on an industrial scale at nearby Bath. Roman coins have been found at other barrows, such as at Uley, Brown Hill, and Rodmarton, all in the Cotswolds, at Pakenham, in Suffolk, and at Mininghow in Derbyshire. Perhaps the Romans were acknowledging WKLB as an ancestral site even in their day, coming to pay their respects, so to speak, and to ask favour from the Gods.

Michael Dames presents evidence that Silbury Hill was a major Roman ritual centre (Dames 2010, p. 54-9), including several sacred wells. Kenneth Watts (in Piggott's excavation report) states that, 'It is possible here that the Romans converted existing prehistoric ritual shafts into wells for their travellers… the shafts or wells provided a ceremonial focal point for worship of the springs and the sacred Kennet'; springs were entrances to the Underworld. The A4 crosses *Pan's Bridge* nearby; Pan was an Otherworldly traveller who rested at streams.

Restoration
Following Piggott's excavation, the chambers were subject to extensive 'restoration', some of which has since been criticised, such as visible runs of mortar, the insertion of stones in incorrect positions, and the infamous skylights, ugly windows set into large concrete blocks: '...irresponsibly restored, with a glass-block roof, it has still succeeded in retaining its sense of sacredness' (Trubshaw 2005). In his defence, Piggott could have backfilled the site, as has been done elsewhere, or left the monument to decay, which has also been the case. At WKLB we have access to an exceptional sacred site due to Piggott's efforts, and the information he gleaned from the rubble and jumbled masses of bones and pottery sherds has helped immensely in our knowledge of Neolithic Britain.

Geophysical Surveys
Modern technology has also been used to probe into the secrets of WKLB. The Ancient Monuments Laboratory undertook earth resistance, magnetometer and electro-magnetic surveys of the ditches in 1991 and the Royal Commission for Historical Monuments conducted an earthwork survey in 1992.
We will concern ourselves here with the results of the geophysical survey undertaken by A Payne and L Martin, on 15-19th January 2001. Their aim was to determine the archaeological limits of the site, by extending further out from the mound than before; they also sought a better definition of the ditches, which are now filled with sediment.

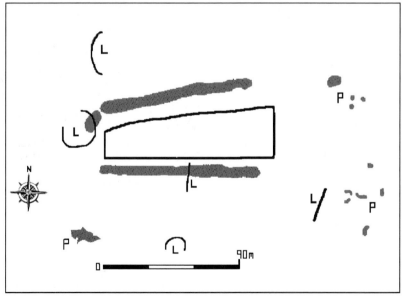

Plan of the magnetometer survey of 2001, showing the ditch and several anomalies. P: pits, L: linear features.
(Redrawn from Payne & Martin, with modern features removed.)

Magnetometry revealed the form of the ditches, 100m long with *outer* edges around 15m out from the barrow. These also extend slightly *beyond* the western end of the barrow and end just short of the front façade at the east end. They found some magnetic anomalies, shown as P in the plan above, which they interpreted as pits. Most were east of the barrow, where field walking revealed fragments of possible prehistoric pottery. The largest anomaly, however, was 45m to the SSW. They thought this particular anomaly suggested an area of burning, or perhaps a tightly constrained group of pits. It was speculated that it might be related to the long barrow in some way, perhaps as a subsidiary structure. This anomaly may also have been connected to a mortuary chamber or ossuary, as discussed by Piggott (1962, p. 75-6). Alternatively, such an 'offering house' could have been a store for ritual material prior to its incorporation into the layers of the secondary deposits. More enigmatic were linear anomalies (L on the plan), which defied interpretation regarding any possible relationship to the barrow. In the past it has been suggested that an earthen barrow may have existed on the site at the west end prior to the chambers being erected (Thomas & Whittle 1986, p. 136). Payne and Martin thought these features, ' … would bear further investigation'.

Virtual impression of a shaman's hut in the vicinity of WKLB,
with Silbury Hill in the background.
(Original model of Neolithic hut in Devizes Museum.)

So it is possible that the barrow did not stand in isolation, but had subsidiary structures, perhaps used by shamans for preparation of the dead prior to their interment. My virtual impression of this 'offering house' or ossuary is above. It is based on an oval Beaker-period hut from Belle Tout, Sussex (model on display in Devizes Museum).

Piggott's investigation was the last major excavation of a long barrow in Wiltshire, and since then only small scale digs have since taken place at

Luckington, Woodford and Mill Barrow (Smith & Brickley 2009, p. 155). Perhaps East Kennet long barrow will be the next 'big thing', if it is decided to excavate what is probably a chambered mound.

Lastly, Piggott had found stems of clay pipes in the refilling of the south-east chamber, which had presumably worked their way in from above, or else left by workmen or farmers who later vandalised the site for building material and bones for medicine. My partner, Sue Wallace, found a small one-inch long fragment of an old clay pipe in front of stone 45 during a site visit in 2010. Even now, it seems, WKLB still gives us gifts.

Fragment of a clay pipe found at WKLB in 2010.

Chapter 9.
Shamanism
And The Meaning of WKLB

'What space is depends on who is experiencing it.'
(Christopher Tilley)

'Even though bodies were sometimes buried in them, that did not
preclude them from having another purpose' (Lucy Wyatt)

I n recent years I have not been content in learning from academics how or
when a barrow or stone circle was erected, or from what material it was
made, or even what people wore or ate thousands of years ago. These are
all very interesting for sure, but my principal interest, following my own spiritual
genesis, has been the *spirituality* of these people. How did they interact with
their ancestors? Were their sacred sites more than mere backdrops to
ceremony? Why did they align monuments with other landscape features? In
particular, what were the **beliefs** of the people of WKLB, and how did they
interact with their local landscape?

Surely chambered barrows held some special place in the hearts and minds of
the clan members who used them. The passages and chambers of these
monuments were very distinct places, detached from the mundane world, and
'… probably associated in the minds of their builders with the spirits of the
dead' (Pollard 1997, p. 37-38). Chambered long barrows resemble caves, to a
certain degree, and this may have been the intention. It has been said that
caves, with their peculiar acoustics that echo and intensify sound, were the
'cathedrals of prehistoric times' (Devereux 2010). At West Kennet, our
Neolithic ancestors sought to create their own cave, in a chalk landscape that
contained no natural ones.

Since the somewhat romantic days of Stukeley and Thurnam, and even since
Piggott's day, archaeology has come along in leaps and bounds, birthing a
new generation of archaeologists, who are taking full advantage of new
technologies and innovative methodologies, enabling updated interpretations

of earlier excavations. Archaeology/science may seem poles apart from shamanism/spirituality, and yet, ironically, archaeology is now confirming an idea that 'alternative' researchers, Druids, pagans and 'fringe' authors have been advocating for years: ***shamanism underpinned the beliefs and daily lives of Neolithic communities.*** It is my guess that daily life in the Avebury area, over 5,000 years ago, was determined by symbolism, ritual, ceremony, spiritual beliefs, a concept of deity, interaction with the ancestors, and by following and honouring the cycles of Nature. As Aubrey Burl put it: 'In unscientific times when reality and imagination blended with the belief of a powerful Other-World of spirits, superstition was a religion. The symbol was the substance' (Burl 1989).

I have never regarded WKLB as merely a 'tomb'. Is a church a tomb because it houses monuments of the dead inside and in the churchyard? Of course not. 'With so few people here, burial was not necessarily its primary purpose' (Wyatt 2010, p. 152). Long barrows were gathering places, before the time of stone circles and henges. Astro-archaeologist John North summed up this state of affairs: 'Not all mounds were used as tombs, even when resembling ones that clearly did, and even tombs served other purposes than burial alone' (North 1996, p. 14).

A shaman officiates over funerary rites, with animal sacrifice, at WKLB. (Detail of painting by Judith Dobie, used with permission of English Heritage.)

So what did WKLB mean to its builders, and to the many generations that interacted with the barrow in the thousand years or so that were to follow?

Shamanism – Meet the Ancestors

Shamans were, and still are, intermediaries between this three dimensional world, with its cycles of birth, life, and death, and some kind of 'Otherworld', the realm of nature spirits, totem animals, and the ancestors. For thousands of years shamans have been entering trance states and 'journeying' to these other dimensions to bring back information of use to their tribe, including knowledge to procure healing. This stems from a primeval belief that part of us survives physical death: 'Their bodies may have returned to the land, but their souls are free, and can be contacted' (Knight 2007, p. 244).

I must add at this stage that when I speak of a 'shaman', I mean either male or female. The term 'shamanka' is sometimes used to specify a female practitioner, but I shall refrain from using it; we do not know if the shamans of

WKLB were men, women, or a combination of both. I get the gut feeling, however, that females may have predominated. I am pulled in this direction by the profusion of 'feminine' and 'Goddess' symbolism at WKLB.

Death is usually seen as a tragedy today – but in many parts of the world it is seen not as 'the end', but as a beginning, and was often viewed so by cultures long ago. People took their beliefs from what they observed in Nature, where death is part of life and is, in fact, an essential component of the continuance of life on Earth. Perhaps the deceased were thought to stay close to the living for a while, and could be contacted at places such as WKLB: 'This holy monument was, and still is, a conduit, a crossing point for a shaman to contact other souls' (Knight 2007, p. 245).

By undertaking trance journeying, a shaman could contact the dead, which could be a powerful recourse. Perhaps only when corpses had defleshed would they have become a 'collective ancestor', having lost any individual identity and made their journey to the Otherworld. It is possible that the interior of WKLB would have been taboo to ordinary folk, not that most people would have ventured into such a dark and highly charged place littered with skeletons anyhow! Inside was the domain of the shaman.

Within Neolithic communities the shaman (male or female) was a powerful figure, and with good reason: 'The shaman was the guardian of esoteric knowledge and the technician of sacred power, whose secret wisdom was of natural laws and psychological dynamics. The shaman knew, and could interpret, the cycles of nature, the workings of the heavens – the cycles of the Moon, the progress of the Sun… ' (Moore & Gillette 1993, p. 70). I believe that to Neolithic people, the world was whole and complete, both wonderful and at the same time frightful, a world that both inspired and threatened, and the shaman had the power to offer the clan protection from wolves, disease, famine, and perhaps even protection from themselves. Their main role, however, was conversing with their predecessors: '… the ancestors may well have been considered 'supernatural' beings. The ancestors may ward off evil, ensure the fertility of the crops and herds and protect the community' (Michael Parker Pearson 1993, p. 42).

Shamans would also have facilitated rites of passage and initiations, aiding adolescents during their transition to adulthood. Today we still have 'rites of passage', such as taking one's driving test or an exam, etc. These are often solitary challenges, involving separation, a test of some kind, and then a return. Tribal cultures today often demonstrate these aspects, including incarceration and exclusion from the rest of community. These rites frequently take place at a special or sacred place – like WKLB was to our Neolithic clan. A person must show their resolve, to pass through a physical or psychological barrier, to be 'reborn'. I have personally experienced this inside the chambers of WKLB, when my shaman teacher, Heather, guided me through a ceremony and into meditation to meet my ancestor, my late father, face to face.

In recent years archaeologists have acknowledged that shamanism was being practiced in the Neolithic. In his authoritative book, *Prehistoric Avebury,* respected archaeologist Aubrey Burl cites shamans and/or evidence of shamanic practices several times. Regarding the 'Upton Lovell Shaman', he concludes it was possible that, '... the unusual burial position and the unique articles of clothing were the remains of a shaman or witch-doctor' (Burl 2002, p. 233). Other archaeologists concur: '... the shamanistic element in prehistoric and early historic tradition in both Europe and Asia cannot be ignored' (Woodward 2001). Shamans were alive and well in Neolithic Wiltshire, and were central figures in their clans. The late Monica Sjoo, artist and visionary, spoke of WKLB as, '... a place of shamanic initiation and out-of-body journeying to communicate with the ancestor spirits that dwell here, within the womb of the most ancient Mother of the tombs'.

Stone Age Trippin'

All around the world today, one of the elements used by shamans to attain an altered state is through the ingestion of mind-altering substances. Speaking of the Neolithic, archaeologist Mike Pitts states, 'It seems we are justified in hypothesising that altered states were indeed a component of some ceremonies...' (Pitts 2000, p. 236).

There are around a dozen 'magic mushrooms' in the UK today, including the Fly Agaric (image below), the Liberty Cap (popular with hippies in the 1960's), Panther Cap, Ergot, and Chicken of the Woods. Fungi expert Dave Shorten has informed me that all these were probably growing in Southern England in the Neolithic (pers. comm.). Hallucinogenic effects usually begin 1-3 hours following ingestion, which can be through drinking, chewing (then spitting out), eating or smoking. There is, by the way, no evidence that magic mushrooms are addictive, which is not the case with another intoxicant which was gaining popularity in the Neolithic, namely alcohol. Some fungi, such as certain species

Left: A Neolithic pot with short legs, which may have been used for the burning of psychoactive plants. Right: The Fly Agaric.

of Coprinus, only become psychoactive when taken with alcohol. Dave Shorten also informed me that the favourite growing medium for the Fly Agaric is on dead or dying birch trees. Archaeology has shown that in the early Neolithic the dense oak and hazel forests of Southern England were being felled to make way for agriculture and settlements. Around these cleared areas, smaller woodland trees thrived, such as ash, elder, and birch - Fly Agaric's favourite host.

The problem with seeking to identify residues of prehistoric hallucinogens is that pottery is systematically cleaned and brushed during excavation or post-excavation work – unwittingly removing any plant residues, psychoactive or otherwise. There are but a few exceptions, which have survived against the odds. The seeds and pollen of the psychoactive plant henbane were found on sherds of Grooved Ware at the Scottish Neolithic site at Balfarg, in Fife. Opium poppy seeds were found in the ditch of a 5,500 yr old long mound in the valley of the River Nene, Northants. At the famous Neolithic occupational site of Skara Brae, in Scotland, a cocktail was made using alcohol laced with the hallucinogens hemlock and henbane – the latter of which is well documented as a trance inducer. At Carrowmore, in Ireland, seven symbolic fragments of mushroom-shaped beads were unearthed.

So if psychoactive substances rarely survive, what of the vessels that may have held them?

Archaeologist Andrew Sherratt suggests that 'Grooved Ware' pots were used for ritual drinks. This kind of pottery, he says, '…has a special quality which set it aside from everyday containers' (Sherratt 1995). Opium and cannabis, which had once been smoked, was in the Neolithic also being prepared as a liquid intoxicant, perhaps combined with alcohol. Archaeologist Peter Furst has concluded that cannabis may have been used for its psychoactive properties, '… long before hemp fibre began to assume economic importance' (Furst 1976). It is now clear that Grooved Ware vessels served, '… a highly specialised social role in addition to that of everyday domestic needs' (Pollard 1997, p. 19).

Neolithic passage graves on Jersey contained many brazier-like objects, thought by some to have been for burning hallucinogens. At La Hogue Bie, for instance, pots with ring-shaped supports were found, thought to be 'perfume-burners' (Joussaume 1988, p. 83). Also found were 19 richly decorated cups with feet that may have been used for burning psychoactive plants. Sherratt suggests that inhalation inside passage graves took place, '… perhaps in the context of mortuary rituals and communication with the ancestors' (Sherratt 1995, p. 28). In some modern cultures cannabis and opium are used in funerary ritual.

Some pots found in Wessex also have short legs, which Andrew Sherratt considers were braziers for burning cannabis. Shown above is a four-footed example from Inkpen, Berks, found with a Bell-Beaker pot (on show in Newbury Museum). This style of pottery was much favoured during the Neolithic in central Europe. An 'incense cup' was also found in a Bronze Age barrow at Woodyates, North Dorset. As happens when fires are lit and incense burnt in a Mayan ritual cave in the Yukatan (Devereux 2011), perhaps a chamber which was smoke-filled from burning incense would soon be a difficult place in which to breathe; this may have led to the 'near death experience' that many shamanic traditions speak of.

Paul Devereux carried out an excellent and invaluable overview of the evidence for the prehistoric use of hallucinogens (Devereux 1997). He has put forward a case that much of the European Neolithic passage grave 'rock art' may be expressions of shamanic experience, images brought back from 'the other side', so to speak (Devereux 1997, p. 141-192). I suspect that during altered states, the faces seen on the stones at WKLB may well have become animated, perhaps revealing spirits held within: 'The walls of the chamber might have extended to mighty proportions while flickering with kaleidoscopic energy patterns before opening up as portals...' (Devereux 1997, p. 57-58). We shall return to 'animated megaliths' in the next chapter.

Devereux also cites the work of British archaeologist Richard Bradley, who speculates a connection between entoptics (images seen by participants during trance) and the images on the Grooved Ware pots used by 'ritual specialists'. This style of pottery spread from Scotland to southern England between 3000 BC and 2400 BC. Devereux concludes that, 'We can envisage a hallucinogen-based shamanic cult... spreading through the British Isles'. Paul, I fully concur!

It has been suggested that psychoactive plants do not cause hallucinations, but rather take away the mental filtering processes of the brain. Shamans in trance see the world as it really is; the editing filters of their brain, which determine how we normally view the world, are removed.

Virtual reconstruction of how WKLB may have looked in the early Neolithic, before the blocking stones, and with a white chalky mound.

WKLB as Clan Icon

In 1986, Julian Thomas and Alasdair Whittle produced, in my opinion, an excellent paper, *Anatomy of a Tomb – West Kennet Revisited*, revaluating the excavations of Thurnam and Piggott. I shall dip in and out of their pages of wisdom during the remainder of this chapter.

Thomas and Whittle note the lengths of the long barrows (WKLB 100m, East Kennet Long Barrow 105m, Devil's Den 70m, and so on) were not merely a means to house the dead, but were a way of **dominating a landscape**. And dominate the landscape WKLB did, its elongated, white mound stretching across the apex of the ridge. Paul Devereux spoke of this: 'When fresh, this feature would have created a stark white marker in the landscape' (Devereux 1992, p. 133). WKLB was no shrinking violet; it was designed to impress!

There is the possibility that 'token' burials were made, representing the whole community, to continue the connection with the ancestors, as well as, '... to symbolise and legitimise rights of access to territory and resources... physical signifiers of connections between particular social groups and the landscapes they inhabited' (Smith & Brickley 2009, p. 87). WKLB enabled a clan to 'lay claim' to the immediate landscape; In other words, local clan members could say to outsiders and potential interlopers, 'Hey, **our** ancestors are up there on that ridge, not yours!' I am not suggesting this was purely for selfish reasons, although a clan's survival would have been of paramount concern. Rather, this ancestral veneration was born out of a sense of indebtedness, an appreciation that the clan owed much to their forebears, who had perpetuated the lineage, and had passed down to them all that they knew.

Thomas and Whittle also speculate that only a few people from any one group would have had access to the interior chambers, '... it is clear that much was potentially gained from the mystification of the relationship between the living and the dead'. The mystique of the site gave the shaman power and high standing. They also suggest that the users of WKLB were closely bound by kinship, perhaps comprising just a few biological families, even if some members were not directly related. They also conclude that is it plausible that the barrow was used by a 'socially pre-eminent group', with burial serving as a community bonding activity (Thomas & Whittle 1986, p. 136), in a similar way that a funeral today 'bonds' relatives and friends in their shared grief. They speculate that only shamans and others high in the social hierarchy would have access to the interior, borne out by the careful arranging of remains by sex and age in the different chambers. The continuance of these practices over many generations was easier to achieve if carried out by a select few.

I believe that most of these 'few' were likely to have been the shamans of the clan, rather than the chieftains or the hierarchical 'upper crust'. Archaeologist Francis Pryor seems to concur: 'We don't know what proportion of society was buried in tombs, and we mustn't leap to the conclusion that those who were necessarily came from the upper echelons' (Pryor 2003). My guess is that many of the skeletons of WKLB were in fact those of the shamans. In some tribal cultures today, the shaman is regarded as equal to the tribal chief.

Some archaeologists have noted that there was a greater investment of effort for 'monuments for the dead' than those for the living. If life was seen as a transient journey to another state of being (like Buddhism) then it makes sense why so much endeavour was given to places that held the dead, and the ancestral spirits there of. J Barratt has described Neolithic life as a, '... process of *becoming,* a movement towards a future state which was described by reference to ancestors or to gods and where life itself might be spoken of as ephemeral' (Barratt 1994, p. 136).

Piggott noted the similarity between WKLB and chambered tombs at Notgrove, Hetty Pegler's Tump, Nympsfield and Tinkinswood, and concluded that there must have been a, '… formal architectural setting for prescribed liturgical and ceremonial performances' (Piggott 1962), which we can compare to churches today: their architecture may vary enormously, but everyone can usually recognise a church as a church. I suspect it may have been important to the clan that their icon, WKLB, was instantly recognised for what it was.

To clan members who lived, farmed, and died around WKLB, the site was a focal point, just as a pub, church or village shop is to a small community today. The monument was as much a part of life as it was of death - inseparable, just as birth, life and death are each essential elements of the cycle of life.

'Samhain', by Rick Kemp, captures the idea of WKLB as womb. Original in colour. (Used with permission.)

The Womb

Over the years, WKLB has been the subject of much speculation regarding any *intended* symbolism. Most of it seems to come under two headings - *Goddess Womb* and *Horns of the Bull*, which seem to neatly offer a balance of the polarities of yin and yang, the masculine and the feminine.

Writing in an archaeological journal in 1921, T Cyriax was very forward thinking when he stated, 'The earth under which men are buried is the mother of the dead… The object of the tomb builder was to make the tomb as much like the body of a Mother as he was able… with burial chambers and passage perhaps representing uterus and vagina. Here myth becomes reality, the old sagas become part of the living'.

Monica Sjoo proclaimed that WKLB was, '… built by early Neolithic peoples to reproduce the darkness and powerful presence of the maternal cave, womb of the Mountain Mother. It represents the Mother of the Dead, the dark Crone of winter and the death of vegetation, the time when the seed germinates within the dark and fertile soil'. Michael Dames restates this association with 'death and rebirth' of the land, suggesting that Ceres (in the form of Silbury Hill) seeks her lost daughter (Persephone) in the Underworld that is WKLB. 'In Winter...' says Dames, '... the Harvest Mother (Silbury) does not vanish from but *into* the earth, into the bone mound, there to receive the dead' (Dames 1977, p. 34). She later emerges with the arrival of Spring. The entrance as a birthing symbol is certainly accentuated by the stones forming the forecourt, which stand as if they are legs spread apart.

Dames sees the five chambers as the 'squatting image' of the Goddess, with two legs, two arms or breasts and the west chamber being the head (Dames 2010, p. 98). Archaeologists J Hawkes and Leslie Grinsell reached similar conclusions (Dames 1977, p. 34). On my two visits to Malta, I too noticed how plans of Goddess temples were in the design of a plump 'figure of plenty', with voluptuous breasts, large hips, and thighs.

Dames notes the similarity of the infilling materials of WKLB and that used for the construction of Silbury Hill. He sees the two sites, '... closely bound together by human eyesight and by a shared feminine iconography' (Dames 2010, p. 98).

Avalon Priestess and author Kathy Jones echoes this: 'The Death Mother is represented in the British Isles in the shape of long barrows... the tomb to which the special dead returned and the Womb from which they would hopefully one day be reborn' (Jones 1994, p. 169). Prof Gimbutas suggests that the immense scale of many Goddess sites may have been an essential element: 'The gigantic size of the Hag is insisted upon or implied by the strength of her appetite' (Gimbutas 1974, p. 205). Elongated goddess figurines found in the UK invite comparison with the protracted length of WKLB.

Bob Trubshaw sees WKLB, '... like a human figure laid down, there are five recesses corresponding to the head, arms and legs. That this is intended to be recognised as a Goddess, the Great Mother, is left in no doubt'. He goes on that entering the entrance arouses the same emotions as the conquest of a lover (Trubshaw 2005, p. 139-40). Nice one Bob!

Archaeologist Catherine Tuck uses remarkably romantic language in describing the symbolism of WKLB, in that it is, '... not just a burial mound but a symbolic body of the mother goddess. Her earthen length lay pure white and supine along the crest of the ridge, the horns of the forecourt protruding like legs between which the passage led into a dark, incubating womb. Ancestors were returning to the safety of her enfolding body' (Tuck 2003, p. 52).

So if WKLB is the Hag Goddess of life, death, and rebirth, it certainly does invite a connection with the ancient Greek myths of Persephone and the Underworld. It is amazing how universal this type of myth is.

Visionary artist Judith Page has poetically described entering the chambers, as, '... almost like Jonah entering the whale, but instead of the smell of digestive juices, it was the aroma of the earth itself'.

The Horns

The 'male' symbolism of WKLB seems to be represented by horns. Even archaeologist Francis Pryor (2003 p. 200) states that, 'The forecourt is flanked by two slightly projecting *horns* of the megalithic revetment' (my emphasis). He goes on to say that, 'You could argue that the forecourt and the ceremonies that took place there were the main point of the monument, rather than the chambered tomb within the mound'.

WKLB plan as a symbolic bull, the stones of the façade forming the horns.

Ceremonies were also taking place *outside*, in front of the entrance, in the crescental forecourt formed by stones 3, 5, 6, 37 and 38 (see plan p. 138). Stone-defined forecourts are unusual in this area, although some Neolithic wooden structures also had horned, crescental designs. The nearest stone-built ones are at the Grey Mare and Her Colts, in Dorset, which I have described elsewhere (Knight 1996), and the Bridestones, over a hundred miles away in Cheshire.

Horns and bull worship was a key element of some Mediterranean Goddess cultures, such as on Crete, Rhodes and Malta. During my visit to Sardinia, I observed that many passage graves had pronounced projections, or 'horns', either side of the entrance, such as at Li-Mazzani, Coddu Vecchiu, and Li-Lolghi (Joussaume 1988, p. 217-19). There is plenty of folklore regarding oxen being associated with powers of prophecy, and strength (and therefore protection) and of course fertility. Dames states that, 'The Stone Age horned graves of Western Britain brings the ox goddess into the architectural ground plan' (Dames 1977, p. 55). He also advocates that some of the forecourt stones resemble a bull or ox (see image p. 132). The concept that a plan of the megaliths of WKLB defines a bull with horns is also developed in *Spirits of the Stones,* by Alan Richardson (2001, p. 151). This further invites a connection with the constellation Taurus, the Bull, which John North and I have found was once aligned to WKLB. Many ox bones were left inside WKLB, so they obviously had ritual significance, as we shall soon see.

Regarding 'male' symbolism, the shape of the mound may be relevant. Why is it so long? Both Thurnam and Piggott ignored the subject. For many years on my tours, I have being telling folks that one explanation for the elongated mound could be that it was a phallus, projecting into the womb of the chambers. I am not alone in this: 'The modelling of a linear mound as part phallic, part womb, may therefore be a necessary prerequisite for the storing of the dead' (Russell 2002, p. 66). As well as being a *symbolic* mound, earth energies and astronomy were also involved, as we shall see later.

So, rather than expressing a preoccupation with death, WKLB expresses *life*. It has been suggested that women may have given birth within the chambers or in the forecourt outside; people came into the world here, and at the end of their days the West Kennet Goddess embraced them, to birth them again. The Alpha and the Omega – the cycle of Life – coming full circle.

We shall return to symbolism in the next chapter, when we look in more detail of how the megaliths of WKLB were carefully chosen to depict clan myths.

Laying the Ancestors to Rest

As well as being a liminal, experiential space for the living, no one doubts that **one** of the many purposes of WKLB was as a tomb, and a transitional place for the souls of the dead. 'The barrow could be seen as a space that facilitated a critical transformation from a transitory corporeal world to that of an eternal spiritual realm' (Pollard & Reynolds 2002, p. 67). To put it another way, it was like passing through the 'Pearly Gates' of Christian mythology.

It may be remembered that the **primary** mortuary deposits at WKLB have recently been dated between 3670 BC and 3610 BC (Bayliss, Whittle & Wysocki 2007, p. 85). This initial use of the chambers may have occurred over just 30 years or less. Then followed a period of 'rather more than a century' when no human bones were left inside the barrow. Then there was a resurgence in use, as bones carbon-dated between 3500-3240 BC were left in the chambers during an infilling which then went on for several centuries.

During these times, the process of defleshing and rotting of a corpse, and the resultant end product of a skeleton, may have signified the end of any personal identification of an individual; they had joined the collective ancestral realms on the 'other side'. 'Ancestors' may not have been remembered as individuals by the living: 'They may be conceived in a generic sense, as part of a 'collective' (Whitley 2002, p. 122). At WKLB there may have been no reverence for the individual dead, but a chaotic assemblage of human and natural debris, perhaps expressing the chaos and mayhem from which new life emerges. Long bones, in particular, were often cast into different chambers from that of the original skeleton. Some skulls and long bones were missing altogether, taken out to be used elsewhere. Similar transference of bones from chamber to chamber was also unearthed at Burn Ground, Gloucs. At Isbister, on South Ronaldsay, Orkney, there were also many bones missing, like WKLB. Of the 340 individuals represented at Isbister, all were incomplete. All this may have been a precursor to the Celtic belief that the soul resides in the head, which in turn perpetuated prolific myths involving decapitation.

Aubrey Burl sees the disproportionately low numbers of bodies in tombs as having two possible causes; either only a small number of selected people were interred, or else a larger number were buried, but that many bones were later removed making resultant counts misleading (Burl 2002, p. 100).

Regarding the primary burials, Stuart Piggott noted that the skeletons were concentrated at the rear each chamber. Clearly the chambers were never filled to capacity and we may speculate that spaces were left vacant for the **living** to commune with their ancestors. Of note was that almost no finds were made in the forecourt or in a 6m (20ft) excavation made in front of the whole length of the blocking stones. This area was kept tidy and 'litter' free in the Neolithic, lending more weight to the theory that the material used to fill up the chambers was highly selective (not just rubbish and debris left lying around outside). The placement of human bones and other artefacts was systematically and symbolically orchestrated.

The male-female and adult-child ratios were not the same in each chamber. All the chambers contained children, but the SE chamber included ten juveniles. Further to this, all the chambers had elderly adults, except the SE chamber, which, as stated, was almost entirely reserved for the young. The highest proportion of the elderly was in the NE chamber, and only the west chamber was male only. Patterning is strongly suggested here; even in death, it seems, people had their appropriate place within the clan.

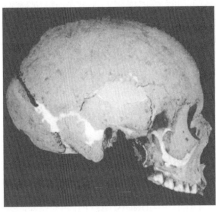 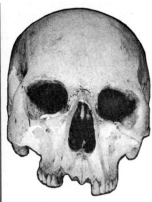

Female skulls found in the SW chamber. The left image shows abnormal elongation. (After Piggott.)

The highest percentage of complete, articulated skeletons was in the west chamber, and it has been suggested that this was the initial part of a west to east transfer of the skeletons, explaining why the assemblages were more jumbled in the eastern chambers (Pollard & Reynolds 2002, p. 68).

Thomas and Whittle (1986) have analysed the distribution of skulls. In the west chamber, all skulls are present (either complete or fragmentary), whereas in the four other chambers, skulls are rare, despite the higher numbers of individuals represented. The skull of a one year-old infant was found on the axis of the west chamber. One year is of course the time of the land's cycles to be completed. In the SW chamber, three skulls had been laid out in a row against stone 15 (see diagram p. 72). They were an elder woman, a younger woman, and a child. These may represent the three stages of womanhood - virgin, mother and crone, as well as the Triple Goddess aspect of many cultures. Skull no. 2 is shown above, on the left, and is abnormally elongated, due to 'scaphocephalic deformation'. This can be caused by premature birth, or by artificially and intentionally shaping the skull, as is still done in some cultures today. Skulls found in Europe, the Middle East and the Americas dating from the late Neolithic show similar, deliberate cranial shaping. Excavations at Harnham Hill (Wiltshire) and Ballard Down (Dorset) also unearthed deformed skulls, which some regard as having been artificially produced. It is possible that a person possessing a *natural* cranial deformity may have been regarded as 'special'. One of the males found inside WKLB also had an extra toe, and suffered from spina bifida. His strange appearance may have led him to be regarded as someone 'out of the ordinary'.

Also noted as 'striking' was the mixture of articulated and disarticulated, complete and incomplete skeletons contained in one monument, which is not usually the case (Thomas & Whittle 1986, p. 134). Bones were moved from one chamber to another – the remains of the 'dead' were being moved around by the living. Thomas and Whittle also note that the largest numbers of stray bones are in the NE and SE chambers, closest the entrance, suggesting that these two chambers were visited more often, and therefore had more disturbances. This also raises the subject of accessibility to the interior, which may have been limited by physical or occult means; today the interior is easily accessible, but there may have been some sort of fence or 'gate', perhaps comprising draped animal hides, restricting entry; there was no sign of scavenging by dogs or other carnivores, whereas smaller animals, such as bats, voles, mice and blackbirds, did find their way in: '... this sealing was only effective against larger intruders' (op. cit. p 135).

The possibility of excarnation in the later phases has also been raised (op. cit. p. 132 & 153), suggesting that missing small bones may have been lost during transit from an excarnation site outside; bodies may have been left outside to decay on platforms, before the skeletons (or what was left of them after scavenging by birds, dogs and wolves) were brought into the chambers. 'Possibly the quickest and simplest way to arrive at a defleshed corpse is simply to leave it exposed to scavengers' (Smith & Brickley 2009, p. 41). There are numerous examples of bones showing the scars of scavenging, such as at Hambledon Hill and Wayland's Smithy. Historically, this custom was carried out in Australia, America, Borneo, and Iran, and continues to this day in Tibet. In 1833, artist George Catlin spent time with the Mandan Indians of North Dakota. He observed how the dead were placed on wooden scaffolds, with their feet towards the rising Sun. After the scaffolds decayed, relatives took the skulls away to an ossuary (Burl 2002, p. 94-95). Back in Wiltshire, a crouched burial at Boscombe Down had already decomposed prior to burial. Some post holes found in the vicinity of passage graves may be a vestige of such raised structures.

Concerning the primary burials, it has been suggested that it should not be assumed that all the mortuary remains were placed in the chambers soon after death: '... they could therefore have died before the monument was built' (Bayliss, Whittle & Wysocki 2007, p. 85). The local ossuary/storage house theory surfaces again.

Some of the skeletons show signs of a violent death, such as fractured skulls, suggesting that the local Neolithic landscape was not as hunky dory as some idealists would suggest. We cannot rule out sacrifice either, be it voluntary or otherwise, to ensure fertility of the land or the tribe. At WKLB, an elderly male was killed by an arrow fired into his throat. Miles Russell incisively suggests that many of the interred, '... may not therefore have been the powerful, the successful, the wealthy, the religious or spiritual leaders' (Russell 2002, p. 69). Offerings to the power of nature and the gods, so to speak, may have been seen as a symbolic act of 'giving back' for 'gifts' given by nature, such as food, water, sunlight, etc. Such practices reinforced the concept that the clans were part of nature, that their priority was not overcoming and subordinating the land, as has been suggested by some. Regarding the arrowhead in the throat, Shaun Ogbourne (of the Wyvern Dowsers) told me, 'If they were not worried about death, why would they fear dying: after all, one gets to meet the ancestors sooner than you would have. And even after death they were still *in* their landscape - the ancestors were everywhere in the landscape'.

Monica Sjoo sees the interred as having a special role: 'There is the possibility that some people that were buried here (in some long barrows no bones have been found at all) could have simply been the guardians of/or the guides to those undertaking initiations within the womb of stones'.

Many separate human bones were found in the secondary deposits, which were deposited over a long period of time, suggesting that the bones of one's ancestors became portable artefacts. This was possibly for use in divination, fertility rituals, and as symbolic totem objects. Pots were left in the secondary

West Kennet Long Barrow by Judith Dobie. The drama of a gathering of the clan for a burial at WKLB is encapsulated. Original in colour. (With permission of English Heritage.)

filling under a variety of circumstances, including deliberate pot smashing and scattering throughout the imported chalk rubble and dark organic layers of the chambers and passage. The human and animal bones of the secondary deposits were not evenly distributed; only in the NE chamber was there a predominance of cattle bones. 'This may in turn be connected with the prevalence of elder individuals in the primary burials of the chamber' (Thomas & Whittle 1986, p. 147).

A spiritual connection also existed between WKLB and Windmill Hill. Some of the bones found at the latter appear to have been taken from surrounding barrows, including WKLB. These consisted mainly of skulls and long bones (Smith 1965b, p 137), which are under-represented at WKLB. 'It seems likely that some of the bones were deliberately brought to Windmill Hill for magico-religious rites...' (Burl 2002, p. 116). The bones in question were not being casually discarded either, but were carefully re-deposited. Paul Devereux sees this type of transference as a moving around of, 'pieces of place... transferring the magic from one area to another' (Devereux 2010).

Michael Dames sees a similarity between the long bones, such as the humerus (upper arm) and femur (thigh bone), with the elongated shape of the mound of WKLB. These bones, '... may well have been regarded as a reference to, or a version of the long goddess' (Dames 1977, p. 44). In many cultures today, the handling of bones is seen as a means to contacting the dead, and, in some cases, of bringing about fecundity and fertility.

WKLB As Ossuary

As well using the term 'tomb', another type of monument that partially describes WKLB is an ossuary. This is a final resting place for human bones, still exercised today in Catholic and Jewish traditions. This often involves burial in a temporary grave elsewhere, and at a later date housing the defleshed bones within a building, well or chest. In Persia, the Zoroastrians used deep wells for this function, some dating over 3000 years old. In the Second Temple Period (516 BC – 70 AD) it was common Jewish practice to place bones in niches of burial caves. Alepotrypa Cave, at Diros, is one of the best-preserved Neolithic sites in Greece, dating 5000 – 3200 BC. One chamber, Ossuary 2, contained the disarticulated bones of at least 20 individuals. A site in Portugal, Casa da Moura, contained an ossuary that dated from the Mesolithic through to the Neolithic.

Nearer to home, this is mirrored by Cathole Cave, in South Wales, which was used by Mesolithic hunters, and later as a Neolithic ossuary. Excavations in 1962 at nearby Llethryd Tooth Cave, NW of the chambered Parc Cwm cairn, showed it to have been an Early Bronze Age ossuary. Nearly a mile in length, the cave is the longest on the Gower peninsular.

William Long discussed WKLB at a possible ossuary way back in 1876: 'It is highly probable that the bodies of the dead were deposited in some temporary grave, and subsequently disinterred for final interment in the complete, or nearly complete, long barrow' (*Wiltshire Magazine*, Vol XIV, 1876, p. 152). It has been suggested that one of the anomalies detected in the geophysical survey of WKLB could be the site of an ossuary.

In a paper on the Neolithic Cotswold site of Belas Knap, Julian Parsons speculates that such sites may have, '... acted as ossuaries, where defleshed bones were placed or stacked in the chambers'. He concludes that, 'It is a sobering thought that, despite the tremendous advances in archaeology since Belas Knap was excavated, the ways in which Neolithic corpses were handled and the whole process of defleshing, burial and reburial, still remains a lively source of debate' (Parsons 2002).

Shamans and initiates ventured into the darkness of WKLB to contact the ancestors and for rites of passage. It is still a powerful place of initiation today.

Is Anybody There?

I suspect that shamans were going into the dark chambers of WKLB not just to deposit the dead, but also to contact the world of the ancestors – *their* ancestors. This was achieved by trance drumming, hallucinogens, or dream sleep. It was then a place more foreboding and claustrophobic than we can even begin to imagine: '… entering a confined space like the West Kennet long barrow is likely to have been intense… perhaps part of the significance of this space was that many of the scents associated with the wider world would have been absent' (Watson 2001, p. 308).

In 1860, John Thurnam measured the height of the west chamber as being, '…seven feet nine inches in clear height', which is much less than today's restoration; it was originally even more claustrophobic, even more like the womb of the Earth Mother.

I have been inside the chambers of WKLB during the night when the last nightlight has died - one's imagination soon goes wild. We must bear in mind that in the Neolithic, shamans and initiates alike would be accompanied by skeletons, skulls with lifeless eye sockets returning their gaze! But what is the point of initiation if it doesn't send one half crazy; we are taken to the edge of insanity, to hopefully return reborn. This is the purpose of rites of passage practices in tribal cultures around the world today.

Based on his work on Irish Neolithic sites, Jeremy Dronfields cites three ways to induce an altered state – migraine, flickering lights (such as produced by waving hands or another object in front of a light source), and the ingestion of psychoactive substances. David Lewis-Williams and David Pearce have also examined means by which altered states of consciousness can be induced; these include the ingestion of psychotropic substances, rhythmic dancing, repetitive auditory input, by means of drumming and chanting, flickering light, sensory deprivation, and fatigue (Lewis-Williams and Pearce 2005, p. 46). Some or all of these may have been involved in shamanic rituals inside WKLB: firstly, we know that hallucinogens were used in Neolithic Britain; dancing, drumming and chanting are usually involved in shamanic journeying today in

Entering the passage today is still a liminal experience, as we pass from the light into the dark, from the known into the unknown.

indigenous cultures, and we have records to suggest this was also the case over 2000 years ago; next, I have already proposed that flickering lights may have animated the faces in the stones – awakening spirits within; sensory deprivation is automatically provided by the darkness and alien environment of the interior of WKLB; and lastly, fatigue: modern shamans often dance, chant or drum for hours, all night, and even for days on end, until their bodies collapse, at which point they 'leave' their body, and 'journey'.

The shamanic experience may have commenced at the entrance. Monica Sjoo suggests that, '… the entrance is a huge vagina of light through which one enters into the deep, almost fearful, darkness of the womb/tomb chambers… This is a place of high energies, a space where all outside influences are cut off and one is left with meditative dream and trance states created and experienced by the lunar right-brain mind in us all'.

Then we encounter the passage, which was, and still is, an important element of the overall experience. 'The passage has the effect not only of limiting access to the main chamber, but also of helping to separate the chambers from the world outside' (Russell 2002, p. 39). This is all part of the liminal adventure of WKLB: we go along the passage, moving from the light into the dark, from the known into the unknown, from the world of the living to the abode of the dead. Inside, there are no familiar objects, no recognizable sounds or smells of the outside world, no significant ranges of temperature: 'There is no sense of reality' (Russell 2002, p. 66). What is achieved is an almost complete disconnection from the world outside, and from the community. One is alone beneath the earth, held within in the dark, intimidating, and unsettling world of the supernatural. In this respect, it may be assumed that some aspect of initiation or rights of passage may have been witnessed within these chambers, '... activity geared to the immatures, or those of slighter build, within society' (Russell 2002, p. 67).

The passage truly is a liminal space. Liminal comes from the Latin word for threshold, *limen*. Robert Moore and Douglas Gillette describe this space: 'From a psychological perspective liminal space is initially deconstructive. It dissolves our previous expectations as to ways of experiencing ourselves and our relationship to the world... we are regenerated, recreated almost from the bottom up...' (Moore & Gillette 1993, p. 108). As I have stated elsewhere, this crossing over to ancestral worlds may be nearer than we think, especially at places like WKLB: 'Your ancestors are never far away, and places such as this are sacred liminal places, where worlds merge' (Knight 2007, p. 248).

There is also a similarity between the passages of chambered tombs and the 'tunnel effect' seen in altered states: '... placing a body in a chambered tomb recalls laboratory subjects' reports on mental imagery's being related to a tunnel-like perspective... when new human remains were placed in a tomb, they and those who bore them were entering a human-made replica of the spiritual, or hallucinatory, world, with its darkness, engulfing vortex, and mental imagery' (Lewis-Williams & Dowson, 1993, p. 60).

At WKLB, both shaman and the dead entered the physical tunnel, i.e. the passage, as an element of their journeying. On a site visit in July 2010, Busty Taylor told me that he remembers that in the 1960's part of the passage roof, between the NW and SW chambers, was around 18ins lower than it is today, that he had to stoop to pass underneath. One had to bow in reverence on the way in and when coming out 'reborn', and such a narrowing would have also enhanced the 'tunnel effect'. Interestingly, fungi expert Dave Shorton informs me that one of the effects of ingesting Fly Agaric is 'tunnel vision' (pers. comm.).

This idea of entering a tunnel or passage as a way of accessing Otherworldy realms is an ancient one, and I do believe the passages of chambered tombs were designed to imitate the "tunnel of light" effects spoken of in near-death and out-of-body experiences. People experience this tunnel phenomena when having near-death experiences, seeing the 'light at the end of the tunnel'. Paul Devereux has described an experience he had in a dream: 'I found myself running along a darkened tunnel... ahead were great archways, or, more precisely, trilithons, forming a kind of corridor. I took off and flew headfirst ... I emerged at the far end and soared upwards into a blue sky' (Devereux 1992, p. 109). Mike Williams echoes this: 'When I was in trance... I left my body behind to move down a tunnel or, at least, that is how it felt to me... the compulsion to go down it is strong' (Williams 2010, p. 33). Earlier, I mentioned folklore of a tunnel said to exist between WKLB and Silbury Hill. Is this a distant cultural memory of a trance 'tunnel', or the path of spirit flights?

John North suggests that the tapering of long barrows may be directing our eyes to a point on the skyline. I also suspect that it may be creating an artificial 'tunnel' effect. A perspective is created whereby the ancestors have gone away to some Otherworld, but could be accessed by calling them back along the line of the mound. Or perhaps the shamans would 'journey' to this tapering end, which represented infinity; the white mound narrows, optically drawing the shaman to the Otherworld.

Today, how we see Neolithic sites such as WKLB is radically different from when they were used. In an article in the journal *Archaeology Today* (2001), UK archaeologist Aaron Watson wrote: 'These megalithic monuments of the distant past were certainly not the remote and silent places we visit today.

Within WKLB, in the early Neolithic, people may have sat surrounded by the skulls and other bones of their ancestors. This must have tested their resolve. (Virtual impression.)

Rather, they may best be understood as gateways through which people of the Neolithic passed to gain access to dimensions far beyond the reality of their everyday lives'. We can perhaps imagine stone faces passing in and out of visibility in the flames of flickering lamps and candles, with bones and skulls likewise becoming animated. The sound of drums, flutes, and chanting echoed around the chambers. Sleep and food deprivation may have preceded trance drumming as the hallucinogens 'kicked in'. Devereux illustrates the scene further: '… environments bathed in supernatural light, their perimeters extended to infinity, and filled with colourful processions of spirits, exotic perfumes and the sounds of other worlds' (Devereux 1997, p. 58).

Some of the activities may not have been so dramatic, however. One ancient means of divination is that of dream sleep, whereby a shaman or oracle seeks messages and inspiration through dreams. Several Greek and Roman temples were places where people undertook dream incubation. In the Old Testament, Jacob rested his head on a 'sacred stone', the ladder ascending to Heaven appearing in a vision. In Islam, pilgrims sleep in the shrine of St George, Cairo, for curative purposes. Although chanting and drumming were important, being still in the dark and deep silences may also have played a part inside WKLB. I can vouch that this can still be true today.

In his excellent new book on prehistoric spiritual practices, Mike Williams paints a dramatic and colourful portrait of shamanic ritual at a passage grave: 'We stand at the entrance to a large tomb. The stones that form the threshold are massive and provide an eerie presence in the flickering torchlight...' He then describes how an old male shaman enters the tomb, following the ingestion of hallucinogens, with drumming echoing around from younger men outside. He emerges from the tomb, '... his arms filled with bones... and he jabbers incoherently at the small group of mourners about us. He then disappears from sight, swallowed up completely by the tomb. It will be some time before he emerges and we wait, in awe of his powers' (Williams 2010, p. 111).

Members of the Neolithic community feast under the stars outside West Kennet Long Barrow, as part of ancestral celebrations. (Mannequins from Kent's Cave.)

Inside WKLB was the domain of the shaman. I think that perhaps most Neolithic visitors would not have even wanted to venture into the darkest depths of the barrow, as it would have been darker and more foreboding than today, even during daylight hours. Try covering up the skylight and entering the west chamber on an overcast day, and you will see what I mean! To most clan members, '... the monument was something to be *seen* rather than entered...' (Trubshaw 2005, p. 144).

Bones were particularly jumbled in the SE chamber, nearer the entrance, inviting the possibility that bones were thrown into the darkness of the chamber from outside by relatives of the deceased. Again, only the shamans would have had the knowledge, permission, and perhaps the courage, to venture deeper within. Speaking of WKLB, archaeologist Nicholas Thomas commented, '... it is not difficult to imagine the elaborate ritual – feasting, dancing and chanting – not to speak of the sense of awe, with which each burial would have been accompanied' (Thomas 1976, p. 16). Interment, or indeed childbirth, would have been a time of gathering, when the families of the extended clan would meet and celebrate with wonder and gratitude for a passing or a birth. Today, a wake is often held following a funeral, with cups of tea and cucumber sandwiches: this is a social event that is an important part of modern funerary custom.

So, after the shaman had travelled to meet the ancestors (in trance or dream sleep), he or she would emerge from the dark interior. Archaeologist Catherine

Tuck comments on exiting from the interior: 'After spending some time within the sombre, airless confines of the chamber, to emerge from the passageway into the light and warmth outside is like experiencing birth itself… community members five thousand years ago surely had exactly the same feeling as they stepped out once more into the Sun' (Tuck 2003, p. 54). The shaman may have been greeted by waiting clan members, who, as the wise one spoke, would have been hanging on their every word.

I often feel as if I too am being born again as I leave the dark of the chambers and step out into the light of day. The effect is sometimes very profound. Perhaps the shamans thousands of years ago may have had even more intense feelings, such as gratitude, even relief: 'I made it back'.

Let There Be Light!

There has been some discussion is to whether, and in what context, fires were ever lit *within* the confines of the barrow. The two excavations did not reveal any burning of the stones, nor any deposits of soot on the capstones. I frequently find myself wiping off black deposits from stones today as a result of thoughtless positioning of candles and nightlights; it seems unlikely then that full-scale fires would not have left any evidence. There is also the problem of smoke when fires are lit in such enclosed spaces. Piggott records that, 'Although burnt fragments of bone were relatively common, and other *signs* of burning and fire, no fire had been made within the tomb at any stage of the filling'. This suggests that bones had been burnt outside the barrow, perhaps as part of funerary rites, and then deposited or thrown into the interior. The charred bones found at WKLB may be due to, '… being returned to, and temporarily removed from, monuments for involvement in rituals' (Smith & Brickley 2009, p. 60). They may have been either charred as a purification ritual or accidentally during ceremonies.

Although there is no evidence that open fires were ever lit *within* WKLB, even

Above: scallop shells had a variety of uses, such as for lamps and receptacles for holding ochre dyes. Right: A demonstration in Kent's Cave of how scallop shells filled with dried moss and animal fat produce a bright and long-lasting light.

though some evidence of internal fires exists elsewhere, such as the Neolithic sites at Notgrove, Hazleton North and Luckington. There is also evidence of fires in the forecourt of Nympsfield long barrow, in the Cotswolds.

Although no fires appear to have been lit on the *floors* of the chambers of WKLB in ancient times, this does not mean the interior was never illuminated.

For instance, lamps can be made from broad seashells, such as oysters and scallops. On a visit to Kent's Cave, Devon, the guide held up a scallop shell and on it placed a small amount of dried moss and fat. She then extinguished the electric lighting and set fire to the moss; the flames were amazingly bright.

Another possibility is that small cups for holding grease or oil may have been used. A Neolithic site at Pewsey included 'chalk cups'. Similar ones found at Cissbury in Sussex (shown here) were definitely burnt: a description of the display states:

Neolithic chalk cup, which may have been used as a lamp. (On display in Devizes Museum.)

'They might have been used as oil or grease-burning lamps' (from label of finds in Devizes Museum). Chalk cups were found at Windmill Hill, as well as oyster shells. Aubrey Burl considers these cups to be too small and too fragile to have been used for lamps (Burl 2002, p. 116), but I do not dismiss this use so easily.

As the Kent's Cave demonstration proved, size is not important, the efficiency of the material being burnt being the critical factor.

Flint knapper Will Lord has also informed me that oyster and scallop shells were also used in ancient times as receptacles for ochre, the natural dye used for decorative body paint, for both the living and the dead.

Light, from any source, illuminates. During a site visit on August 1, 2010, drumming, chanting and 'tuning in' by a group

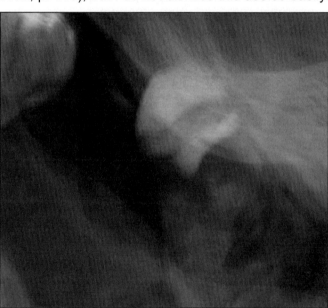

Incense smoke and a face with a 'beak', caught inside WKLB. Surreal scenes such as this may have been significant to ancient shamans.

was preceded by shaman Heather Heaton smudging the interior using smoking sage. Soon afterwards, flash photography caught the resultant thin intermingling wisps and filaments of smoke. The example shown above also reveals a beaked face (on stone 12). Effects such as this would not have gone unnoticed. Did shamans see similar spectacles as messages from the gods, or perhaps even interpret them during divination?

The most profound lights to illuminate the inside of the barrow were of course that of the Sun and Moon. At certain times of the year their light entered the west chamber, and even the side chambers received their fair share, as they still do today. We shall look more into this aspect in Chapter 15.

The Symbolism of Animals

Excavations of the chambers and passage by Thurnam and Piggott revealed the remains of roe deer, red deer, horse, badger, pig, sheep, goat, dog, jackdaw, blackbird, and probably wolf. It is possible that at least some of these assemblages were totem animals of clans or individuals (Burl 2002, p. 103), or at the very least were elements of ritual. Chris Tilley sees *particular* monuments and *particular* domesticated animals as having social identities to clans, and that the burial of these animals at a monument incorporates these things together (Tilley 2007, p. 343).

I have suggested elsewhere, in my novel *Thirteen Moons,* that the totem animals of tribal cultures are primarily animals and birds that were either still living in their area, or had been previously: 'Choosing indigenous totems, ones that belong here, shows you are connecting to your ancestors and the ancient spirit of this Land… the object of this exercise is for people to connect with their native landscapes' (Knight 2007, p. 137-138).

Horned Animals

Cattle, and oxen in particular, seem to have been of vital importance to the clans of WKLB. After all, the beast pulls the plough, it breeds to increase the herd, and its horns symbolise power and fertility; this was certainly the case with other prehistoric bull cults around the world, famously with the Minoans. I have recently seen the images of two bulls carved on the walls at the temple at Tarxien, Malta (see image p. 132 - inset). Some cultures today still carry out bull sacrifice, such as on Madagascar. Oxen (which are often castrated bulls) also have a long history connected with prophecy.

In Neolithic Wiltshire there existed a close association on a deeper level between people and cattle, '… evident in the special treatment often afforded to cattle bone upon deposition' (Pollard & Reynolds 2002, p. 43). Ox bones are often found in long barrows. Those at Horslip, South Street, West Woods, and Beckhampton Firs did not contain any human burial remains, but did contain votive offerings that included ox horns and deer antlers. Ox skulls were ritually left at other Wiltshire long barrows, such as at Sherrington and Manton.

At Windmill Hill, the greatest number of animal bones found were cattle, in numbers that suggest more than mere consumption was involved. Pollard and Reynolds suggest that, '… forest animals were being identified with, or as, spirits, carrying a close association with the human dead and a certain kind of ancestor … animals were thought of as more than just resources' (Pollard & Reynolds 2002. p. 44). Regarding WKLB, large ox bones were noted by Thurnam in his excavations of the west chamber, and Piggott found more, some perforated, in the other chambers. The bones were not evenly distributed either; the NE chamber contained the largest number, greater in fact than any other animal. It was this chamber that contained the highest number of elders, suggesting some association. Fragments of ox skulls and mandibles were over-represented in WKLB, these being most favoured in ritual it would seem. It has already been described how the plan of WKLB can be seen as a horned bull (see image p. 92).

This invites a link with the constellation of Taurus, the Bull: It is, '… reminiscent of old cults that would have seen the dawn or evening rising of stars within the Taurian cluster as heralding the spring or autumn respectively, and adjusted their lives in the appropriate way' (Richardson 2001). Goddess priestess and

My impression of a young woman, carrying an ox skull, entering the inky blackness of WKLB during her rite of passage. This may have been a traumatic experience.

author Kathy Jones also comments that, '…magnificent stones were placed across the front of the ox-horned forecourt' (Jones 1994). Michael Dames, too, sees the 'Divine Ox' symbolism at the barrow (Dames 2010, p. 102). He sees two of the blocking stones as representing a bull. Are they pulling the plough, he asks, represented by the long mound of WKLB?

We shall return to the symbolism of the WKLB megaliths soon. Some of the pierced ox bones found inside WKLB may have been used as simple flutes or whistles (see Chapter 10).

Sheep were also well represented inside WKLB. Most were disarticulated and probably the result of feasting. Nevertheless, they were thought valuable in a ritual sense to be left inside with the ancestors. An exception to this was an almost complete skeleton of a sheep found in the secondary layers in the NW chamber: 'This animal must have been introduced into the tomb in a fleshed condition well before the blocking... it seems unlikely that the animal crawled in by itself to die' (Thomas & Whittle 1986, p. 147). A sacrifice to 'the gods' seems possible, or perhaps it was left as food for an ancestor's consumption in the afterlife.

Deer

The deer is another animal held in special esteem by our Neolithic clan at WKLB. Red Deer and Roe Deer were both indigenous to the area at that time, and were somewhat larger than their equivalent today. Both species are also well represented in the finds at Windmill Hill. Roebuck antlers were found by Thurnam in the west chamber of WKLB, and also by Piggott at the entrance to the NE chamber. Unlike other deer, roebuck grow antlers through autumn into winter. This may explain their presence in a 'Winter Hag tomb'.

Shamans adorned antler-clad headdresses to contact the spirits of herds for hunting and divination. Skeletons with antlers resting on their skull or shoulders have been found in Wessex barrows, and it has been suggested that deer were even captured and farmed for their antlers (North 1996, p. 5).

Also, John Thurnam found boar tusks in the west chamber. Reverence of horned animals and horned archetypes was to continue in much later times,

Above: Man has had a long spiritual relationship with deer. Right: Old drawing of a Siberia shaman with deer antlers, beating his drum as part of his trance ritual.

expressed as Pan, Cernunnos, Dionysos, Herne the Hunter, the Minotaur, Thoth, and a host of others. Druids wrapped themselves in the hide of a bull for divination and seership rituals, similar to those carried out by Native Americans with bison (Knight 1998, p. 81-82). Horned beasts represent the male, yang energy and male Divinity, to balance the yin, female aspect of the Goddess, the Earth Mother.

This spiritual marriage of yin and yang, male and female, was perhaps further expressed in the west chamber, the heart of the womb, where, next to an antler, Thurnam found a rib lying between two chalk ball-like sarsen nodules –

The roe deer antler found at the entrance to the NE chamber during Piggott's excavations. (After Piggott.)

perhaps representing the phallus and the testes.

I was particularly interested in seeing both deer and possibly the wolf mentioned in the excavations at WKLB. These are my two totem animals. The story of my connection with these is told fully in my novel *Thirteen Moons – Conversations with the Goddess* (Knight 2007 & 2010 ed.).

It is perhaps worth noting that Lapland shamans give their reindeer the fungi Fly Agaric and then drink the animal's urine, which increases its potency as a hallucinogen. It makes me wonder if Neolithic shamans were doing a similar thing here, with domesticated cattle, sheep and even captured deer. This would be an additional explanation as to why these creatures were venerated.

Shells

Ornaments convey aspects of ourselves, often showing who we are, and what we are 'into'. Pendants made from perforated shells were found inside WKLB, most of which were marine gastropods, presumably brought east from the Severn estuary or north from the Solent: *Nucella lapillis* and the whorled whelk

Perforated shells and beads unearthed inside WKLB. (On display in Devizes Museum.)

Nassarius reticularis are represented, and the cowrie *Cypraea,* which was perforated twice. There was also a small spiral pendant made from the periwinkle *Littorina littorea,* and tiny tusk-shaped *Dentaliurn.* Some of these are displayed in Devizes Museum (image left). Terence Meaden sees these as examples of the spiral as a Goddess symbol, which is widespread across the ancient world: 'The followers of the Cult of the Goddess worshipped every manifestation of the spiral

– her epitome – in Nature and art' (Meaden 1991, p. 152-161). He also reminds us of the auditory effects experienced when a spiralled gastropod shell is held to the ear: 'I can hear the sea' is one exclamation children give about this effect. Meaden comments that this adds to the symbolism of birth and death, as one hears, '... the sound of the creative breath' (Meaden 1991, p. 155).

Inverted pot P12 from WKLB, showing how, according to Dames, it resembles both a skull and Silbury Hill. (On display in Devizes Museum.)

The Symbolism of Pottery

Neolithic pots had sacred as well as mundane meaning: 'The production of a pot was regarded as a spiritual as well as a manufacturing art' (Meaden 1991, p. 196). The total number of sherds (fragments) found in WKLB was in excess of 850 (Thomas & Whittle 1986, p. 144), representing at least 250 individual vessels, although an accurate total cannot be assured. You may remember that the sherds were not randomly spread throughout each chamber, implying conscious selection of decoration and shape. It is suggested that although this may be due to chronology, specific meanings of pot decoration and style related to differences in age or sex of the human bones, or other criteria (Thomas & Whittle 1986, p. 144). Pot smashing may be indicative of the cycles of life and death; a pot is born from the earth, like people, so perhaps the breaking and scattering was mirroring the scattering of the human bones.

Close-up of bell beaker B8 found in NW chamber, showing geometric designs. (Also see image p. 73.)

Michael Dames makes a comparison between the shape of some of the late Neolithic pots found in WKLB and that of Silbury Hill. When these round-bottomed pots are inverted it has to be admitted that they do resemble the mound. Indeed, the pots were deliberately broken and scattered around the chambers around the time Silbury was constructed. Dames also notes the similarity in shape of some of the rounded pots and the human skull, suggesting that drinking from such an inverted pot may have been a ritual to ensure health, the skull being, '…the most evocative container'. A tradition of drinking from skulls persists to this day. Indenting made by grains, and 'plough furrow' marks, adorn these pots, which may well have been ritualistic, magic vessels, a '… forerunner of the Iron Age magic cauldron, and the medieval Holy Grail' (Dames 1977, p. 47-52). Pottery ornamentation was not merely decorative; it was imbued with sacred meaning.

This links us with the famous bell beaker from WKLB. The pot in question was designated B8 by Piggott, and was found nearly complete in the uppermost layers of the secondary deposits of the NW chamber, close to the capstone. Interestingly, it had been carefully placed upside-down. This style of pottery is typical of the later-Neolithic, becoming common by 2500 BC. By this time most pots were *not* being broken, as they had been before, possibly because they were too valuable. B8 measures 20cm (8ins.) tall and is 17.5cm (7ins.) wide across the lip. Terence Meaden sees the pot as '… a holy vessel, rich in expressive ornament' (Meaden 1991, p. 195). He regards the ornamentation as expressions of the Goddess; the lozenges or diamonds represent the fertility powers of the Goddess; the zigzag motifs representing lightning; the sloping lines representing rain and fertilising waters; the background of horizontal lines being the lower regions of the waters, such as springs and lakes; 'The whole is a sacred vessel decorated to the glory of the chief divinity of the age – the fully fecund Great Goddess' (Meaden 1991, p. 198). Lozenges and diamonds are widespread motifs of the Neolithic and Bronze Age; an incredible gold lozenge/diamond-shaped breastplate was found at Bush Barrow, near Stonehenge. It may also be that lozenges were amongst symbols observed during shamanic trance, and later immortalised on pottery.

Elaborate decoration such as this is more common on the Continent. However, an 'incense cup' found in a round barrow at Woodyates, North Dorset, was also inscribed with lozenges/diamonds. The design occurs on pots in Brittany, accompanied again by sloping lines and zig-zags; I have seen for myself lozenges and zigzag lines carved on the megaliths of the Neolithic complex in the Boyne Valley, Ireland, on kerbstones at Newgrange and Knowth, and at Fourknocks (see Brennan 1994). On Anglesey, one stone in the chambers of Barclodiad Y Gawres is decorated with lozenges (Meaden 1991, p. 127-28). It is of note that at the Brittany passage grave of Gavrinis, dated 3500 BC, some of the decorated pottery contained traces of cannabis. The chamber stones of Gavrinis are decorated with abstract 'trippy' images, possible records of trance journeying.

The Flint Stones

Many fashioned flints were found scattered around the interior of WKLB. As well as being useful and vital tools, flints may also have had mythic and spiritual meaning: 'Inscribed with rich biographies, axes helped define relations between people and the ancestral world' (Edmunds, 1999, p. 42). Particularly finely crafted, polished flint axes and arrowheads may have been, '… emblems of position and identity' (Pollard 1997, p. 21). The WKLB flints included 125 flakes, four scrapers, an awl (hole puncher) and a leaf-shaped arrowhead. In 1859, John Thurnam made special mention of a particularly skillfully worked flint (see figure below and front cover). He saw this flint as, '… a beautiful thin ovoidal knife, three and a half inches long, which may have been used for flaying the animals slaughtered for the funeral feast' (Thurnam 1860). Michael Dames has also recently suggested that the flint is ritualistic, '… a possible flint image of the hooded winter Hag' (Dames 1977, p. 34). The flint certainly has the hint of facial features on the upper left-hand side. I D Wakefield saw a similarity between the shape of this flint and the form of the *Silbury Water Meadow Hag,* a simulacrum defined by fields, topography, and a river (Wakefield 1999, p. 59). Chris Tilley has recently suggested that natural flint simulacra found casually on the land by Neolithic farmers may have been collected and deposited at sacred sites as spiritual artefacts (Tilley 2007, p. 339-342).

A very poignant discovery was made in the west chamber by Thurnam. The skull of the one year-old found against the west wall was accompanied by three delicate flint flakes, one of which was transparent. Language and sentiments do not fossilize, so we can but guess at the emotions going through the minds of those who left the skull of this child, and the flints, inside the chamber's dark depths.

Flint tool, possibly representing a left-facing 'hooded winter Hag'. (After Thurnam.)

The Times They Are a Changin'

Even in the late Neolithic, bones were still being taken out of the chambers. For instance, a male femur taken from the SE chamber was left in the forecourt. The articulated skeletons of WKLB were part of the primary burials, whereas the disarticulated, jumbled bones (and cremations in the NE chamber) of the secondary deposits signal a change in practice and belief.

Thomas and Whittle also discuss why the monument's use lapsed in the later Neolithic after a thousand years of 'on and off' use. It is possible, they say, that after this length of time the living could no longer associate with such distant relatives, of whom they had no personal knowledge: 'Group rituals thus ceased to be concerned with unity with the ancestors, and became concerned with respect for the past' (Thomas & Whittle 1986, p. 139). It has been proposed that by the later Neolithic the focus had turned towards the memory of particular *living* people, their material wealth, and perhaps individual achievements during their lifetime (Pollard 1997, p. 56). Gone were the days when 'anonymous ancestors' were paramount. As time progressed, the number of burials in most long barrows fell dramatically, often to a mere one or two, and this trend was to continue into the Bronze Age with the Beaker round barrows. This may be further proof that an age of hierarchy, ego and 'grandiose' chieftains had arrived.

The latter period of West Kennet marks a transition from the old to the new, from the outmoded to the newly fashionable - the meaning of the barrow became very different. People were perpetuating the memory of the dead by scattering into the chambers token votive offerings from feasts: '.... The remains of the ancestral departed are overtly connected with the remains of fires and feasting' (Thomas 1991, p.76). The ancestors within the chambers were now less accessible as, *over several centuries,* the infilling took place. Was this a sign of final protection of the ancestors within, or the rejection of them, the closing of a barrow that had lost its meaning? This we may never know: 'It remains to be established whether this was final protection for the ancestors of a still dominant group, or the closing down of a redundant monument... ' (Thomas & Whittle 1986, p. 153). Dames sees the infilling as an act of, 'protective reverence' to the ancestors who had, after all, given the people farming, weaving and pottery (Dames 2010, p. 102). Perhaps the slow filling of WKLB even replicated the silting up of a stream or river as it nears the end of its life.

The final sealing of the tomb occurred as Silbury Hill came into use, which may indicate a symbolic connection. Layering of organic material and chalk was used in both monuments, perhaps to ensure a continuity of purpose and symbolism. Stone 45 was erected to mark 'closure' of WKLB, entombing its bones, flint and pottery for the next 4000 years. It has been suggested that such blocking stones were intended as 'spirit traps', preventing spirits from leaving and entering. The result was that the womb was closed, the birthing Goddess made barren, her uterus blocked.

This final 'closure' of the monument had been more gradual than Piggott had thought, and the site remained important: '... West Kennet was a focus of interest throughout the Later Neolithic... the tomb was finally blocked in the period that saw the elaboration of the major monuments of Avebury and Silbury Hill' (Thomas & Whittle 1986, p. 153).

WKLB may have fell into disuse because of social change. Ancestral places were being replaced by huge monuments, such as Avebury, Stonehenge, and Silbury Hill. The 'new elite' may have abandoned the ancestral places for their new exotic

Stone 45 marked the final phase of WKLB in the Later-Neolithic.

Beakers and other prestige goods. Group solidarity was now being expressed in terms of massive monuments and huge megaliths. These projects involved the whole community, controlled by a well-structured hierarchical system. Perhaps the new tribal leaders held power over an increasing population through these grandiose undertakings of monument construction; no more solitary shaman in dark chambers.

Yet the stones and mound remained prominent on the landscape: 'Long after the tomb ceased to be used for burial, it must have continued to function as a focal point… for us today it is hard to envisage such loyal devotion to a low ridge of earth and stone, but that is only because we are ignorant of the beliefs perceived by those who revered it' (North 1996, p. 77-78).

Many centuries later six Roman bronze coins were left near the blocking stones, possibly for later recovery. Pollard and Reynolds (2002) raise the issue that they may have been votive offerings, left at a place the Romans recognised as an ancestral resting place, a place of the gods, perhaps even an oracle locality.

During our drumming evenings at WKLB, I guide groups into the chambers to get a brief, if much diluted, version of what went on thousands of years ago. Even without psychoactive substances, the participants co-create an atmosphere, a group energy, a bonding; and they are also partaking in theatre, they are performers, just as the shamans once were. Those attending often feel 'heady', from effects of drumming and chanting in an enclosed space. This can often be powerfully felt and can initiate visions, cause upwellings of emotion, and connections with other realms. We call to the ancestors once more, and in doing so may glimpse the dark regions of our own inner being. The following words mirror those souls who, long ago, ventured into the dark recesses of WKLB, as they took their own leap of faith:

'Come to the edge, he said. We are afraid, they said.
Come to the edge, he said. They came to the edge.
He pushed them off… and they flew'
(Guillaume Apollinaire)

Chapter 10.
Acoustics and Sacred Sound

'The hills are alive with the sound of music.'
(Rogers and Hammerstein)

Until recent years, archaeologists had paid scant attention to the role sound and acoustics may have played in the design and use of Neolithic monuments. Paul Devereux helped redress the situation, kick-starting a wider and livelier debate in the subject with his seminal book, *Stone Age Soundtracks* (Devereux 2001). He demonstrated how prehistoric caves, tombs, hypogea and other enclosed monuments have powerful acoustic properties, which may have originally enhanced experiences in such places. Since then, several archaeological studies have been undertaken, some of which are still ongoing, to ascertain the acoustic properties of Neolithic chambered sites, and the effects of acoustically designed monuments on their users. As today, sound was important: 'It seems unlikely that the world was silent in prehistory. Sound was present in all aspects of peoples' lives - from speech to the manufacture of stone tools' (Watson & Keating 1999).

During my drumming and chanting sessions inside WKLB, people often comment how the sounds of a particular drum or flute vary when played in different chambers, and even in different parts of the same chamber. I cannot believe that Neolithic people designed WKLB to be acoustically resonant for the dead! So was it for the living? Let us first look more closely into sacred sound, how it can be produced, and to what end.

The Human Experience of Sound
Sound has probably played an important role in Mankind's ritual and spiritual activities for thousands of years. Even on a mundane level, prehistoric hunters used sound to great effect when hunting game, especially as they listened for noises made by their prey; the sounds of Nature would have been appreciated, imitated, and sometimes feared – a rumble of thunder or the howl of wolves in the distance; but also the rushing of a life-giving river. Speech was borne out of a desire to verbally communicate with our peers, such as when we first stood up on two legs and romantically cried out 'Ug!' to a potential mate!

114

Regarding the creation of sound vocally, the pitch of human speech is at present generally 110-130hz for males, and around 200-230hz for females. Children speak at a much higher pitch, about 300hz. Singing can of course produce a great variety of pitches. People of the Neolithic were, on average, slightly smaller than today, so it may be their the pitch was also higher.

In terms of receiving sound, different frequencies can activate or switch off different parts of the brain. Paul Devereux has remarked how at 110hz activity in the left hemisphere of the brain (the 'logical' side) reduces, and by 130hz it returns to normal (Devereux 2010).

The sounds produced by musical instruments not only have aesthetic effects, but also have an impact on bodily senses and functions (Needham 1967, p. 610). Some very low and very high frequencies, such as those of dog whistles and bat clicks, are beyond the range of the human ear. But that does not mean that such 'infrasound' and 'ultrasound' does not have an influence on the human brain, and indeed other parts of the body.

Recent evidence suggests that drumming may improve the immune system and may have psychological benefits (Williams 2010, p. 36).

Stone Age Soundscapes

Research suggests that people were hitting rocks and flints to produce sound way back in the Palaeolithic, long before WKLB. According to Riaan Rifkin, rock gongs were used at prehistoric sites in South Africa (see *Antiquity*, Vol 83, 2009, p. 585-601). In certain African cultures today it is believed that spirits are released when standing stones and rocks are struck. At Deccan, in India, stone outcrops covered in petroglyphs give out sounds like a gong or bell when struck (Devereux 2010).

At the autumn 2010 *'Stars and Stones Forum'*, near Bury St Edmunds, master flint knapper Will Lord demonstrated how sounds produced as flint is struck, during knapping, get progressively higher in pitch as the fragments get smaller. It made me wonder whether or not flints may have been used as sound producers back in the Neolithic. Many flints, of various sizes and designs, were found during the excavations inside WKLB. Were some of these struck for acoustic effect?

Cymatics is the study of waveforms, and research has shown how sand grains on a taught membrane will create patterns when music and sonic noises are played. Many of the resultant patterns, such as spirals, geometrical shapes and crosses, are seen in Nature, such as in snowflakes, seashells, and starfish. Sound vibrations are actually the creative force of Nature. Knowledge of acoustics may have helped shamans connect with the vibrations of the Universe.

Quartz seems to have ultrasound properties, as well as pulsing/vibrational qualities, which make it valuable in modern industry and science. Interestingly, the sarsens of WKLB are composed of silica, the base component of quartz. Although their individual grains are very small to the naked eye, the megaliths of WKLB could be regarded as gigantic quartz crystals! The dense nature of these stones means that they reflect, rather than absorb, sound.

Left: The Neolithic chambers of the Hal Saflieni Hypogeum, Malta, which have notable acoustic properties. Right: The interior of Newgrange, Ireland, where a corbelled roof and narrow passage influence the acoustic resonances of the monument.

Curvature helps focus sound, notably demonstrated at the Hypogeum and temple complexes in Malta. At Stonehenge, several of the sarsens are concave on their inner faces, possibly to focus the sound of a drum or chanting shaman. Crescental forecourts at the entrance of many passage graves may have been amphitheatres, to focus and enhance the sound produced by participants during ritual. I believe that corbelled roofing, seen at Newgrange and on Minoan Crete, as well as here at WKLB, was designed to hold and reverberate sound - it was like being inside a giant bell!

In 1994, the P.E.A.R. Group, directed by physicist Dr. Robert Jahn, set out to test acoustic resonance and standing wave behaviour at megalithic sites, such as Newgrange and Wayland's Smithy. Jahn found that these ancient chambers sustained a strong resonance at the 95 - 120hz frequencies, which is well within the human vocal range. In subsequent testing, stone rooms in ancient temples in Malta were found to match the same resonances, registering at the frequency of 110 or 111hz. Victor Reijs has recently found similar results on two other Irish tombs. This turns out to be a significant level for human brain activity and receptivity. Whether it was deliberate or not, the people who spent time in such settings would have noticed these vibrations impacting on their minds, quietening the logical aspects of the brain.

Similar effects were recorded in the Hal Saflieni Hypogeum in Malta. Work by the Old Temples Study Foundation (OTSF) suggests that sound and a desire to harness its effects may have been just as important as vision in the design of the temples in Malta: 'We may be hitting on one of those 'lost secrets',' says Linda Eneix, President of the OTSF. Science Officer at the Hypogeum, Joseph Farrugia, describes unusual sound effects: "There is a small niche in what we

116

call 'The Oracle Chamber', and if someone with a deep voice speaks inside, the voice echoes all over the hypogeum. The resonance in the ancient temple is something exceptional. You can hear the voice rumbling all over'. As anyone who sings in the shower knows, sound echoing back from tiled walls can be amplified and can produce unusual effects. This is magnified several times in stone chambers: 'Standing in the Hypogeum is like being inside a giant bell,' says Eneix. 'You feel the sound in your bones as much as you hear it with your ears. It's really thrilling!' (OTSF website).

On a recent visit to the Hypogeum with a private party, we let our guide go off for a coffee, and members of our group chanted and overtoned inside the resonant underground chambers, accompanied by my drumming. The sound and echoes produced were incredibly powerful. Referring to the Hypogeum, Paul Devereux has noted that, '... some echoes produced could be heard for 25-30 seconds', and that the site is, 'acoustically remarkable' (Devereux 2010). Jennifer Berezen recorded her emotive album *Returning* in the Hypogeum; this song is chanted at the end of all our evenings at WKLB.

Further work by Devereux and Jahn on Neolithic underground chambers suggests that deep male chanting may have taken place within these places (Devereux & Jahn 1999, p. 666). Other acoustic studies have come to similar conclusions (Watson & Keating, 1999). Of course, one could speculate that deep-chanting *women* or even musical instruments, such as large, deep drums, could produce sounds of that frequency range. We shall return to the issue of drums shortly.

An ongoing research venture, The *Landscape and Perception Project*, is being coordinated by Paul Devereux, as more acoustic work on sacred sites is being undertaken. As part of this work, Devereux has demonstrated the acoustic properties of the Bluestones at their outcrop in the Preseli Mountains. When struck by a small 'hammer stone', some rocks issue a clang, like a bell. This makes me wonder about WKLB. Some of the primary skeletons were overlaid with flat slabs of stone, which were balanced on the bones. Were these simply to protect them, or were they also there for their acoustic properties? Were they struck to create sound - messages for the ancestors? Food for thought.

The Acoustics of WKLB
Despite positive results on the acoustics of other Neolithic sites, we have problems in applying scientific, acoustical studies to WKLB. Here, the internal structure is not as it originally was, and therefore, the acoustic properties cannot be as they once were. For instance, the capstone of the SE chamber was dragged away prior to the 1955 excavation, and was reinstated by Piggott. With all due respect to him and his team, I very much doubt if they will have placed it in *exactly* the same position it was in 5,500 yrs ago. Also, one of the capstones in the west chamber is absent altogether, its place being taken by a hideous concrete roof with skylights. In 1859 John Thurnam measured the height of the west chamber as being, '...seven feet nine inches in clear height', which is much less than the height of the skylight today. The original, more enclosed, space would have further enhanced its acoustic properties. Another

skylight was also installed near the east end of the passage. So this leaves only the NE, NW and SW chambers in anything like their original state. Even potential acoustic surveys in these may be fraught with difficulty because of 'seepage' of sound waves, out through the entrance, the lintel of which was raised slightly by Piggott, or through the glass of the three skylights, which were certainly not designed with acoustics in mind!

I believe that the passage and chambers of WKLB *were* designed to achieve an interface between participants and the properties of sacred sound, the main motivation being to initiate trance. Drumming, chanting, singing and wind instruments may also have been used inside WKLB, in conjunction with the ingestion of hallucinogens, to help achieve 'out-of-body' experiences. In an article in *Archaeology Today* (2001), archaeologist Aaron Watson considered that, '… many Neolithic monuments possess unusual acoustic properties that give sound strange, otherworldly aspects. We cannot be sure that acoustic properties were exploited thousands of years ago, but it seems highly likely that they were'.

WKLB Hot Spots

Acoustic 'hot spots' have been noted in relation to rock art sites in North America, Australia, and Western Europe (Devereux & Jahn 1996, p. 665), and in Scottish passage graves (Watson & Keating 1999).

I have found similar acoustic 'hot spots' inside WKLB, which I believe may have been exploited by our shamans. I suspect that these occur where *standing waves* are produced; these are caused when waves of sound from a source are reflected back from an object and interfere with them, making them appear stationary, in effect cancelling them out. These manifest as areas of high or low volume, and have already been identified in other Neolithic chambered sites, such as at Newgrange. The most profound, consistent, and powerful hot spot in WKLB is immediately in front of stone 22, the 'Skull Stone' (see image below & p. 136). This stone is very smooth and rich in iron, and even when speaking in front of it one's voice goes 'deeper', and a brief echo can often ensue. But when a shamanic drum is used here, the effects are startling. The drum goes louder, deeper and richer in tone. On our drumming evenings I tell people to take turns in spending time in front of this stone, to experience the changes in the human voice and of the drum.

On my day tours I sometimes ask people to stand in the corner of the west chamber, between the 'Skull Stone' and stone 23, whilst I drum up and down them with my shamanic frame drum, interacting with their aura and chakras. Frequently, those on the 'receiving end' tell me they felt the vibrations passing through their clothing and pulsating through their body. Sometimes, they can shake uncontrollably, and even have muscle spasms. David Griffiths, from New South Wales, Australia, told me, 'I felt the drum beat hitting the front of my body and penetrating within. I felt pulsing inside my body'. His partner, Cheryl, '… saw spirals while Peter drummed up and down my body, I was inside a fine gold coil or spiral, which was energetic and alive… and gold spheres floating within the spiral'. Interestingly, the sound of my drum can actually vary depending on the individual recipient. Sufi teacher and mystic Haxrat Inayat Khan wrote how sound and drumming can physically effect people, '... sound has an effect on each atom of the body... the sound of the drum goes directly into their whole system, bringing it to a certain pitch' (Khan 1996).

A phenomena I have noted several times is that when I beat my shamanic drum in front of stone 22, an 'overtone' is produced, a simultaneous background note of higher pitch. Several other people have heard this. I bring this to your attention because although I have played my drum at ancient sites across Europe and the USA, WKLB is the **only** place where my drum 'overtones' in this way.

This 'hot spot' was also experienced independently by American sound healer Susan Elizabeth Hale. When a male companion stood between stones 21 and 22 and sounded a vocal bass note, she experienced the following: 'I

The author drumming in front of stone 22, with stone 23 to the right. This is an acoustic 'hot spot' in the west chamber of WKLB.

heard overtones emanating from his low drone. Coming from different places... I could not locate the source of the sound. His voice filled the chamber in an unusual way, now here, now there... in front of me then far away, disappearing and then reappearing' (Hale 2007, p. 62). She has also informed me that a combination of male and female chanting might have been used, '... to commune with the ancestors and enchant the land' (pers. comm. 2010). I plan to work with Susan inside WKLB during her 2011 visit to the UK.

On a site visit in 2010, dowser Maria Wheatley expressed to me her view that the corbelled 'beehive' roofing of the west chamber enhanced the acoustics, as well as channelling a rising energy vortex. The 'beehive' structure at Carn Euny, Cornwall, resonates at 99hz, and Paul Devereux has noted the peculiar sound qualities of the beehive-shaped Greek mausoleum at Artreus, which he thought might have been an oracle chamber (Devereux 2010). On a visit to the

Neolithic sacred well of Santa Cristina, in Sardinia, I experienced the powerful acoustic properties of its corbelled, beehive-shaped structure.

Concerning WKLB, Maria also confirmed, without prompting, another acoustic hot spot I had found previously in the passage between stones 18 and 25, where a 'richer' sound is often experienced. Author and researcher Jackie Queally also experienced this hot spot when she stood there whilst I drummed in front of the 'Skull Stone'. So this particular hot spot is active not just for a drummer or chanter standing there, but also for a *receiver/listener*, even when the sound source is elsewhere.

In the corner of the SE chamber, in front of stones 9 and 10, is another such place, although this hot spot is less defined and noticeable than the others, and sometimes may be absent altogether.

During many years of visiting WKLB, I have noticed that drums and voices can be more resonant in damp conditions, or following rainfall. During some dry

The author, Karen James (flute) and didge player Les Miles experience the acoustics of the west chamber, August 2010. (Image: Sue Wallace.)

summer spells, the west chamber can be very 'flat' and quite non-resonant. On May 27, 2010, Sue Wallace and I made a late afternoon site visit. I drummed in front of stone 22, but the drum and the chamber was 'flat', with no pronounced resonance felt or heard. But as night fell and the air cooled and we began to see our breath, the sound became fuller and deeper. An hour after sunset, just after moonrise, my voice and drum both became deeper and 'richer' within the west chamber, and echoes were produced. This happened again on our drumming group night of July 26, 2010, when the acoustics in front of the 'Skull Stone' noticeably improved after the rising of the full Moon. On that occasion, the stone developed condensation, with tiny droplets of water running down its surface. This also enhanced the appearance of the stone as a skull! Another example of this was on the afternoon of Oct 4, 2010, the day after a fierce weather front had crossed the county, bringing with it heavy rainfall; drumming in front of the 'Skull Stone' produced the deepest and loudest sound I had ever experienced inside WKLB, the drum sounding several octaves deeper than normal. Condensation and drips from above were again on the stone, as well as puddles on the chamber floor. When I drummed up and down Sue, she felt very powerful vibrations, resulting in dizziness.

During another full Moon gathering, on Sept 23, 2010, attendee Julie Umpleby had an experience which may have been initiated by drumming: 'When we started drumming I saw a huge serpent emerge through the portal stone [stone 22] that connects with other dimensions. When I placed my forehead on it, I immediately saw a diamond grid network arise from 'far away' in the darkness travelling along a timeline and bringing ancient knowledge and wisdom through'. On the same evening, another of our number, Rick, crouched down and overtoned in between the 'Skull Stone' and the 'Living Head'. The rest of us spontaneously began our own chants, oms, hums, and low toning, accompanied only by a single, quietly beating drum. It was a truly magical moment that affected everyone profoundly. There were three male baritones present, which contrasted and balanced the chanting of the three ladies; what a magical moment in time. Were similar events being played out in WKLB thousands of years ago?

Let us now look at the theories regarding various musical instruments known to have been around in the Neolithic, and their uses and possible effects they may have produced inside chambered monuments.

Drums and Percussion

The use of drums is very ancient. Back in 1912, A E Crawley, wrote: 'The music of the drum is more closely connected with the foundations of orally generated emotion than that of any other instrument. It is complete enough in itself to cover the whole range of human feeling'. Scenes on the ancient walls at Thebes, in Egypt, show drums being used in ceremonies, and they were in use in Europe as long ago as the 5th millennium BC.

Recently, Lynda Aiano (under the Dept of Archaeology, Exeter University) has studied the acoustic properties of Neolithic pottery. Some previous researchers had suggested that people used clay drums, developed in Northern Europe from small pedestal bowls. Aiano identified over 300 pots and sherds that could have been used as drums. These pots are characterised by a goblet-shaped hollow vessel fashioned from clay with lugs around the sides, for tying on laces that held the drum skin taut. She found them to be most common in Germany, Denmark, and Poland (see www.eurorea.net). Of the sixty clay drums that have been found in Germany, about 50% were unearthed at megalithic sites (Devereux 2001). Some pots bearing lugs were excavated at Windmill Hill, and we should not take it for granted that these pots were used merely as cooking vessels.

The British Museum has an exhibit of three elaborately carved 'chalk drums', dated c.2600 – 2000 BC, found in the 19th Century at Folkton Wold, North Yorkshire. They are between 10-15cm high and 8-12cm wide and were found in a round barrow next to a child's skeleton. They are cylinders, with raised central areas at the solid end, decorated with carved eyes, concentric circles, lozenges, spirals, and other geometric designs. Although found with a child, Dr Terence Meaden concludes that, '... these objects are no toys... one might expect such objects to be part of the magical equipment of a religious leader... indicating the importance of the child' (Meaden 1991, p. 143). A recent reappraisal of the objects has concluded that, '... the strongest resemblances, taking the drums as a whole, are to the decoration found on Later Neolithic Grooved Ware pottery. There is a nod in the direction of the geometric decoration on Beaker pottery' (Middleton, Young & Ambers, 2004). Indeed, the lozenges or diamonds on the drums invite comparison with those on beaker B8 at WKLB (see images p. 73 & 109).

Chalk drum found at Folkton Wold in North Yorkshire, with lozenge/diamond decoration.

It was recorded that drumming in the Camster Round tomb (Caithness) could be heard from inside the neighbouring Camster Long, 190m (c.625ft) away. What is interesting is that this was far beyond the point at people *in between* the sites could hear the drumming (Watson & Keating 1999, p. 330). Paul Devereux speculates that this drumming effect could have been regarded as having a supernatural quality, '... perhaps viewed as the movement of spirits from one site to another' (Devereux 2001, p. 99).

Watson and Keating also noted how drummers were affected by certain fast beats, resulting in some of the participants experiencing changes to their speech, breathing, and raised pulse rates. Mike Williams comments that, 'It was drumming that enabled me to enter trance. The regular beat of the drum slowed my brainwave pattern and caused hyper-quiescence' (Williams 2010, p. 33). I can confirm this at WKLB, where I have found that a quite fast beat, around two beats per second, influences me physically. At times I have felt very 'heady', and one has to ask what effects were experienced in here in the Neolithic, when drumming was supplemented with periods of sleep and food deprivation, and the ingestion of hallucinogens!

It is possible, therefore, that chambered 'tombs' may have been designed to heighten the sound of the drum to achieve some exact required frequency; drums and architecture combined to become a tool used by the shamans to help facilitate trance states (see Williams 2010).

On Sept 22, 2010, drumming at WKLB could be heard from Silbury Hill, as well as from the river valley floor between the two sites. On a calm night the sound of a drum can carry for miles, as we communicate with the landscape.

Wind Instruments

One of the most beautiful and evocative sounds I hear inside WKLB is when a flute player joins us for our evening gatherings. The sounds produced by flutes are delicate, pure, and evocative. But is there any evidence that wind instruments were used in the Neolithic and, more to the point, in the vicinity of WKLB?

J V S Megaw has undertaken a study of prehistoric flutes and whistles. The oldest possible flute found so far might be that of a bone perforated by 2 holes unearthed at a Neanderthal site in Slovenia, dated 40,000 years ago. Perforated reindeer phalanges were found in the Upper Palaeolithic deposits of La Madeleine in France (Megaw 1960, p. 8). A 35,000 year-old flute, made of a 20cm (8ins.) long vulture's wing bone with five holes, has recently been unearthed in the Hohle Fels Cavern in SW Germany. From the same site came two fragments of flutes carved from mammoth tusks. Nearer home, cave deposits in Kent's Cave, Devon, yielded a hare's bone perforated with six holes: 'These flutes provide yet more evidence of the sophistication of the people that lived at that time' (Prof Chris Stringer, Natural History Museum).

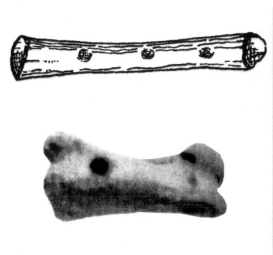

Prehistoric wind instruments. Top left: Bird bone with three holes, found in a barrow in the Avebury area (after Dean Merewether);
Bottom left: Perforated reindeer bone whistle from La Madeleine in France (after Megaw); Right: Ox toe bones from WKLB, at Devizes Museum.

Mesolithic flutes are represented by a long perforated animal bone from the Baltics. Neolithic bone flutes, however, have now been found in China and around Europe, such as in Germany, Poland, and the Baltic States. British finds have been made for some time: Sir Richard Colt Hoare found a carefully smoothed swan or crane tibia with a single finger hole during excavations of the Normanton group of barrows in Wiltshire. In the 19th century, Dean Merewether found another flute (as then unrecognised) in a 'low barrow near Avebury', which was made from a bird bone (Megaw 1960, p. 9).

Megaw stresses the problems in finding the harmonic evolution of bone flutes, as the sounds produced were determined by a great variety of lengths, number of holes, and materials. He also suggests that 'effects' rather than 'music' may have been what were required. Perhaps the objective was to produce noises, strange to our ears, which might have mimicked animals or birds, or else other sounds to enhance trance experiences: 'There is the open question as to what degree music was a matter of purely personal enjoyment; but music has ever accompanied the sacred rites of past recorded times no less than the present' (Megaw 1960, p. 13).

I soon noticed the similarity between the image of the perforated phalanges (toe bones) from La Medeleine and those found by Piggott in the secondary deposits at WKLB (image above, displayed in Devizes Museum). Are we talking here about simple whistles/sound producers? Aubrey Burl comments on six perforated ox toes: 'These finger-long bones had off-centre perforations the thickness of a pencil through them. They may have been whistles to summon up the dead or to comfort them, or perhaps symbolic figurines of Death herself' (Burl 2002, p. 131). He adds that these pierced bones may have been used, '... by witch-doctors'.

So we have the possibility that during the late Neolithic, perforated ox bone 'whistles' were brought into the chambers of WKLB to produce sound, probably by shamans to summon the ancestors. I met post Graduate researcher Claire Marshall at a recent conference. She is currently making faithful replicas of prehistoric musical instruments, and testing their acoustic properties. Regarding replicas she has made of the WKLB perforated ox bones, she informed me that when the holes are blown into, high-pitched sounds around 1700khz is produced, '...inaudible, like a dog-training whistle' (pers. comm.). This range is well above the normal human audibility limit, which is around 20khz (20,000hz). Ultrasound is used today in therapies and in hospitals, such as to scan unborn babies.

At the other end of the scale, at around 2-5hz the effects of 'infrasound' can also affect the human mind and body, such as producing difficulty in speech, chest vibrations, and pressure in the middle ear (Devereux 2001, p. 52). The human ear has a lower limit of perception of around 20hz. It is also worth noting that below 4hz the brain is at the level of Delta Rhythms, associated with both deep sleep and higher levels of consciousness.

Drums may also activate so-called Helmholtz Resonances. These are sounds caused when air blows into, or across, an enclosed space, similar to the effect produced when an empty bottle is faced into a strong wind, or when one blows across the top. Aaron Watson has commented that the Helmholtz effect might be produced as a result of drumming inside chambered barrows, as the air inside expands and pushes out into the passage; between each beat, the air then rushes back, elastic–like, into the chambers. This constant alternation causes an increase in amplitude – the volume is raised even though the drummers are beating as before: 'It is feasible that a megalithic tomb may be activated in this manner' (Watson 1996). Ancient musical instruments expert Corwen Broch informs me that the WKLB ox toe 'whistles', '... may be

Helmholtz resonators, perhaps designed to be spun around on cords. The use of such instruments might well generate standing waves and be binaural in an enclosed space' (see also www.ancientmusic.co.uk). 'Binaural' effects can be produced when different frequencies are received by our left and right ears. This produces an inaudible 'beat', which our brains cannot detect, yet can affect us physiologically. Binaural beats have been found to enhance telepathy, hypnosis, out-of-body experience, and lucid dreaming. Now we can appreciate why Neolithic shaman were interested in acoustics.

The human voice can add further dimensions to sounds issuing from bone flutes, just as the vocal cords of a didge player can affect the sound produced. Who knows what sounds, both vocal and non-vocal, our shaman ancestors produced to summon up the ancestors, their totem animals, and the like. Perhaps certain key sounds, high- or low-pitched, affected the consciousness of the participant, inducing sought-after sensations and altered states of consciousness: sound was all part of the shamanic 'trip'.

Drumming within the dark recesses of the acoustically attuned chambers of WKLB can be a powerful experience.

Sound and Shamanism

Drumming, dance and chanting are essential elements used by modern indigenous tribal shamans seeking the state of ecstatic trance. And of these, drumming seems to be almost universal: 'Drumming is the most common of ritual instruments' (Devereux 2001, p. 41). The drum is often the tool that helps the shaman cross over to the spirit world and in many cultures is a sacred object in itself. Steady, rhythmic drumming has been proven to have effects on the brain and some recent experiments have found that controlled drumming can help the brain 'dive' into the low-frequency theta range, associated with trance and deep meditation (Devereux 2001, p. 48-49)

Enclosed spaces, such as inside WKLB, created sound effects not normally experienced in everyday life, adding to the mythos that such places were 'supernatural' and Otherworldly domains. Sarsen stones reflect sound, rather than absorb it, creating amplification and echoes in the process; this may have been interpreted as stones 'talking back'. Echoes played an important role at many sacred sites across the ancient world; 'To a shaman, an echo is a communication between the shaman and the landscape' (Devereux 2010). I have myself experienced how echoes are produced when one speaks into some of the deep cavities in the megaliths at Avebury. Echoes are involved in many legends and myths around the world, often involving a cave or cave-like environment, where such effects may have been regarded as an interaction with otherworldly spirits. I suspect that echoes may have also played a role inside WKLB.

I am suggesting that acoustics may have been an inseparable component of the shaman's *experiences* at chambered long barrows. I am not alone in this view: 'These places may not have been simply a technology for producing visual and acoustic experiences, but a means of creating different worlds altogether' (Watson & Keating 1999, p. 336). At Dwarfe Stane, a rock-cut tomb in Scotland, Watson and Keating used their voices to achieve a certain resonance and found that the massive blocking stone, and the air itself, seemed to 'shake vigorously'. They comment that, '... one person can induce many tons of stones to appear to come alive'. This links us to the stone simulacra at WKLB; I have witnessed how their features become animated and 'alive' under certain lighting and sound conditions.

On the full Moon drumming evening held on Sept 23, 2010, participant Julie Umpleby informed me that, '... throughout the drumming and meditation I was seeing many symbols in the stones - serpents and animals'. It seems to me that the designs of cave and rock art are connected with ancient shamans. Several researchers have previously proposed a link between trance drumming and carvings at Neolithic monuments.

On a very blustery day in November 2010, I was inside WKLB with a guest of mine, Frann Haykin. Just after I had ended a short session of drumming, the blustery wind outside the entrance sounded like distant drumming! We both heard this. I wonder if a shaman inside here thousands of years ago may have interpreted this as a Divine message, a sign from Spirit.

Paul Devereux (although referring to Newgrange) describes what may well have taken place at WKLB: 'Did some Neolithic shaman or shamanic elite take a mind-altering infusion and sit within the inky blackness of the awesome chamber, perhaps among the ancestral bones, intoning deep chants until the very walls reverberated, waiting to receive the ecstatic golden blast of soul-searing solar light...' (Devereux 1997, p. 187). He also concludes with what I have been saying for years at WKLB: '... If these chambers were designed solely for the silent dead, it is odd that they should repeatedly be found to be so ideally suited for the performance of the living human voice' (Devereux 2001, p. 89). Good point Paul.

Rodney Needham of the University of Oxford has looked into the role of drums and why sound produced by striking a drum is so widely used by shamans to communicate with the Otherworld. 'Just why does he beat a drum, and why is this banging noise essential if he is to communicate with spiritual powers?' He also notes that, '... drums are used not only to establish contact with spirits, but also to repel them, but this is still a form of communication with the other world (Needham 1967).

Archaeologists are now acknowledging the significance of acoustically charged places and the activities of the shamans who used them: 'These chambers may have served as centres for social or spiritual events, and the resonances

The volume and intensity of several drums in the west chamber can be powerful, sometimes leaving people 'heady' and emotional.
(Image: Alex Smith.)

of the chamber cavities might have been intended to support human ritual chanting... the resonance frequency lies within the human vocal range' (Cook et al 2008, p. 95). It is concluded that, '... the acoustic properties of ancient structures may influence brain function' (op. cit. p. 96). The Eagle has landed, the penny hath dropped.

I have had personal experience with 'journeying' following shamanic drumming. My shaman guide, Heather Heaton, helped me to contact my late father, whose ashes were scattered at WKLB. I was on my back on the floor of the west chamber, with Heather drumming around me. I soon sank into a deep meditation and met my father on the other side of the 'Skull Stone'. I shall share what he said to me later, as it is relevant to our unfolding future.

I also know from personal practice that rhythmic drumming induces a state of 'automatic pilot', where one no longer has to concentrate on the act of beating; the mind is free to roam, or to 'sink' into another place. Visionary artist Monica Sjoo saw West Kennet long barrow as, '... a space where all outside influences are cut off...' One can envisage a shaman, drumming in the dark void of the west chamber, isolated and alone - yet not alone.

Rodney Needham concludes, rightly so in my opinion, that, '... there is a significant connection between percussion and transition' (Needham 1967, p. 611). *Transition* is *liminal*, a passage from one state or condition to another. Weddings, funerals, New Year, coming of age, graduations, are all such occasions. He considers that one state of transition is, '...to change location, so that the passage from one social or mystical status to another is symbolised by a territorial passage' (op. cit. p. 612). In the case of WKLB, the 'territorial passage' is quite literally that, the passage of the monument, and the 'transition' is the liminal crossing from the world of the living to the world of the ancestors.

It has been said that buildings and landscape influence people through a combination of their senses (Watson 2001, p. 297). It could be argued by skeptics that the acoustic effects in WKLB are simply a fortuitous side effect of architecture originally intended to serve quite different purposes. But I find it impossible to envisage that the acoustic effects, at the very least, would have gone unnoticed, and, once experienced, would have been disregarded. I believe it was sound that actually brought the chambers to life!

As well as flutes, whistles and shamanic drums, musicians take other instruments into WKLB that were certainly not around in Neolithic Wiltshire. These include didgeridoos, djembes, violins, gongs, Tibetan and crystal bowls, sitars, and other modern 'imported' sound producers. Personally, I have no problem with this. Many of these instruments have been proven to help achieve altered states in their own culture, both in the past and today. So bring 'em on, I say! In fact these instruments all serve to demonstrate how pure and effective the acoustic properties of the chambers can be, and in themselves may move people emotionally: 'The sound you can achieve with a didge in the main chamber is amazing', is how one online blogger put it. Nevertheless, at the end of the day, it was the drum, flute/whistle and the human voices that were the tools used here thousands of years ago.

In the next chapter we will at times return to acoustics, and how particular phenomena were triggered by drumming inside WKLB recently.

I would also like to add that it is not all about making a noise! Despite all the wonderful and powerful drumming, chanting and toning I have experienced over the years, some of the most potent and emotive experiences I have had inside WKLB were when I was silent, still, and receptive, taking 'time out' to listen to what the site had to say to me. There is indeed a power and a sanctity in 'the sound of silence'.

Chapter 11.
Stone Faced –
Symbolism of the Megaliths

'The spirit of life dwelt permanently, it seemed, in these rigid rocks.'
(Michael Harrison)

Human beings have a deeply intuitive tendency to project human features on to non-human aspects of the environment, perceiving images in 'inanimate' objects. We see dolphins and dragons in clouds, human likenesses in root vegetables, and faces in the bark of trees. We may even talk to our car or computer as if it can understand us.

Art, architecture, the stars and planets, rocks, hills, trees and even human body parts, may acquire metaphorical significance. Large rock outcrops, especially, have been the subject of anthropomorphic reverence and superstition for thousands of years, on every continent. Rather than seeing the planet as an uncle or a brother, we speak of 'Mother Nature' and 'Mother Earth'. Standing stones were often thought to be alive, or formerly so, a practice that has been cross-cultural and almost universal.

For many years, during my travels around Europe's sacred sites, I have observed megaliths that appeared to display faces, male and female symbolism, and Otherworldy creatures. Initially, I had put these down to either 'chance', or else were due to weathering. Two books were to change all that. In 1992 Paul Devereux's *Symbolic Landscapes* came out, suggesting that many of the Avebury stones had been deliberately chosen because of the images they displayed; the sarsen stones had not been *carved* into simulacra, but people had *deliberately selected them*: '… they have not been formed by human design, some may have been *recognised* by human intent' (Devereux 1992, p. 152). Devereux called them *Dreamstones,* suggesting that people were observing them to 'engender imagery'.

This charged my interest and my imagination, and led to me to demonstrate several simulacra around Dorset. Some of these included Neolithic barrows, such as at the Hellstone, the Grey Mare and Her Colts, and at Corscombe (Knight 1998 and 2000).

The second impetus came in 1999, when Terence Meaden published, *The Secrets of the Avebury Stones,* in which he took the whole issue of simulacra and anthropomorphs to a new level. Meaden suggested that the *vast majority* of stones in the Avebury area had symbolic meaning, and that at certain times of the day or year, '… the unseen spirits of the stones come to life'. He goes further than Devereux, advocating that some stones were even *modified* to enhance particular features, '… involving the dressing and merging of an array of contours' (Meaden 1999, p. 69). In the megaliths of the Avebury area, he found many facial features, vulva and phallus symbolism, and otherworldly creatures, '… every surviving stone… if not already sexually symbolic… has a head upon it, usually in profile' (Meaden 1999, p. 37). I had the privilege to be shown many of these heads by Terence during a site visit, and I was immediately convinced.

Since then I have found other imagery in the stones, as have others, and no doubt further ones may be awaiting our perception. On my regular tours of Avebury, I also demonstrate to the attendees how the outer circle comprises alternating 'male' and 'female' stones, borne out by masculine horned/phallic imagery, and the feminine yoni, breasts and diamond shapes. The designers and facilitators of Avebury, which I suspect were priestesses, were expressing in their temple what they observed in the Cosmos around them – the balance of yin and yang.

I believe that the ancient shamans at WKLB may have also 'connected' with their megaliths, perhaps to trigger their imaginations, or maybe even to kick start a psychological 'opening up' of their mind. Cheryl Travers, from NSW Australia, sat in one of the side chambers after I had drummed around her. She told me, 'I sat cross-legged and pushed my back against one rock, as if I could reach through to the other side – to the ancestors. It was dark and deliciously cool. The rocks whispered to me and the air stirred around me. I was feeling the land itself seep into every pore of my being… something was ignited within me'.

Archaeologists are somewhat on the fence over the issue of whether the simulacra we see in stones are the result of *intended selection,* or pure coincidence. Aubrey Burl sees them as, '…surely coincidental... the features are very probably fortuitous' and that he had observed some himself, '… after a glass or two of Wadworth's 6X' (Burl 2002, p. 217). This seems to be a bit cynical and sweeping, and a little confusing, particularly as earlier in the same book, when referring to suggested 'male' and 'female' stones, he states that, 'The implicit symbolism, similarly often to be seen in stone circles, is very relevant to these ancient people and their ceremonies' (op. cit. p. 118).

Perhaps there is a middle ground. As the very *earliest* megaliths were erected, this may have been done without any *initial* preference to form and feature. But perhaps it was *soon* recognised how some of these stones resembled this, that and the other. This may have kick-started a whole new focus, perhaps even birthing mythologies concerning these stones. The stones, after all, were gifts from the landscape, from the Goddess, and may therefore have been seen as expressions of, and a means to linking with, the spirit of the land.

Spirit Stones

Man has a long history of associating stones and rocks with deity, spirits and ancestors. 'Ancestral powers and histories are sometimes vested in trees and stones, and spirits of the dead may be seen in their forms' (Edmunds 1999, p. 21). In certain African cultures it is believed that spirits are released when certain standing stones and rocks are struck. Aborigines in Western Arnhem Land, Australia, believe that local quartzite holds the spirits of the ancestors within. Around the world are many megalithic structures that contain stones with holes in or through them, some of which are known as 'spirit holes', conduits through which beings from other dimensions cross over into our world. Relics of a Neolithic belief that megaliths contain spirits may be represented today in the widespread folklore that witches, beasts, people, and even the Devil, were transformed into stones, petrified forever in solid rock.

But did the people of Neolithic Wiltshire believe that the stones themselves were inhabited with spirits? Terence Meaden certainly thought so, when he suggested that: '... stones were, to a greater or lesser degree, thought to be inhabited by ancestral spirits, somehow locked into the stone... prayers and offerings were used to persuade the entrapped spirits to intercede for the community' (Meaden 1991, p. 183). I suspect he may be right.

WKLB Imagery

So what of WKLB and simulacra? It is interesting that when I take people around the monument they often see, unprompted, faces and creatures in the stones. Surely our ancient ancestors would have also seen these. I guess it is all about *intentionality*. Were the simulacra *selected for their imagery* by the builders of the monument? I have a hunch that several of them were!

(The plan at the end of this chapter will aid the location of the simulacra described below.)

We turn to Terence Meaden again, who discovered and first described many of the images on the WKLB megaliths (Meaden 1999, p. 102-108), where he highlighted nine left-facing heads at WKLB. I lean heavily on his research, but also add my own revelations over several years, in all weathers and under varieties of illumination.

Terence Meaden demonstrating the 1m high vulva symbolism of stone 45, which is the long, slightly shaded area to his left.

External Imagery

Mention of stone 45, the 30-50 ton 'blocking stone', has already been made several times, concerning its purpose and the age of its erection. But it also displays symbolism that even the casual observer may notice. Standing in front of the stone and a little away from it, a huge left-facing head will be discerned. There is an eye, some say two, staring southwards towards Milk Hill and,

The 'Forecourt Ox/Bull' at WKLB, formed by stones 43 and 45, proposed by Michael Dames.
Insert: Bull mural at Tarxien Temple, Malta, for comparison; the outlining dots have been inserted by the author for clarity.

ultimately, to Stonehenge. Low down on the south side a nose protrudes, adding to the imagery. The whole stone has a 'female' appearance, a wide symbol of fecundity and plenty (Michael Dames sees the stone as a '12ft-tall Hag'). Running down the centre of the east face is a vertical mark, a depression over 1.5m (5ft) long and 50cm (20ins) wide at its maximum. The best time to see it is late-morning, when the Sun is catching the face of the stone at an acute angle. It shows up well in the images on p. 112 and 131. Sculptors have confirmed to Meaden that it was channelled out by axe grinding and pecking of stone tools. The deepest depression indents into the stone about 12.5cm (5ins) and is seen as a, 'vaginal entrance'. Above is a lesser depression, which marks a, 'clitoral region' (Meaden 1999, p. 107). These features were only exposed when Piggott re-erected the stone after it had been facedown for perhaps centuries. Meaden sees it relevant that the vulva faces east, enabling the rising Sun to 'impregnate' it. Several researchers have previously commented on the

Side-ways head at entrance. The head may not be in its original position, but the features may have led to its selection in the Neolithic.

female symbolism of chambered long barrows, some describing them as 'womb tombs'. The vulva symbolism would be appropriate for the closing of the monument - feminine symbolism expressed for eternity: 'The rediscovery of this fertility image has considerable consequences for rebirth theories and the spiritual motivation behind the construction of long barrows' (Meaden 1999, p. 108). Touché Terence.

Michael Dames has advocated that stones 43 and 45 form the shape of a bull or ox, his 'Forecourt Ox', with stones 44 and 46 being the legs, reaching towards the entrance. He sees these 'Bull Stones' as a stylised image of the Divine Ox, an embodiment of strength, who pulled the sacred plough (Dames 1977, p. 53-59). He also sees a link between this imagery and the crescent-shaped 'horn' design of the megaliths already spoken of (see image p. 92), as the late-Neolithic people identified with the beliefs of their forebears who built the barrow. This bull image may have been associated with early spring rituals as, '… the Great Goddess emerges miraculously out of death *via* the sacred bull' (Gimbutas 1974, p. 236). We have already seen that oxen had a ritualistic significance at WKLB, and other sites around the world mirror this. On both of my two recent visits to Malta, I observed the beautiful Neolithic carvings of bulls at the Tarxien Temple, which are also Neolithic (see insert above). In Manitoba, Canada, a rock rising from a riverbed is called Bison Rock, as it resembles that animal; the rock is sacred to the local Indians.

When standing in front of stone 45, symbolism can be seen on the west face of stone 2. There is a small west-facing head, with prominent eyebrows, nose and open mouth, which looks to the right, towards the setting mid-winter Sun.

Left: Left-facing profiled head on stone 36. Right: Left-facing head on stone 25, that appears part ram, part human. (Images: Sue Wallace.)

133

Chambers of Faces

Moving into the forecourt, behind stone 45, Meaden identified a left-facing head on stone 46, and another to its left on stone 36, with a rather large nose and slanting eye. The latter is directly in front of you when you enter the forecourt (image above). Dames regards stone 44 as a Goddess stone, with an eye near the top of the trapezoidal-shaped megalith.

Standing at the entrance, you will see a small stone on the left side that has been wedged under the lintel. It has an elongated head, on its side, and looks for all the world like some alien creature! (image p. 132). We cannot be sure, of course, if this is in its original position, and what the intention was, if any, of the people who selected it. But today, it seems to guard the entrance, perhaps welcoming visitors who have come with the right intent.

Venturing further into the passage, one's imagination really kicks in, as weird-shaped rocks present themselves, to tease and cajole the senses. And whatever image you see is meant for you. Perhaps thousands of years ago this was also the case. Different individuals would have seen different faces in the stones, and perhaps each image would have been 'correct' and valid for them. Each stone had its own story to tell to every individual.

Stone 25, which forms the wall of the NW chamber, is a wonderful simulacrum (image above). It may have been carved, as Terence Meaden notes: 'Stone

25, at whose base is a cleverly crafted head of an animal, apparently a ewe' (Meaden 1999, p. 102-3 and colour plate). It is a left-facing profile, a bas-relief no less, and the worked surface is paler than the general colour of the reddish sarsen. The horns are very suggestive of a ram or goat, whereas the facial features are very delicate. Is the image representing the shape-shifting of a shaman?

Opposite the ram's head is stone 19 (image left), a tall megalith that defines the entrance to the west chamber. Note how it juts out into the passage, restricting access to the chamber to a gap of only 50% of the average passage width. I suspect that the reason for this is two-fold: the stone restricted the entry of light into the west chamber from the Sun and the Moon. We shall return to this later in Chapter 15. Secondly, by jutting out into the passage, stone 19 appears phallic, with red stains, undulations, and striations adding to the symbolism. The location of phallic stones within

Stone 19, showing the phallic symbolism that was achieved by positioning it jutting out into the passage. Also note the 'ear'. (Image: Sue Wallace.)

chambered mounds is well documented. I have noted several on my travels to Neolithic sites in Brittany, as well as at temples in Malta. Sexual symbolism was expressed elsewhere in the Avebury area, such as the 30 chalk balls and 4 phalli found at Windmill Hill.

So even at a 'womb tomb' it would appear that the male element is present, the balance again of yin and yang – Nature personified. It has been suggested that other chambered long barrows have both 'male' and 'female' stones, such as the two of the forecourt at Wayland's Smithy, at the Bridestones, and at the Grey Mare and Her Colts (Knight 1996, p. 114). Two archaeologists have concluded that the megaliths of the Avebury area had to, '…conform to certain required shapes, and to this end were selected as near to the required form as possible' (Keiller & Piggott 1936). Meaden has dealt extensively with the sexual symbolism of megaliths in the Avebury area (Meaden 1999).

Half way up stone 19 is a curious feature that looks like a large ear. Perhaps we can call this the 'Listening Stone'! On the other side of the stone, visible from the west chamber, is a deep, dark eye, which is very evident and is in deep shadow when illuminated from below (image p. 184 and cover).

In the SW chamber, there are three cup marks at the top of stone 14 which, although natural, may have determined why the stone was selected. Meaden sees these holes as representing the triple goddess. It is interesting that this was the chamber where three females skulls were found in a row.

The 'Living Head' and the 'Skull Stone'

In my opinion, the rear of the west chamber displays two of the finest uses of simulacra in Britain. On p. 47, I mentioned how stones 21 and 22 depict left-facing, profiled heads, first described by Terence Meaden. The symbolism is representative of life and death, this world and the next: stone 21 displays a

Left: Stone 21, the left-facing 'Living Head' of the west chamber.
Right: In the dark, shadows are deepened as the head is illuminated from the side.

'Living Head', with eye, nose, facial creases, ear, and a hint of a chin. Stone 22 is an iron-rich 'skull', rounded, smooth and often glistening with condensation. Here we have, I believe, features of this world and the Otherworld, on either side of the barrow axis. These stones were involved in an astronomical event I shall detail in Chapter 15, whereby the rays of the Sun entered the west chamber around equinox, illuminating the heads.

For now, let us concern ourselves with how stones 21 and 22 may have been involved with the symbolism, theatre, and the actual experience of shamanic trance. On my drumming evenings, the west chamber is illuminated by nightlights placed *carefully on the floor* in the *centre* of the chamber. In the flickering light the faces in the stones become animated, with eyes moving in and out of shadow. It makes me wonder how these features would have

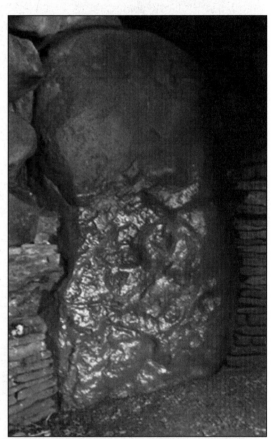

appeared to the Neolithic shaman, who may have already endured days of chanting and drumming, sleep and food deprivation, and the ingestion of psychoactive fungi! The right-hand image above conveys a little of how mystical and eerie the simulacra of stone 21 appears with flickering illumination from an acute angle. We have taken flashlights into the chambers and have seen how features of the simulacra stand out when shadows are accentuated. Did the shamans see these ethereal images as intermediaries between this world and the next? '... people considered the rock itself as a membrane through which the spirits could pass' (Williams 2010, p. 40).

Stone 22, the left-facing 'Skull Stone', is very significant on several levels. To me, the skull symbolism represents the dead, the ancestral realms. John Thurnam found an unusually well preserved skeleton in front of the stone. Due to its rich iron content, the stone is often covered in condensation droplets, enhancing the skull effect.

Stone 22, the 'Skull Stone', in the west chamber, showing the glistening effect due to condensation.

Astronomically, light from the rising Sun around equinox would have shone on the stone – and still does! (see image p. 185). Lastly, I have already described how the stone marks the most pronounced acoustic 'hot spot' inside WKLB. Surely all this cannot be coincidental.

Meaden notes how the back of stone 21 (the 'Living Head') is angled steeply downwards, pointing to the mouth of stone 22, '... as if to suggest rebirth from the dead' (Meaden 1999, p. 104).

These two stones may also have sexual significance, as Terence Meaden and I have observed on other stones at Avebury, and elsewhere. Others have confirmed this observation; for instance, Angie Lake has posted comments (www.megalithic.co.uk, July 7, 2007) telling of how she saw stones 21 and 22 as having sexual symbolism. She observed that, '... the feminine symbolism appears as the indentation on the left-hand stone [on stone 21] facing you...

Left: Dry-stone walling in the passage, next to 'ram's head' stone. These small stones are an original feature of WKLB. Right: The author with flashlight, checking out how the megaliths change appearance under different lighting angles. (Images: Sue Wallace.)

and the phallic is the whole of the stone to the right [22]... the wetness enhanced its appearance'. She continues that stone 23 also, '... looks a little like a face'.

Dry-stone Walling

Both Thurnam and Piggott recorded 'dry-stone walling', filling the spaces between many of the large sarsen stones. This comprises well over a ton of Jurassic limestone and oolite brought from the area of Bath and/or Calne. Visitors have often expressed to me how they thought the stones were part of the restoration. But no - they were already in situ when the barrow was closed in the late-Neolithic.

The use of this type of dry-stone walling is unusual, and Piggott cites only five other long barrows in North Wiltshire that incorporate such 'imported' stones, including Adam's Grave, Horslip, Easton Down and Kitchen Barrow. Pieces of the same shell-laden oolite were also found at Windmill Hill, and at a Neolithic occupational site on Waden Hill, next to the stone avenue (Dames 1977, p. 98). Grains of this oolite were used as filler in pottery found at both Windmill

137

Hill and WKLB. The introduction of this stone makes little sense if it was just a building material (Russell 2002, p. 73). Joshua Pollard and Andrew Reynolds suggest that symbolism played a part in the selection of this material, that it was chosen because of, '… aesthetic qualities, perhaps its whiteness [when fresh], which was akin to that of bleached ancestral bone', and that it was, '… held to contain the essence of ancestral or spiritual beings' (Pollard & Reynolds 2002, p. 73). It has also been argued that the wavy lines present in the dry-stone walling represent water, itself a medium of transition; symbolically, perhaps the waters from local springs and the River Kennet were being brought up the hill to the ancestors.

Is it also possible that these 'foreign' stones were imported from an area seen as some ancestral or mythic Motherland? Were the builders of WKLB bringing with them tokens and memories of a land they formerly occupied, where oolitic rocks are part of the landscape? Paul Devereux calls such imported objects, 'pieces of place', and that the act of transporting objects from one area to another is, 'transferring the magic… like medieval relics' (Devereux 2010). This may have been part of the mindset involved in bringing bluestones from the Preseli Mountains to Stonehenge, or in the megalithic sites of the Boyne Valley, which house stones from the Carlingford Mountains to the north and the Wicklow Mountains to the south.

Perhaps the megaliths displaying simulacra already had their own myths to tell when they were still lying on the landscape, stories that may have ultimately become integrated into WKLB. The living stones were transferred into the living womb of the Goddess, and perhaps with them the qualities and legends they held.

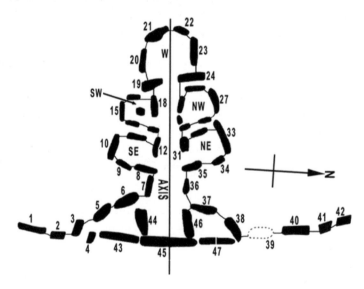

The numbering of the stones in 1955 by Stuart Piggott, as an aid to finding the simulacra described above.

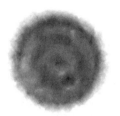

Chapter 12.
Psychics, Shamans
and Paranormal Phenomena

'There is another level of physical reality, not
normally detectable by conventional instruments, some of
which we may be able to image under appropriate conditions.'
(Prof. William Tiller Phd, Standford University.)

I suspect that inside WKLB thousands of years ago, shamans and initiates were experiencing both the explainable and the enigmatic, the accepted and the inexplicable. And so it is today, as people observe, hear, and sense unexpected phenomena they cannot understand. In addition to this, many people go into WKLB today with the *intention* of experiencing such things, to gain knowledge and information from the 'Other Side', just as may have happened here thousands of years ago. I know from personal experience that much can be learnt from such pursuits.

As well as my own experiences and thoughts, based on my site visits, I offer here a variety of testimonies made over many years, as part of my 'holistic' approach to the study of WKLB. I do this without judgement, and often without comment, unless I have something relevant to offer. I leave readers to make up their own minds on the incidents reported to me and those from other sources, just as I have done.

I must state from the onset that the viewpoints expressed in this chapter are not necessarily those of the author. An open mind may be an asset here, as we deal at times with information that may seem akin to things that go 'bump in the night'. I **do not** include in that category the information I have received from some well-respected acquaintances of mine in the world of the paranormal, as well as my friends in the field of shamanism; these are people who are gifted in the ability to be able to sense and feel what I cannot. I invited several clairvoyants, psychics, channellers, and other 'sensitives' to investigate WKLB, and have recorded their experiences.

As I have gained knowledge about shamanism and psychic phenomena, I have come to the realisation that this physical body I call 'me' is but a small part of what I am, and that this physical universe is only part of something much bigger, something quite immeasurable. Perhaps I am approaching the mindset of the ancient users of WKLB: their Universe was a dynamic place, alive with non-physical entities, in a landscape bristling with myth and life-force – part of a living Earth. This is the cosmology of the shaman.

I shall begin with phenomena and reports that I have gathered from elsewhere, those that I was not personally involved in. I do not offer these as a definitive list, far from it, but as a selection of the varieties of phenomena, some of which show similarities. I welcome any further information for possible inclusion in future editions. To this end, in 2010 I initiated the **WKLB Ancestors Project**, to co-ordinate records of phenomena seen at and near the barrow; this has already yielded important information, some of which is detailed below. This is an ongoing project, which in the future will include taking scientific instrumentation to the site. Watch this space!

Examples of Modern Phenomena

Psychics and channellers have been 'connecting' with WKLB for many years, and some of these have even been filmed. In 1996, for instance, *Desperately Seeking Something*, a TV series looking at spiritualists across the globe, saw presenter and travel-writer Pete McCarthy joining members of the Golden Dawn Occult Society inside WKLB for a trance session.

The following is an extract from correspondence sent to me by Susan Elizabeth Hale, the internationally renowned musician, over-toner and sound healer from the USA: 'Walking to the far end of the chambers [i.e. the west chamber], I breathed in its space, giving voice to not only what I was feeling, but to what I heard within. The sounds were mournful, expressing dissonance. Low sounds gave way to high harmonics that I saw with my inner eye as diamonds. I left feeling spacey... I was later told that I was receiving an initiation, but that it wasn't complete, that the power of the space was more than I could handle'. On a subsequent visit, 2 years later, Susan 'saw' more diamonds and experienced the strange acoustic effects I described earlier (p. 119). I would also refer you back to the 'diamonds' inscribed on some of the pots in WKLB (see images p. 73 and p. 109).

Elizabeth and John Fox are the founders of the *Sirius Group*, and are self-confessed 'practioners of magic'. They went to Avebury in the 1980's, and in a vision witnessed a Beltaine procession going down the avenue of stones, men coming from The Sanctuary and women from WKLB; on reaching Avebury stone circle they would make love. On John and Elizabeth's visit to WKLB they went to the west chamber and saw a vision of the people who had used the place long ago: 'tall... Mediterranean in appearance... they wore short kilts'. In the SW chamber, they noted the stone which now lies on the floor, and Elizabeth had the strong impression that this was a 'birthing chamber', where important babies came into the world. She lay down on the floor and immediately her head started to spin until she almost lost consciousness.

Researcher and artist John Palmer slept in the chambers of WKLB one night, only to be awoken by a light moving around in the passageway. He went outside and witnessed a moonlit landscape that was totally different from the one that had been there when he had gone inside at dusk.

The next story was emailed to me by John Grigsby, telling me of his experiences on June 5/6 2010. 'I often go down to Avebury in the summer and sleep out in the avenue if the weather is good. I decided to sit on top of Waden Hill around 11.00pm and look down on West Kennet long barrow on the opposite side of the ridge'. Next morning he, '… returned to watch the Sun rising over West Kennet. After a few minutes I noticed a black shape moving alongside the barrow, from its stone entrance in a westerly direction. My first thought was that this was an individual who had spent a night in the barrow, or an early visitor. It didn't take long for it to cover the entire length of the mound, whereon instead of turning back or climbing the mound, it continued in a westerly direction along the crest of the hill. However, it began to dawn on me that this 'figure' was moving at quite a speed – about twice as fast as I would expect if it was someone walking, and it was moving smoothly, so wasn't someone running. Next it started to come down off the ridge, at which point I realised that I was looking at something about half the height of a man, but wider, and moving steadily at quite a speed. There were cows and calves in the field in front of it and so I could gauge its size as roughly that of a calf. I own two greyhounds and so know how dogs move, how they look when they run, the way they move in circles and sniff the ground; this creature was nothing like that – it was heading with intent towards the thin strip of woods to the south of Swallowhead Spring. It neither deviated from its course nor stopped to look around or sniff. All I know is that it wasn't a man, it was too big for a fox or badger, it was moving fast and purposefully, fairly low to the ground, but at a distance from me that made it hard to make out what kind of animal it was. My guess would be some kind of big cat or wolf-hound sized dog, although its behaviour wasn't typically canine. After reaching the trees it disappeared from sight'. This apparition reminded me of the folklore of the spectral dog seen at WKLB at mid-summer.

On June 6, 2002, 'Rachelwych' posted a comment on Julian Cope's website: 'In the early 90's I went with a group of shamanic students and we gathered inside and chanted. The quality of the air seemed to grow thicker and the energy inside seemed almost electric. The acoustics were marvellous!'

It has been said more than once that WKLB was, and can still be, an interface between this world and ancestral realms. Yet it is often felt by 'sensitives' that the site is very 'earthed' and 'grounding', and always has been. Solara An-Ra, a channeller, healer and alternative therapist, considers that, '… West Kennet Long Barrow was always a magical place. There is not a more grounding place – no place closer to the womb of Gaia – which I know in this country' (www.solara.org.uk).

The late visionary artist Monica Sjoo also spent time inside WKLB: 'I have slept and dreamt within this long barrow, on a dark Moon night in July 1991, meeting some extremely primordial ancestor-beings in my dreams'.

141

Here is a story that implies WKLB is still a place to receive knowledge, a portal that can act as a 'trigger'. During a lecture I attended in Glastonbury in August 2010, archaeo-astronomers Philippa Glasson and Nicholas Mann told the audience how, a few years earlier, they had gone to WKLB to offer their thanks to the ancestors for the knowledge that had been revealed to them regarding their discoveries at Glastonbury. They felt that the, 'ancestors were pleased' with their offering of red ochre. But then they received wisdom from the ancestors: '…the insights and keys we received in a few seconds took the next two years to unravel'. This input of knowledge is about to reach fruition in Mann's book (Mann 2011).

After arriving home from a visit to WKLB, visionary artist Judith Page saw flashes of the site, envisioning a man, woman, and a child, whom were all crying due to the fact that their remains had been disturbed.

Paddy Slade tells of her encounter with a group of young men who had just scrawled graffiti on the stones. In her rage at seeing this she struck one of the stones, which released energies that whirled around the chamber before exiting through the entrance. A brief time later, she passed the same youths, whose car had been involved in a collision. So BEWARE!

On April 21, 2007, members of the Twilight Shadows Paranormal Group conducted an investigation at WKLB. Some felt 'uncomfortable' and 'tingly' in the SW chamber and one of them developed a severe headache, which disappeared on leaving the chamber. They all felt 'warm, protected and safe' in the west chamber. A séance was then conducted; after a while, some of the group heard a female voice, as if coming from the forecourt, although they could not make out definite words. Footsteps were also heard behind them, which was strange as they all had their backs to the stones! Two knocks were heard, as the temperature in the chamber dropped and the air became 'charged' (www.twilightshadowparanormal.co.uk).

Following a vision, Birger Mikkelsen, a Sami shaman, felt urged to make a drum, the *World Drum*. The message it carries is to change our ways and develop a more spiritual connection with the Great Mother. After its first rite in 2006 at the Norwegian Parliament, it travelled to more than 60 groups on four continents. In April 2008 it came to the British Druid Order. Members did a ceremony and played the drum at Dragon's Hill, and then Avebury, before bringing it to WKLB. Inside they beat the drum, as the Druid Greywolf recounts: '… the drum began to sound, and other drums sounded from the stones around us, and a hundred voices began to sing a high, keening song. The ancestors were with us. The Great Mother was with us' (Greywolf 2008).

This singing phenomenon is complimented by a story told to me by Maria Wheatley. In April 2010, an acquaintance of hers, an elderly gentleman named Leslie, heard 'beautiful female singing' whilst in the west chamber. Apparently he was very moved by the experience.

In 2009, a male 'hedge druid' named *Gwas* went to WKLB to dowse and connect with the site: 'Question after question emerged, and each time I worked rapidly towards finding the purpose of each chamber… and the order they should be visited…. I finally arrived at a complete vision of how a person could undergo a spiritual transformation by passing through each chamber in turn – and the time you should spend in them'. His results are summarised thus: one must first go into the NE chamber, '… for energy cleansing and grounding'. One should remain there for seven minutes; Secondly, the NW chamber, which is about, '… knowing and stating one's purpose', a process that takes one minute; then into the SE chamber, which is about contacting, '… the Guardian Spirit, getting permission to undergo the transition', which he was told takes seven minutes; the fourth encounter is with the SW chamber: 'Energising oneself ready for the rebirth/transition chamber'. This takes about three minutes. Finally, one goes into the W chamber: 'The chamber of rebirth and transforming' achieved, apparently, through, '… acoustic resonance'. He dowsed as to whether he could partake in what he had been shown, but on that occasion the answer came back, 'NO!' With reluctance, but showing great respect, he took it no further.

In the 1970's, hereditary witch Paddy Slade was in her garden in Somerset, working simultaneously and remotely with other members of her coven, who were at other geographical locations. Suddenly they all, 'found themselves inside' WKLB. During her experience Paddy saw 'The Lady', who was calling to a stone and asking if his brethren were ready to awaken; yet another stone, '… had been watching me steadily'. This may imply that the prehistoric shaman also had interactions with the megaliths, and that the stones 'come to life', or at least appear to, when invoked to do so. Paddy also describes seeing many people and beings, including 'Dryads, green and shining, … and Herne, his antlers gleaming'.

Brenda Wallace has communicated to me an experience of hers (email, Nov. 2010): 'One winter evening, in January 2005, I went along, alone, and sat in the chamber in the back for a long time in a sort of meditative state. I stood up and started singing, which I continued for 15-20 minutes. I then felt spirals of energy like electric shocks running up both legs, through my body, and down both arms, exciting my fingers, and actually giving off light. I nearly danced back down the hill (I am normally quite unfit) and for several days I had incredible energy and exhilaration! I wish I could repeat that experience'.

I do not expend too much time and energy on conspiracy theories, but this next story is interesting. On a site visit in July 2010, Maria Wheatley told me the story of how she had an encounter in the mid-90's with, as she put it, 'Men in Black'. It was lunchtime on a rainy day and she had come up to the barrow along the former, much narrower, path that used to serve the site. It was very muddy and by the time she had got to the top her footwear was very muddy too. She sat on the mound and closed her eyes to connect with the site, only to feel two firm pushes on her shoulders from behind. She looked around and there stood a man in a black suit, black tie and spotless black shoes, which were shiny and clean! Rather sternly he said to her, 'You don't want to be here now, do you?' Maria felt threatened and left hastily.

In 2010, I showed David Griffiths, from NSW Australia, around WKLB and drummed around him. He had been having nightmares since childhood about wolves prowling and snarling outside a cave in which he was sheltering, frightened. That night, after visiting WKLB, he had another dream, this time very different, in which he was inside WKLB and the wolves were outside, but that they were now silent and not menacing at all: 'I no longer fear wolves, and I have come to feel that the wolf is my totem animal or ally... they were welcoming me on my spirit journey... I am connecting with this land of my ancestors'.

On October 4, 2010, I was drumming on top of the west chamber, watching the sunset with Sue, my partner. At the moment of sunset, Sue was physically pushed about two feet backwards. She felt a rush of energy from the Sun come along the axis of the mound. She had been doing tai chi moments before and had felt really grounded.

Site Investigations and Drumming Evenings

To list all the profound experiences that attendees have experienced over the years at my drumming evenings would fill a small book in itself! For now, I can only include below ones that I feel are especially important. However, I do include *all* the documented details of the special site visits held as part of the *WKLB Ancestors Project*, and any subsequent revelations following these visits. You may well see some similarities between these experiences, as well as links to some archaeological finds and theories outlined in previous chapters.

July 25, 2010

During a full Moon shamanic drumming session, one of the 15 people present, Amanda Barnett, told the group that she had had a vision of a bird of prey just above the 'Skull Stone', as well as seeing an orb and a spectral face in front of the same stone. The bird image is interesting, as on our regular visits to WKLB, birds of prey, such as buzzards and kestrels, frequently fly above us, sometimes approaching quite close; the buzzard is one of my totem animals. Amanda also felt that the apparitions were, '... the ancestors coming forward to be with us'. Another drummer present, Jean-Ann, told me how she 'drifted off' and for several minutes and saw, '... a vision of a procession of people coming out of the chamber'.

Aug 1, 2010

During the afternoon-early evening of August 1, 2010, a site visit was made as part of the WKLB Ancestors Project. This commenced at 4.30pm, on what is the old festival of Lughnasad. Those present were Sue Wallace (dowser), Joyce Henry (Angelic realms channeller), Katrina (who connects with ancestral realms through incantations), Jackie (clairvoyant), Chrissy Murray (a psychic shaman), Heather Heaton (psychic shaman), Pauline Smith (a psychic), Les Miles (didge and flute), Karen James (flute), and the author. We were in the interior of WKLB for well over an hour, sometimes together, and at other times separately. I made a point of not prompting the participants with any information that might have biased them in any way.

Chrissy Murray knelt in the west chamber, but initially felt and saw nothing, but when Katrina joined her and started overtoning, Chrissy envisioned, 'a young man in pitch darkness, terrified... he never came out of there!' She then heard chants, but could not make out where they came from. She also saw "layers" in the chambers, which makes me wonder if she was picking up on the layering of the secondary infilling. She also felt that WKLB was a family place and had a vision of children playing in and out of the chambers.

Katrina sang her 'West Kennet Song', which she had especially composed, whilst facing the 'Skull Stone'. I had not told anyone of its acoustic hot spot or symbolic significance, and yet Katrina soon found that she was 'shaking like a leaf'. She also had visions of spirals.

Jackie said the spirits did not like the blocking stone there. She also envisioned a wolf, and a small man who used to sit looking out of the unblocked entrance, and a small girl, who she felt was the man's daughter. I was particularly interested in the apparition of a wolf, as it is one of my totems.

On the site visit of August 1st 2010, channeller Joyce Henry attempts to connect with other realms inside WKLB.

Joyce Henry felt the site was not designed for angelic connections, that it is 'too earthy', and she could not as easily contact the angelic realms as she normally could: 'It is a place of the Earth Elementals – the Land Whites are here'. In the west chamber she saw a swirling mist/energy and also a 'black mist'. In the passage she felt energy lifting upwards, and sensed that the passage was energetically blocked, and that it needed to have energy and light coming down it again.

When Heather Heaton was in the west chamber she felt as if a tall male wanted to 'embody' her and that he was the guardian, watching over the site. Twice she had a vision of chevron-like images on the floor of the west Chamber.

Some of us then beat our shamanic drums in the west chamber, and Chrissy then saw images of men sitting cross-legged drumming, and an energy in the centre moving like a snake, twisting and turning upwards through the ceiling. She also felt that drumming and flute playing was 'right for in there'. During this drumming I personally felt dizzy, nearly losing my balance a couple of times. Later, Karen and Les joined in with the flute and didge in the west chamber (see image p. 120). After our drumming/flute/didge session, three of the women came into the chamber and all felt dizzy, so much so that one of them, Heather, had to go outside. She felt that the 'West Kennet Gateway' was opening up again because of the work being done here.

Whilst I was in the west chamber, talking to the group about how my late father's ashes had been scattered at WKLB, Pauline Smith envisioned him standing behind me, placing a hand on my shoulder. (On a drumming evening prior to this, Pauline had 'seen' my father follow me out of WKLB, and felt he wanted me to know that I had, 'done the right thing'.)

Analysis of digital images taken during this gathering show peculiar light phenomena, which we shall deal with soon below.

Psychic channellers Julie Umpleby and Ann Menzies-Blythe inside WKLB.

Sept 23, 2010

This was one of my scheduled full Moon gatherings, which was also at the equinox. Eleven people were present for an evening of drumming, chanting, overtoning, meditation, and earth healing. During the quiet meditation time, a 'higher being' was channelled in by Ann Menzies-Blythe. His name was Albon. His role had been to, '…wait for a connection'. The following is a transcript of the dialogue spoken by Albon, speaking through Ann:

'Time lines - the lines of Time, of the energy through the beginning to the end.
In past times this was kept ritually.
As time has passed the old has faded in memory and focus.
It is time to bring the connection through to the Now, as we all, past and present - start to see the future... there is a choice.
Peter is part of the lines of the time continuum;
*   without his attention, the focus would be lost.*
In some way, the connection has been made.
Thank Peter for his faith, his intuition, and instincts to hold the continuum,
It is vital to continue.
Who I am? Albon - lost in time.
I am the guardian of the Hill and the Barrows - I was Master, priest and shaman, in your understanding.
I vowed to wait until The Time.
My ancestors stretch to the Phoenicians and Egyptians, and here in Wessex.
My insights were offered to the people coming out of the Dark.
We have undertaken the Dark again, yet the Light is ahead -
I am here.

Julie Umpleby sensed Albon as being the grandson of a Phoenician tin trader, and that his grandmother had been a Wessex wise woman. Albon was the head shaman for WKLB, East Kennet long barrow, and Stonehenge and that he had stayed here to hold the wisdom for those who were to follow, to pass it on to us.

Ann also channelled the image of Albon, and her drawing is reproduced here (the original is in colour). He has a beak-like nose and a thin face. The feather in his hair is that of an eagle; the disc on the top of the staff has the Sun on one side and the Moon on the other; there are two serpents on the pendant, and he wears a necklace bearing the 'infinity symbol'.

At the same event, Julie Umpleby connected with the site and had the following insights: 'The blocking stone [no. 45] is also a communication stone and forms part of a greater communication network - it links with Stonehenge. This stone links with the portal ['Skull'] stone within the deepest chamber, and brings the information through from the past and broadcasts it through the network of stones across the landscape'. 'The Skull Stone...', she continued, '... is an access point through which the timelines are maintained... this stone, for me, felt like an inter-dimensional portal through which the wisdom of the ages and the ancients is maintained and brought forward'. Julie also saw, 'spirals, ovals and circles, serpents and animals'.

Channelled drawing of 'Albon', by Ann Menzies-Blythe. (© - used with permission.)

Another attendee, Rick, then knelt down between stone 21 and 22, and overtoned. This led to the rest of the group joining in with our own ad-lib hums, ohms and other toning. It was a beautiful moment in time that lasted for several minutes – no one wanted to stop. As we were doing this powerful chanting, Sue Wallace felt a cold rush of air pass around her. Rick later said he had wanted to let out the cry of an eagle. After the final meditation, one of the party shared that her father and two

147

brothers had died; yet she felt that in WKLB she had finally found a safe place in which she could grieve.

November 11, 2010
This was another visit for the WKLB Ancestors Project. Frann Haykin, a 'light-worker and channeller', went with the author up to WKLB on what was a cold and very windy afternoon. In the west chamber Frann felt the lesson for her was not to be in fear - she had challenged herself by merely coming into that dark and enclosed space. She added that WKLB should be approached with humility and gratitude. People should also, 'enjoy it in there, be light in there'. She added that, 'We should also stop categorizing about the purpose of WKLB, as it already knows what it is – let us discover it!'
I had told her about the scattering of my late father's ashes, and how I had been contacted by him previously, and yet had not felt his presence in recent weeks. Frann replied, 'He is giving you some space; he does not want to stand in your way. He has just backed off a bit, for you to work things out for yourself'.

November 21, 2010
This was another specific site investigation event, on the evening of the full Moon. Present on this occasion were Julie Umpleby and Ann Menzies-Blythe, both psychics and channellers, plus Sue Wallace and myself.
In the west chamber we stood forming a small circle, and Julie tuned in and brought in 'Diamond energy'. After visualising a diamond, she saw a shaft of light come down vertically into the chamber. As had happened in September, Albon 'came in' and again spoke through Ann:
> 'There is a reason for the four of you coming together here.
> The work is bigger than you think…
> a conjoining of the work of all of us…
> connecting the ancestors with now… history and future.
> Time is compressing into the Now.'

During this channelling I had difficulty keeping my feet, as I wobbled all over the place, feeling more than a little heady in front of the 'Skull Stone'; this was one of the most powerful physical experiences I have had inside WKLB.
Then I drummed, which was very powerful with a deeply resonating sound (it was a very damp environment), after which Julie Umpleby said, 'When you started drumming, a huge red serpent emerged through the portal stone that connects with other dimensions'. She also visualised Albon as a leader, serving people from all over, a conduit for stellar and ancestral channels, orchestrating a 'bringing together'. Julie also saw symbols, such as concentric circles and zigzags. She said that spirit told her to, '… go into the broken timelines to bring them back for healing and cleansing'. Ann later said to me that, '… it's all about re-activating what had been open before… a healing needs to happen'.
During Ann's channelling with Albon, Sue heard a stone-like clunk, and then a series of clunks, '… like in the Indiana Jones movies, when the pulling of a

lever sets in motion a whole series of cogs, which open something secret and hidden'. She also envisioned images of symbols painted on animal skins, which were being taken up to WKLB in a procession; the skins were stretched and held taught on wooden frames.

At the end of our session images of orbs were 'captured'.

Ann and Julie both see stone 45 as a 'communication stone' (and that there is another at Stonehenge). They say that energy coming into the chambers is being transmitted out across the land. Later, they were delighted when I showed them images of the diamonds/lozenges on the WKLB pottery, and at Newgrange, which they had not been aware of. Sue explained to them how standing stones are like acupuncture needles, accessing energy nodes.

Tom Graves and Liz Poraj-Wilczynska have recently made a good point about the visions people get at sacred places: 'If you imagine something it is real... What we may perceive about 'imaginary entities' at a place are also just as real - with everything that that implies' (Graves & Poraj-Wilczynska 2008, p. 84-85). Did our distant ancestors literally 'imagine' beings and forces into being, through the power of the mind! Can our mind manifest these things into reality? Thoughts, after all, precede manifestation.

Meeting My Ancestor

I have said previously how we are all related the builders of our Neolithic sacred sites, and that by taking this on board we may forge closer connections with these ancestors, and with the sites they left us: 'These places were not built by our ancestors, but rather by our relatives' (Knight 2007, p. 245). On a personal note, I have also mentioned how my father's ashes were scattered at WKLB. I have felt his presence on more than one occasion since his remains were returned to the Great Mother. He has appeared and/or spoken to me in my thoughts, during shamanic journeys, and in meditation. During one of my sessions in the west chamber with my shamanic teacher

My mother and late father, my immediate ancestors. My father has connected with me inside WKLB.

Heather Heaton, her drum helped to take me down into a deep theta state. Physically I was still lying on the floor, yet my mind had passed through the 'Skull Stone', encountering my father on the other side. He told me that I have a responsibility to the ancestors... *because I am an ancestor*. He explained that everyone is an ancestor, but that for a short while 'the living' are on our side of that stone, in physicality. He went on to tell me that the ancestors of thousands of years ago do not know of our modern times, so that I have a responsibly to take knowledge back *for them*. It's a two-way exchange of information, and not all about take, take, take. He also told me that one day, when I have passed over, people may well come into WKLB and pick my brains (God help 'em!). I had never looked at it in that way before – I am an ancestor. We all are.

It also made me realise that I may have been in WKLB before, thousands of year ago. I do not know for sure. But it may explain why I have such a deep connection, love, and respect for the monument, and for the people who built and made use of it. Perhaps I am being over romantic and fanciful; however, it has to be said that although I have been to sacred sites all over Europe, Egypt, and elsewhere, WKLB is the **only** sacred site where I **feel** I have been before – a long, long time ago.

I now know that the ancestors are within reach, which I suspect was the mindset of the users of WKLB back in the Neolithic. This is how the Goddess put it to the hero in my novel, *Thirteen Moons:* 'Your ancestors are never far away, and localities such as this are sacred liminal places, where worlds merge. The seen and the unseen converge here, as they can at any site of ancestral power' (Knight 2007, p. 248). When we connect with the ancestors, it really is a two-way communication between ancestor and ancestor. As the Goddess also stated:

'Be mindful that to honour your ancestors
is also to honour yourself' (Knight 2007, p. 246).

Light phenomena
Unexplained lights are periodically captured in images taken inside and outside WKLB. These can take various forms, such as luminous streaks, balls of light ('Orbs') and misty/nebulous apparitions. I took my first orb photo here on an old 35mm camera film back in 1991.

US author and folklorist Gary Varner took a photo of, '… a white, textured object apparently in motion… in the 'empty' chamber', concluding that it was not a result of light leak. Chief Druid Emma Restall Orr was shown the picture and considered such images as, '… spirit energy emerging from the Earth' (posted May 16, 2002 on www.authorsden.com).

Marina Graham, a local photographer carrying out a survey of the site, told me of an apparition she had witnessed inside WKLB: '…a nebulous form, an image resembling Osiris'. She also told me how another photo she had taken inside showed two unexplained 'black rods'.

Artist Rick Kemp was on top of WKLB one evening a few years ago, whilst a group of people were inside: '… a lady began wailing. She sounded as if she was entering a trance… As I concentrated on the Moon I suddenly became aware of tiny points of light dancing around it. I was so surprised that I just stared without taking any pictures… I have photographed the Moon on numerous occasions and had never ever seen anything remotely like this' (email June 12, 2010).

Orbs

Balls/spheres of light are quite frequently captured by cameras inside the dark interior of WKLB. These are the controversial Orbs. Many people have dismissed them as reflections, specks of dust, or droplets of water on the lens; some may well be, but a growing number caught by digital cameras cannot

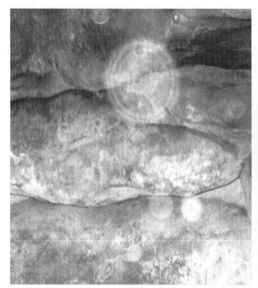

Orbs captured by a digital camera inside WKLB after drumming. (Image: Diane Gall, used with permission.)

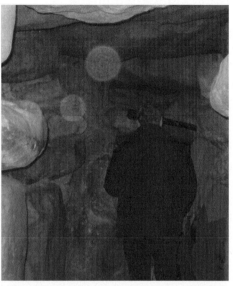

Two orbs floating in the passage of WKLB during a drumming evening in June 2009.

possibly be the result by the aforementioned explanations. Images of luminous spheres have also been caught on video over fields where crop formations have manifest.

I offer here a few of the many images that have come my way over recent years, some of which were taken by people who had no previous knowledge of the subject. Some have manifest during tours I led, or during our drumming evenings, or else during or after reiki circles and meditations. (Another can be seen with the author, whilst dowsing, on p. 162.

I offer no judgement regarding

Two orbs captured on the evening of the summer solstice, 2009. (Image: Sandy Walker.)

these. However, should 'Orbs' prove to be genuine paranormal phenomena, it does beg the question as to whether Neolithic shamans saw similar manifestations, perhaps interpreting them as spirits, fairies, divination visions - or perhaps even the ancestors themselves.

Moving Light Phenomena
For hundreds of years, psychics, clairvoyants, and other 'sensitives', have spoken of seeing ethereal objects and entities, things that others around them could not. Did the greater sensitivities of Neolithic shaman enable them to see, sense, feel and even communicate with 'something' or 'somewhere' we cannot generally access today. I have certainly had the feeling whilst inside WKLB that

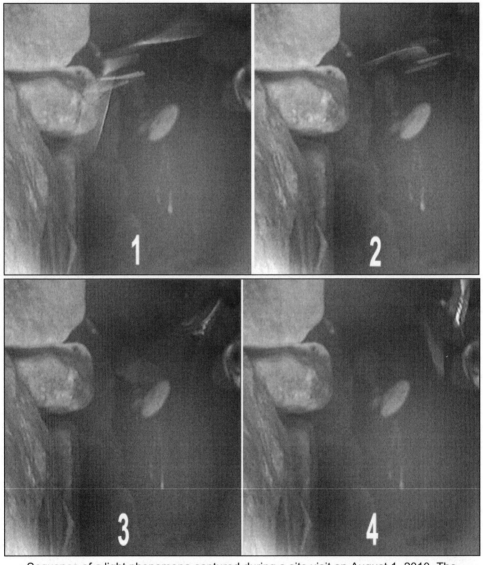

Sequence of a light phenomena captured during a site visit on August 1, 2010. The sequence lasts just a few seconds. (The white oval shape in the background is a drum). (Images with permission of Chrissy Murray.)

I was not alone, even though I physically had been. Today, many people, myself included, see stationary or moving objects or lights in the corners of the eye, in their peripheral vision, only to find nothing there when they turn their head. I suspect there may be dimensions and entities that just 'flicker' into our reality, when conditions are suitable, or when they have been 'requested'… or perhaps **when we are receptive**.

I think one such phenomenon occurred during the site visit on Aug 1, 2010, a gathering I have already discussed above. Analysis of a digital video sequence revealed several 'frames' that show a nebulous, semi-transparent object moving across the passage from left to right, before disappearing in front of, or into, a stone. It changes its form several times, and yet the sequence shows it to be a single object. As with the orbs that are captured, this phenomena manifested during a period when a group of sensitive people were on site, chanting, drumming, meditating, forging channels through to other realms. A close-up from the sequence (below) shows the apparition to be the shape of a bone joint. Image 3, above, shows a very clear 'wake' and 'ripples' in the original, that can just be made out in this reproduction. The images in their original colour format show variations in colour and hue, more than can be replicated here.

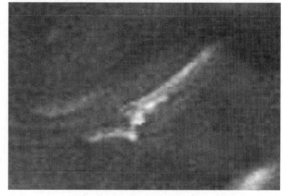

Did the apparition appear in response to our presence and to our activities? Or was the object just 'passing through', doing its own thing, so to speak? The sequence is the most impressive I have seen at WKLB, and I feel honoured to have been present.

A possible link between light phenomena, earth energies, and geological faulting is discussed in the next chapter.

Close-up of image 3, showing structure reminiscent of bones.
(Used with permission of Chrissy Murray.)

Crop Formations

The phenomena of 'crop circles' is a very controversial one, a vast and often mind-blowing field that is, mercifully, beyond the scope of this book. Regarding the 'genuine versus hoax' debate, it is perhaps enough to say that I accept that over many years there have indeed been numerous 'hoax' formations. But there have also occurred a vast number of huge, complex patterns that could not possibly have been made, in my humble opinion, by a gang of people in the dead of night wielding planks of wood!

Several crop formations have manifest in the fields around West Kennet and are dealt with in depth on specialised websites, and in a plethora of books. I will deal here with just two formations, both of which caught my attention and my curiosity, and which I feel have symbolic messages that are linked to how I view WKLB today.

July 13, 2004

To me personally, this formation says 'balance'. It shows the rays of the Sun and the crescent Moon, with the axis pointing towards the megaliths of WKLB. The symbolism is lunar and solar, yin and yang, God and Goddess, which may be one of the messages for how we need to interact with WKLB. The balance of male and female skeletons found inside WKLB brings us a message that it is a place for all, regardless of sex, religion, and ideology.

Karen Alexander, a leading crop formation researcher, has sent me her interpretation: 'This formation illustrated the Sun with its many illuminating rays. Within the laid crop of the crop circle was a small additional swirl representing the planet Venus as it crossed the face of the solar disk as it indeed did on the 8th of June 2004. This is a rare astronomical event as this only occurs four times in a period of 243 years. The next transit of Venus will be on the 6th June 2012' (text © Karen Alexander). Venus, of course, is the Goddess of Love.

Crop formation, July 13, 2004. This image of the Sun and the crescent Moon occurred within yards of WKLB, which is seen beyond. Silbury Hill rises in the distance.

(© Steve Alexander - used with permission; see also: www.temporarytemples.co.uk)

July 28, 2007

This formation has obvious symbolism linked with WKLB. It is a wonderful 3-D image, giving the impression that we are looking down a passageway that leads to an area of light in the distance. This so reminds me of the 'tunnel-effects' seen in trance and near-death experiences I described on p. 100. I feel we are being drawn into the depths of WKLB, into its mysteries, towards a comprehension of new knowledge.

Karen and Steve Alexander gave me their interpretation on the formation: 'This crop circle soon became known as the Temple, the Tunnel, or the Gateway. This crop circle marries the square and the circle. The square of the inner temple design is neatly enclosed by a containing circle. This crop circle shows one point perspective. One point perspective is used in design to create the illusion of three-dimensional space on a two-dimensional page or canvas. Once again a crop circle appeared close to an ancient site, which is very

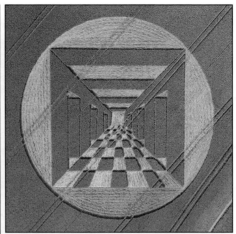

Crop formation of July 28, 2007.
The 3D effect mirrors the chambers
of WKLB, which is seen beyond the
formation in the left image.
(© Steve Alexander - used with
permission; See also:
www.temporarytemples.co.uk)

common in crop circle history. The marriage of the ancient and the modern perhaps?' (text © Karen and Steve Alexander).

Even today, it seems, the land gives us mysteries – just as it has always done. In her book *The 13th Step*, scientist, healer and mystic Jude Currivan (PhD) began and ended a worldwide journey in the valley in between Silbury Hill and WKLB, on the spot where a solar-like crop formation had manifest in spring 1998. In 2003, at the end of her trans-global planetary healing pilgrimage, she and others gathered there, at the 'seed-point', for a ceremony and meditation, to help the awakening of the planetary grid, '… at the moment of the Harmonic Concordance' (Currivan 2007, p. 213-216). This is just one example of how people today are connecting with the landscape to help manifest planetary healing. We shall look into this aspect further in the final chapter.

'The otherworlds are domains that can be accessed by all.'
(Mike Williams)

Chapter 13.
Earth Energies, Dowsing and Sacred Geometry

'Draca sceal on hlaew, frod, fraetrum wlanc.'
The dragon shall be in the tumulus, old, rich in treasures.
(Beowulf)

The paranormal lights discussed near the end of the previous chapter links us nicely with this one, as we seek to discover what processes are causing some of these phenomena. Strange lights, Orbs and apparitions would suggest the barrow is not just a collection of inert, old stones and a long, bumpy mound of earth. Forces are flowing across and through the landscape that would surely have been sensed here thousands of years ago, and may even have influenced the location and design of WKLB. Many ancient cultures, and modern aborigines, speak of 'power sites', as well as 'serpents' moving across the land. What is it they are referring to?

Many barrows are linked with tales of dragons, or dragons guarding buried treasure. Are these myths in fact speaking of the planetary life-force, flowing across the landscape, surging through these ancient mounds?

From the ancient Celtic *Cad Goddeu* manuscripts comes the line, 'I have been a snake enchanted on a hill'. Prof Gimbutas, in *The Language of the Goddess*, observes that: 'Throughout the Neolithic the snake is clearly a benevolent creature… a manifestation of the Goddess'. Dowsers today frequently refer to dowsable energy flows as 'serpents' or 'dragon currents'. William Stukeley's name for the collective Avebury sites was *Temple of the Dragon,* which contained The Sanctuary at the *Head of the Serpent.*

There are many books, websites, and societies where one can find out more about dowsing and earth energies. Personally, I have found dowsing to be a wonderful tool for demonstrating that there are unseen forces operating within and across the landscape. For me, this is no more difficult to accept than the concept that other invisible forces are also present in our Universe, such as gravity, X-rays, radio waves and infrared; we cannot see them, but they are there all the same. Has anyone ever seen gravity? What, for instance, does a thought look like? Water companies, farmers, the military, and even archaeologists, are today using dowsing to locate unseen targets.

I will concentrate here with the work done by individuals and groups on WKLB in particular. I have divided this section into two parts, although they are inextricably connected, as everything is (dowsing proves that!). First we shall look at WKLB as part of the bigger picture of landscape energies, and then at the barrow in detail, including a survey by my local dowsing group.

WKLB and Landscape Energies

As I have shown, WKLB was very carefully positioned on the landscape. This was due to several factors, I believe, and one of these was that the locality felt 'special' or 'powerful' in some way. Psychic Julie Umpleby told me that, 'West Kennet Long Barrow, for me, is a definite power spot as part of the greater Wessex landscape alignments' (email Sept 25, 2010). Scientist and mystic Jude Currivan speaks of the Avebury landscape as, '... an energetic and symbolic omphalos, or navel' (Currivan 2007, p. 211).

Dowser Sig Lonegren suggests that places such as WKLB helped solve an energetic problem due to the seasons: 'When we settled down and became farmers we had a problem – we had to make do all year 'round with the power centres that were in our local area. We then had to find ways to enhance the Earth Energies at times when they were not at their peak... There seems to be a solid connection between the introduction of farming and our first permanent temples built on sacred space' (Lonegren 1986, p. 36).

WKLB stands on the Mary current of the famous St Michael Line, the celebrated alignment that stretches right across southern England. Hamish Miller and Paul Broadhurst did the classic work on this alignment, spending years following hundreds of miles of dowsable energies (Miller & Broadhurst 1989). Two primary energy currents follow the axis of the alignment; the Michael flow passes through phallic stones and churches mainly dedicated to St Michael; the Mary flow passes through predominantly 'female' sites, such as wells, springs, churches dedicated to St Mary, and *Neolithic chambered sites.*

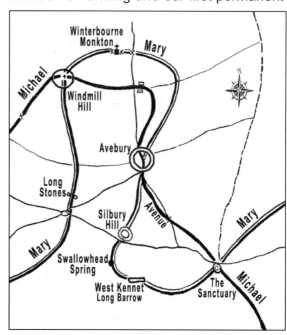

Map of the Michael and Mary currents of the St Michael Line in the Avebury area. (Redrawn from Miller & Broadhurst, with amendments.)

157

The two currents weave a dance around Avebury, passing through several key sites. On leaving Avebury, the Michael current flows up the avenue to The Sanctuary, whereas the Mary current goes over Waden Hill, through Silbury, up to WKLB, then to The Sanctuary, where it crosses the Michael flow. It is relevant that the majority (though not all) of chambered barrows have been dowsed to be primarily on 'feminine' energy flows, which ties in well with the concept that they are 'womb tombs'.

Miller and Broadhurst describe their dowsing of the Mary flow from the Sanctuary to WKLB: '… it was confirmed that the new serpent was found to pass right through the monumental megaliths of its façade at a diagonal angle, leaving to run down the valley' (Miller and Broadhurst 1989, p. 108). The flow also passes through the Swallowhead Spring. Although this is the best known,

and most thorough, work regarding the landscape energies around WKLB, it should be borne in mind that these are main 'veins and arteries', so to speak; there are other energies flowing in and out of WKLB.

In 1991, dowser Dennis Wheatley, with his daughter Maria, dowsed an energy flow thought to be associated with an earthen avenue that once existed, linking the mound and the spring (see map right). On a site visit in 2010, Maria informed me, '… it is about

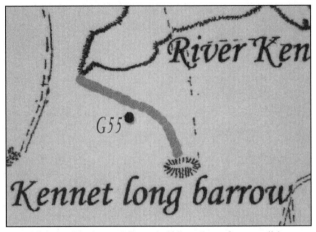

Map by Maria and Dennis Wheatley of a possible former avenue dowsed by them. It links WKLB and Swallowhead Spring, passing close to site G55.
(© Maria Wheatley, used with permission.)

12-15 paces wide, heading downhill as if mirroring the river - the giver of life bringing energy to the barrow'. She added that it partially follows narrow geological fissures in the Earth's crust, and terminates near the west chamber. Guy Underwood termed these flows *aquastats*. Maria concludes that, '… It was either the ceremonial way to approach the barrow, or a Spirit Path for the souls of the departed to use – or indeed both'.

This is complimented somewhat by the findings of archaeologist Caroline Malone, who noted a faint cursus-like feature running past the NW end of the barrow in an old aerial photograph.

WKLB Energy Dowsing
Regarding WKLB itself, the structure may have been designed to enhance and experience the energies of the site to the full. John Michell found that Chinese feng shui practitioners held great stead in connecting with their ancestors, and positioned their tombs with great care. He found that one task regularly undertaken by geomancers was the location of potential tomb sites: 'In finding

a burial site a geomancer first located the main currents, yin and yang, that crossed the area where the tomb was to be sited' (Michell 1983, p. 60-61).

It may be remembered that the mound at WKLB is layered. Pat Toms, of the British Society of Dowsers, has commented, '… when different types of substances are brought together particular etheric influences arise' (*Dowsing Today*, Sept 2006). Researcher and author Gary Biltcliffe found that geological layering was relevant to the energies and sanctity of the Isle of Portland (Biltcliffe 2009, p. 5-9). Many other ancient cultures built structures with a combination of silicon- and calcium–based rocks. In the 1930s to 1950s, physician Wilhelm Reich found that this blend of organic and inorganic layering accumulated a benevolent, healing force he called *orgone*.

Dowser Guy Underwood found a 'dew pond' SW of WKLB, which was nearly obliterated in his day (pre-1970's). These features, according to him, are always located within primary spirals of energy, marking important *blind springs*. In general, he found that long barrows require one or more blind springs, most having a powerful one beneath the highest part of the mound. The energy pattern for a long barrow is the presence of two aquastats running between two blind springs, '… enclosing the long oval space between them' (Underwood 1972, p. 79); blind springs are the energetic centres where primary energy flows converge, and from which they also emerge from the earth. Underwood found that a blind spring was, '… the esoteric 'centre' of the Old Religion, as well as being the actual centre of its monuments (op. cit. p. 79). The dowsable effects of these points are usually in the form of either a right- or left-handed *geospiral*. Maria Wheatley found that WKLB is situated over a geospiral with seven coils (Wheatley 2002).

American sound healer Susan Elizabeth Hale comments that, 'There are places on the earth, often where ley lines and underground water streams converge, that emanate powerful vibrations. These vibrations alter our sense of ordinary reality and put us in contact with the numinous – with mythic reality and greater mysteries that cannot be named' (Hale 2007, p. xiii).

It has also been suggested that 'power of place' is very much connected with energies that may be experienced. Archaeologist Aubrey Burl surprisingly concurs: 'There are reasons for believing the function of these barrows was to harbour powerful forces rather than merely to contain the respected but lifeless bones of the family's forebears' (Burl 2002, p. 95).

Psychic surgeon Chris Thomas heaps praise indeed on WKLB, saying that at one time it was the site of one of the most powerful vortexes on the planet! He suggests it was built by a chieftain who wanted the energy upwelling to link him to the stars.

As long ago as 1935, dowser R Boothby commented that, '… every long barrow had an underground stream running its full length' (*Journal of the British Society of Dowsers*: vol. 2). Michael Dames suggests that the dry-stone walling, which is sometimes undulating, may represent local rivers, but may also be symbolic of underground water underpinning the site.

'Hedge Druid' *Gwas* describes the entrance stones as, '… huge lower teeth clamping the mound in a pit-bull jaw lock'. The view inspired him: 'I felt like there must have been many a shaman, warrior or nobleman who wished to be buried here, in sight of Silbury Hill'. He dowsed a spiral of energy just west of the two concrete covers: 'I was in a zone outside of time and space and the rods moved lithely in my hands'. He also comments how he had also photographed images of Orbs at the very same spots in the chambers where, '... the centre of spiralling energy was dowsed' (see www.hedgedruid.com).

In the previous chapter we looked at several accounts of lights and energies that had been experienced inside WKLB. Some of these weird happenings may be connected with earth energies. Photographer John Hague visited WKLB in June 2010, and reports that, '... for some mysterious reason my camera went on the blink... when I got back to the B&B quite a few photos were lost... weird!'

On the Aug 1 2010 site visit for the *WKLB Ancestors Project,* shaman Heather Heaton told me that when she arrived (after a Lughnasad drumming session with another group) the energies were so powerful that she was dizzy and her head was spinning. She told me that the place can, '...overload the senses", and that it, '... marks an upwelling from Mother Earth... the energy comes up from deep underground to provide energy for the land'.

Artist and visionary Monica Sjoo observed that, '... this is a place of high energies, a space where all outside influences are cut off and one is left with meditative dream and trances states created and experienced by the lunar right-brain mind in us all'.

BSD member Gunther Schneck has kindly sent me the results of his dowsing at WKLB. He states that there are two important energy crossing points, or nodes, at the site. He found that, '... the west chamber has the first node point... the second in the middle... [between stones 12 and 31] and four energy connecting lines pass into each of the four side chambers' (pers. comm.). Gunther feels that the first node may be a, 'mental healing point', whilst the second is a, 'physical healing point', a possible location for treating cancer. He speculates that people may have spent time in the

Site visit with Maria Wheatley and Busty Taylor on July 3, 2010.

chambers purely for its physical curative properties. He also thinks that some of the bones that were removed from the chambers may have been ground down and the resulting powder ingested, because the bones had absorbed this healing energy. William Stukeley spoke of a local doctor who appears to have been doing this (p. 62). Schneck concludes by saying that we could regard WKLB as a, 'Stone Age treatment centre and pharmacy'.

Dowsing Site Visits

July 3, 2010

On this occasion, Sue and I were joined by dowser Maria Wheatley and Busty Taylor. I invited Maria after reading her description of WKLB on the BSD website: 'At this atmospheric barrow there is a form of vortex energy which is startling and dramatic… watch as the rod spins wildly'.

Maria confirmed Hamish Miller's claim that the Mary current of the St Michael Line came into the chambers, '… at a diagonal angle', around 45 degrees, through NW and NE chambers, passing out of monument through stones 6, 7, 44 and 45. Around full Moon this may even encompass stones 36 and 40. I found that the edge of it also impinged on the SE chamber too. Maria told me of a powerful vortex that spirals out of the ground in the centre of west chamber and goes straight up through the roof. She said the roof may have originally been corbelled (to enhance the energies, as at Newgrange) and I could see some surviving evidence in this; some of the higher stones stick out more than those below (like an igloo). You may recall from the last chapter how some people had felt and envisioned energies passing upward in this chamber.

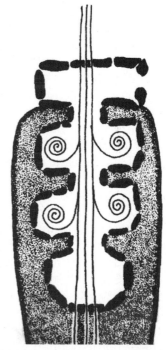

A triad of water lines with branch spirals, as dowsed by Dennis and Maria Wheatley
(© Maria Wheatley, used with permission.) Not to scale.

Maria also gave me a copy of a plan (right) of the dowsing she and her father, Dennis, had done at WKLB: 'Coursing along the central axis is a water line composed of a triad of hairlines of no appreciable width'. Dowser Tom Graves also found three well-defined water-lines flowing along the mound of Belas Knap, Gloucs (Graves & Poraj-Wilczynska 2008, p. 130-131).

Also shown here are four 'branch spirals' going from the passage into each chamber, which is shown in her recent pamphlet (Wheatley 2002). She also spoke to me of the 'preservative qualities' of tombs that have branch spirals. Richard Colt-Hoare had found remarkably preserved skulls in barrows that were later dowsed to have branch spirals. She concludes that the spirals, '... physically set the design of each burial chamber'. This is a good example of what dowser Guy Underwood called 'geodetic engineering', whereby earth energies were integrated into megalithic sites. Underwood concluded that, '... the justification for the [side] chambers is that the central geodetic line inside the barrow has thrown out branch or 'habitation' spirals on one or both sides. It appears that the existence of such a spiral made the site auspicious either as a habitation for the living or as a grave for the dead' (Underwood 1972, p. 80-81). I interpret 'habitation' as being the time spent by shamans in these chambers.

July 27, 2010

Sue Wallace and myself dowsed the mound and chambers using L-rods and pendulums. We dowsed spirals in the chambers and flows of overground energy traversing the length of the mound, from east to west.

The image shown here was taken in the west chamber. It was only later that we noticed an orb behind me (arrowed). In the image I am dowsing a powerful anticlockwise spiral of energy, which came out of the ground and went through the roof, literally! Without prompting, Sue confirmed the direction of this with her pendulum. This energy spiral has been confirmed by other people quite independently. Dowser Tom Graves has also noted energy moving in a 'twisting motion' in the *west* chamber of Belas Knap, in the Cotswolds.

The author dowsing in the west chamber on July 27, 2010. The arrow marks an Orb that was later spotted in the photo. (Image: Sue Wallace.)

I also confirmed the three lines going down the passage, and that the Mary flow came in at an angle through the NW and NE chambers and left the site through stone 45, heading off at about 45° to the SE (also see site survey below).

Sue and I also dowsed along the length of the mound. I located seven bands of overground energy flowing along the mound, parallel with the axis. I don't think that these corresponded with the ones that Maria Wheatley had dowsed. Sue picked up on some wide energy flows that crossed the mound diagonally at two points, seeming to 'mimic' or 'echo' what the Mary current was doing at the chamber end.

We also took along an 'electro-smog detector', designed to identify black spots and harmful concentrations of electricity in the home. Inside, cut off from the outside world, the detector was totally silent. At the entrance, it immediately began to 'buzz', presumably detecting interference from the masts on Morgan's Hill, and perhaps elsewhere. This demonstrated to us just how well the interior is isolated and insulated from outside influences.

I felt, however, that we needed the help of more experienced dowsers to do justice to WKLB, so help is what I sought.

October 9, 2010

This site visit was composed of fellow members of the Wyvern Dowsers. At my invitation thirteen people attended the survey, which lasted about two hours. The hill was misty and the skies were overcast; the Moon was 3 days old in Virgo, and Venus was moving in retrograde (just for the record!). Everyone was given two plans, one showing the whole site, the other the chambers in detail. No information about previous dowsing at WKLB was given to attendees.

Later analysis of the maps and accompanying comments proved most interesting. Dowsing is a very individual process, however, and conflicting results have led to criticism down the years. But dowsing is not about 'science' – it is about **experience**. I suspect that dowsing results between participants vary because everyone is unique, with different vibrations, physiques, abilities, and mindsets. Dowsing can open up a two-way communication between us and the landscape around us, and this experience is different and unique for all of us.

All that being said, several of the plotted energies and comments on hot spots and physical effects, *did* coincide and these deserve special mention.

Members of the Wyvern Dowsers on the site visit of October 9, 2010.
The flags mark out the courses of dowsed energy flows.

163

Members of the Wyvern Dowsers during the survey at WKLB on October 9, 2010.

Inside

Virtually **all** of the participants dowsed or physically sensed spiralling energies in the chambers, several of them in **all** of the chambers. The split between clockwise and anticlockwise movements of energies was split almost evenly. This may be because several people did not specify if the energy was flowing **up** out of the ground, or **down** into it.

Some of the participants confirmed the dowsing results of Maria and Dennis Wheatley, regarding energy entering the passageway and then flowing as branch spirals into each side chamber.

The biggest agreement of data was in the west chamber; many participants felt a strong energy spiral coming out of the ground and rising upwards. This compliments the experiences and visions of several people in the previous chapter. In the same chamber, three individuals felt strong energies immediately in front of stone 22, the 'Skull Stone', one person becoming, 'very shaky', another feeling, '...a clockwise rocking sensation'. This is one of the acoustic hot spots found previously by others and myself. Sib Cole dowsed two powerful energy spots between 18 and 25, another acoustic hot spot.

A brief drumming session was carried out by myself halfway through the dowsing session; during this one participant present, Pat Cannings, felt, '... filled with energy, spinning, rocking, vibrating... out of body, out of time'. She also witnessed a brief flash of light.

On a more general note, various participants experienced wobbly moments at certain spots, as well as spinning pendulums, and some visions. Chris Hinton saw a 'white form' in the SE chamber, between stones 10 and 11, where she also sensed an increase in energy. She also felt that the chamber belonged to one family. Whilst the drumming was going on, a crystal pendulum she was holding, which had previously been stationary, suddenly started to become very active, only to be still again after the drumming ended. She also saw a flash of light and had an impression that there had been flickering torchlight long ago. Standing in the west chamber, next to stone 19, Chris, '... visibly shook' and in between stone 19 and 24, '... could hardly stand still'. This spot is identical to where Pat Cannings had recorded 'strong energy'.

In the NE chamber Chris Hinton also had feelings about bones: 'Here I felt bones, that they were used in magical ceremony perhaps to promote the qualities of the deceased which may have been special, perhaps cremation ash sprinkled into a drink'. Val Midwinter recorded this space as having, 'positive energy'.

It is interesting that Tom Graves and Liz Poraj-Wilczynska found that different chambers in the Neolithic chambered site of Belas Knap had also afforded them very different feelings, individually, and regarding movements of energy (Graves & Poraj-Wilczynska 2008, p. 124).

Regarding the Mary current of the St Michael Line, three participants picked up on the energies of the flow, finding it either in the passage, the west chamber, or both. Some diversity of opinion exists, it would seem, as some dowsers feel the Mary current flows the length of the passage, from west-east, whilst others dowse it as coming into the interior through the NW and NE chambers, before exiting through the entrance. This is what I found on the July 27 site visit, and on this occasion. It could be, of course, that the line has split into smaller flows or 'ribbons', which is apparently quite commonly found along major energy flows. Perhaps with dowsing there is no 'right' or 'wrong' (a real 'bummer' for the logically minded!)

Outside and the Mound
Several members picked up the Mary flow as it left the site via stone 45. We marked the edges of the dowsable energies with flags (right). At one point, an underground stream crossed Mary, almost at right angles. This seemed to join another flow that

Flags denoting the limits of the dowsable energies of the Mary current outside WKLB.

165

Sib Cole had dowsed coming out of the entrance. The two converged and went off down the hill in a northerly direction.

Regarding the mound, five exterior plans were handed back completed. Underground water was detected by some, and Sib Cole and Shaun Ogbourne agreed that a powerful underground stream runs under the axis. Is this one of the determining elements of why the mound is so long? Shaun showed us where another underground water flow passed diagonally under the mound, just west of the chambers. At the very western tip of the mound he also told us about an overground flow of energy that he felt very uneasy with, that it had, '… nasty, polluted energy'.

A few yards to the east of this, a little way in from the west end of the mound, Shaun showed us where he had dowsed a geological fault passing under the mound at around a 40° angle to the axis. Paul Devereux has demonstrated how ancient sacred sites are often located on or very close to faults in the Earth's crust, as well as a correlation between faulted areas and strange earth-lights and other unexplained phenomena (Devereux 1989). In Wiltshire, 'UFO's' have been famously seen at Warminster, as well as at Mere, both close to where faults come to the surface. Devereux speculates that perhaps many of the strange lights seen in our skies are not alien spacecraft, but are in fact 'Earth Born'. He poignantly concludes that, '… like planetary messengers, the dancing lights in the sky may be leading us back to the world we so readily disregard - Planet Earth' (Devereux 1989, p. 202). Nice one.

An Interview, a Pint, and an Open Fire
After the site visit, Sue and I adjourned to the local watering hole, the Waggon and Horses, with Shaun Ogbourne, Chairman of the Wyvern Dowsers, for a well-needed warm by an open fire, and some liquid refreshment! Shaun kindly answered a series of questions I put to him, as well as commenting on related matters. On the issue that the mound had possibly been extended, he told us that as the site progressively drew more energies to it, the mound was extended accordingly. He agreed with Piggott's findings that pre-barrow activity went on there: 'WKLB was a place of healing and ceremony in the Mesolithic, when people were travelling through the area'. When I raised the issue about the patterning on the B8 Beaker pot, he replied, 'The lozenges on the pots mirror the patterns of the energies in the chambers'.

Asked about Neolithic shamans venturing into the dark chambers, Shaun replied that, '… initiation and rites of passage are best done in confined places, such as caves or cave-like spaces. And in those days, you were doing initiation in WKLB not out of fear; the main reason for going into trance was to speak to the ancestors, and to be told by them what your journey would be'.

He also implied that being the shaman of the clan was not all a bed of roses: 'Regarding divination, shamans were under real pressure to come up with answers in times of hardship'.

When I finally asked him about the use of the site today, Shaun replied, 'Today it is still a good place to focus our healing, to radiate it down the water lines and overground energy flows. The confinement of the chambers helps us focus'.

Some people may be disappointed that I have not produced one or two 'definitive' plans of the earth energies of WKLB. I believe that such things are impossible to create. Two issues come into play here. Firstly, everyone experiences and interacts with the earth, the land, its energies, and themselves, differently to everyone else. I am sure that Hamish Miller would have been the first to admit that the energy flows that *he* mapped would not necessarily have been experienced in exactly the same way by others who followed. Secondly, dowsers over many years have found, and I can confirm this, that dowsable energies vary enormously regarding strength, width and even depth, with the cycles of the year, the phases of the Moon and whatever the Sun is doing in the sky – if it is above or below the horizon, as well as the levels of solar sunspot activity. With such variables, I believe it is impossible to produce a 'definitive energy map' of any site. All that can be said of such ventures is something like this: This is what was found at one particular time by one particular person – no more no less. This invalidates nothing or no one. To me, it merely shows what the ancients knew thousands of years ago, that the Earth is alive! She moves, she changes, and there is constant flux. More than anything else, dowsing has help me appreciate that the planet we are blessed to live on is indeed a magical place, and that the interaction we have with it is individual and unique.

We will now look at an aspect of WKLB that links many aspects we have already broached upon – sacred geometry.

Sacred Geometry

The premise that ancient sites were laid out with the principles of sacred geometry in mind is now virtually mainstream. The architecture of churches, cathedrals, temples, and other secular buildings has been studied at great length and were found to have been built to specific proportions, to enhance both experience and the earth energies. Surveyor Alexander Thom, for instance, demonstrated that Avebury's stones incorporate sacred geometry (Thom 1967, Frontispiece & p. 89).

I have dealt with this subject in some detail in *The Wessex Astrum: Sacred Geometry in a Mystical Landscape* (Knight & Perrott 2008), which does not need repeating here. The Wessex Astrum hexagram will be discussed again in the next chapter, in terms of landscape alignments involving WKLB, so perhaps we can confine ourselves for now with the long barrow itself.

Although 'alternative' researchers have for years advocated that sacred geometry is an integral part of many sacred sites, a recent study by an *academic* asserts that our Neolithic ancestors possessed a sophisticated knowledge of geometry rivalling that of Pythagoras, 2,000 years before the eminent Greek. Five years of detailed research has led respected archaeologist Anthony Johnson (of Oxford University) to the conclusion that Stonehenge was designed and built using advanced geometry (Johnson 2008). He demonstrates how an outer polygon was laid out using the geometry of the square and the circle, and advocates that knowledge of geometry was an imperative part of wider European spiritual belief, driving the building of Stonehenge to highlight such expertise. Johnson declares that the Neolithic complex was designed and erected as a result of methods used to construct simpler monuments during the preceding centuries. This knowledge was regarded by prehistoric clans as arcane wisdom or magic, which in turn conferred a privileged status. 'It strongly suggests', says Johnson, '… that it was the knowledge of geometry and symmetry which was an important component of the Neolithic belief system… '.

Stuart Piggott, as a result of his 1995-6 excavations, noted how the chambers, forecourt and blocking stones of WKLB stood inside a perfect isosceles triangle, whose height was twice the length of the base, the latter of which is 9.75m (32ft). He noted that, 'If a triangle is drawn, it is found that its sides run through the stones forming the rear walls of all four lateral chambers, and that three of the stones involved (no. 10, 27 and 33) are coincident in angle with the triangle's sides, the fourth (15) only slightly divergent. The west chamber falls symmetrically within the converging sides, its rear wall being 20ft from the apex'. He tellingly concludes that, 'It is clear that some kind of a regular plan was envisaged, presumably to definite units of measurement and with a knowledge of ratios, and that building followed this plan so far as practical difficulties in handling large masses of stone allowed' (Piggott 1962).

Later, astro-archaeologist John North discussed how the faces of many of the stones comprising the chamber walls are parallel, and that there are also several right-angles. North noted how four of the stones (A in the figure right) are, '… almost perfectly aligned with the axis'. This implies accurate positioning, as the axis is an invisible line, unmarked by stones.

There was a time when the chambers were roofless, when WKLB was under construction. Speaking about this stage before the capstones were put in place, North states that, '… it is easy to make conjectures concerning slight changes of plan, forced on its builders by their materials' (North 1996, p. 77). The shapes and the positions of the stones could therefore by fine-tuned, or even replaced by more suitable ones, because the basic geometric design

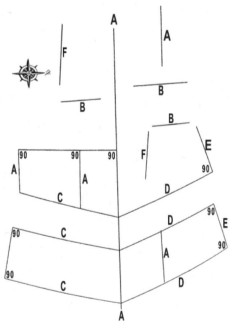

John North's plan of the construction lines of WKLB, based on the faces of the stones. Parallel faces are given the same letters, and 90° angles are also shown. (Redrawn after North.)

168

was in place, enabling refinement before the chambers were enclosed by the capstones and the mound. Looking at WKLB today, it is difficult to get an idea of the sacred geometry involved in the monument. But when the site was being constructed, the standing stones featured in the diagrams above would have been open to the skies and could be tweaked to perfection.

One of the basic foundations of sacred geometry is the Golden Section or Golden Triangle. This triangle comprises angles of 72°, 72°, and 36° (totalling 180°). This triangle is involved in the construction of many sacred sites around the world. Gary Biltcliffe has found that some churches on Portland, Dorset, were located to form Golden Triangles (Biltcliffe 2009, p. 73-74). I found it interesting that a Golden Triangle encloses the chambers of WKLB.

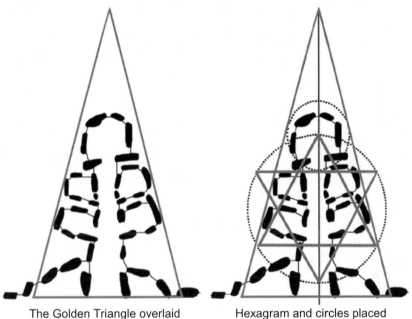

| The Golden Triangle overlaid on the plan of WKLB. | Hexagram and circles placed over the plan. |

This can be developed further by a hexagram: lines defining it go through the centres of the four side chambers; the two axial points of the hexagram are both on the axis, in the centre of the west chamber and in the forecourt. A circle can be drawn around this hexagram, and smaller one also encloses the west chamber, bounded by the lines of the Golden Triangle.

If Prof Johnson is correct in his assertion that knowledge of sacred geometry at Stonehenge was perfected during the construction of earlier monuments, then WKLB could have been one such place. It certainly pre-dates Stonehenge, and is less than 20 miles to the north.

Our distant ancestors observed mathematics and sacred geometry all around them in Nature; it was a natural progression, perhaps even an act of reverence, to incorporate number and proportion in their sacred sites.

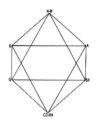

Chapter 14.
Landscape Alignments

'Long barrows were emphatically arranged in
lines of three or even four.' (John North)

Long has it been suggested that the location of ancient sites may have been chosen to deliberately align them with other points on the landscape, including sacred sites. Archaeologists have generally expressed scepticism of such landscape-wide configurations, which is ironic, considering the first one recorded, involving Stonehenge, Old Sarum and Salisbury Cathedral, was noted by scientist Sir Norman Lockyer in 1906; this has since been extended to Bredon Hill and Pershore Abbey (Furlong 1997, p. 263). Much of the criticism has been part of the inherited backlash by academia, in the 1920's, on the work of Alfred Watkins and his proposed *ley lines.* If there has been any 'softening' of attitudes it has usually been concerning proposed *astronomical* alignments, which seem to be more acceptable. These include an extension to nearby sites of the famous summer solstice alignment at Stonehenge.

In *Ancient Stones of Dorset* (Knight 1996), I demonstrated several alignments involving Neolithic sites, such as the Dorset Cursus with local long barrows, (op. cit. p. 56), and those relating to Mount Pleasant Henge, Maumsbury Rings and Allington Avenue Long Barrow (op. cit. p. 137).

The intervisibility of barrows was noticed by William Stukeley back in the 18th Century: 'I observe the barrows of Hakpen Hill and others are set with great art not upon the very highest part of the hills but upon so much of the declivity or edge, as that they make appearance as above those in the valley'. Alfred Watkins was to observe this in the 1920's: '… mounds were planted in very special positions for sighting, not on the highest point unless the ridge were a narrow one, but just a shade down the slope, to be seen from all parts of the valley below' (Watkins 1927, p. 25). In *Prehistoric Avebury*, Aubrey Burl seems to concur: 'Often barrows stand on the skyline because the builders set them not on the summit of hills and ridges but slightly down the slope where they would be visible from below' (Burl 2002). Was this positioning because they would make good points from which to survey the land, in much the same way that Ordnance Survey triangulation pillars are intervisible today?

Local Alignments

Some local alignments have already been discussed, such as the impressive line-of-sight examples in Chapters 4 and 6. Resulting from an in depth study of local sites, I consider the following alignments to be accurate and, more to the point, intentional and fundamental to their placement:

(A) Involving Neolithic Sites Only:

Windmill Hill -- Silbury Hill -- WKLB.

WKLB -- Silbury Hill -- Horslip long barrow.

Long stones barrow -- Swallowhead Spring -- G55 -- WKLB -- East Kennet LB
    (solstice aligned).

Avebury Henge -- WKLB -- Adam's Grave long barrow.

Silbury Hill -- 'Silbaby' and Waden Spring -- Palisades Enclosures -- The
    Sanctuary.

East Kennet long barrow -- Palisades Enclosures -- 'Silbaby' -- Avebury
    Henge.

Windmill Hill -- Silbury Hill (east side) – WKLB (west end) -- Knap Hill (summit).

Windmill Hill -- 'Silbaby' -- East Kennet long barrow.

(B) Involving Neolithic and Bronze Age sites:

Harestone Circle and Cove -- WKLB -- Silbury Hill.

WKLB -- Palisades Enclosures -- Overton Hill tumuli (solstice aligned).

Beckhampton Penning stone circle -- WKLB -- Palisades Enclosures -- Overton
    Hill tumulus (grid ref: 118692).

Windmill Hill -- Silbury Hill (summit) -- G55 -- Knap Hill (tumuli at SW end).

Marden Henge -- Beckhampton Penning stone circle -- Silbury Hill -- Avebury
    Henge

I think it inconceivable that these alignments, which include some sightlines, were not part of the original conception and positioning of these sites. The incorporation of Bronze Age sites into existing alignments involving Neolithic sites shows site continuity; people in later times still saw the earlier sites as important. I offer no map of the above alignments, as I think it would be an

171

admirable exercise for the reader to plot these. You may be amazed at the results; before your eyes will manifest Man and landscape in harmony.

Ironically, one of the advocates for the *intentional* alignment of Neolithic sites in the Avebury area was astro-archaeologist John North. In his classic work, *Stonehenge - Neolithic Man and the Cosmos,* North shows how long barrows around Stonehenge, on Cranborne Chase (Dorset), and around Avebury, are very accurately aligned. He suggests that these groupings define local clan territories. Of the 28 long barrows he mapped in the Avebury area, he found that ALL are aligned with at least two other long barrows, and sometimes more

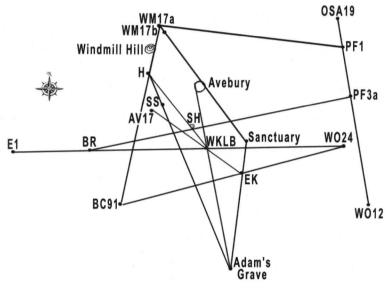

Alignments involving Neolithic monuments in the Avebury area, based on the work of John North. All involve three or more sites, and/or right angles. Some long barrows are shown with their official numbering, based on their parish. Abbreviations:
WM = Winterbourne Monkton; H = Horslip barrow; SS = South Street;
EK = East Kennet Long Barrow; E = linear enclosure; AV = Avebury;
BR = Beckhampton Rd barrow; OSA = Ogbourne St Andrew; PF: Pitton and Farley;
WO = West Overton; SH = Silbury Hill; BC = Bishop's Cannings.
(After North; some other long barrows have been omitted for the sake of clarity.)

(North 1996, p. 170). More than this, North found several perpendicular alignments, whereby a line heads off (from a barrow) at around 90° from one alignment to another barrow. He gives eight examples of this, and the range of all of them, amazingly, is between 86.7° and 89.77°. I have only shown a selection here, involving the immediate landscape of WKLB, and some further out with actual sightlines. This data is impressive by the fact that most of these long barrows were never intervisible! The ones that *are* intervisible seem to involve the right angles. North comments that, 'These are surely witness to the custom to be found repeatedly in long barrow design, that is, the custom of seeking out lines of sight at right angles... there is not a single long barrow that cannot be somehow accommodated by the scheme' (op. cit. p. 171-172). Paul

Devereux has commented on one of these: 'It seems as if the builders of the great mound [Silbury Hill] respected the Horslip-West Kennet sightline with some precision' (Devereux 1992, p. 150).

Some of John North's alignments shown above are three miles long, and the skill of Neolithic surveyors has to be admired when one considers how undulating the terrain is: *several of the barrows are not intervisible*. Some of the orientations are astronomical, but others are not. Alignments may have been achieved by the lighting of fires on calm days, the smoke from which would rise vertically, visible from another site over an intervening hill. Perhaps the object of these alignments was more symbolic than purely practical, as the clan shaman articulated their appreciation of how everything is connected in Nature. They perceived their monuments as part of the landscape, not simply buildings placed upon it; their monuments express their cosmology.

John North must have sensed archaeologists shouting 'ley lines – stone him!', for he comments on this, attempting to quell their deepest fears about the non-intervisibility of many aligned barrows: 'It would be unfortunate if this were thought to cast doubt on the reality of the alignments, and even more so if readers were to turn tail and run, at the thought that this marks the slippery ley-line slope, for the fact is that long barrows were emphatically arranged in lines of three or even four' (North 1996, p. 166).

It has been suggested in recent years that alignments between sacred sites, particularly barrows, might be vestiges of 'spirit flights' of shamans over the landscape (Devereux 1992, p. 85). Several ancient and modern cultures have the concept of straight line 'flight' when shamans journey to meet their ancestors. I too think it feasible that the alignments of the long barrows mark out-of-body journeys of the shaman between one ancestral site and another. I remind the reader of the exchange of relics and artefacts, including human bones, between Neolithic sites around WKLB.

It needs recording here that dozens of crop formations have manifest *precisely* on these lines over the past 15 years. Cynics may argue, of course, that with so many alignments covering such a relatively small area, inevitably some would be on these lines. I make no judgement on this – I simply pass on the information as 'food for thought'.

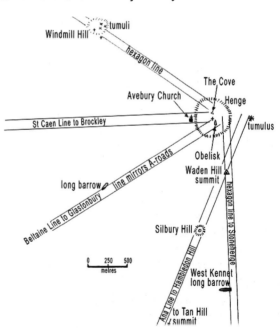

The 'corridors' of the hexagram and hexagon lines of the Wessex Astrum as they converge on Avebury (Knight & Perrott 2008, p. 130).

Stonehenge to Avebury Alignment

This alignment has been discussed previously, by authors such as Robert Coon, John Michell, Robin Heath, and myself. Robert Coon's landscape hexagram he called the *Wessex Star* involved a Stonehenge – Avebury line (Coon 1993), which runs through WKLB.

The *Wessex Astrum* hexagram is the huge landscape figure involving arguably the 'big three' ancient spiritual centres of Wessex – Glastonbury, Stonehenge and Avebury (see map below). This also has a Stonehenge to Avebury line, the *central axis* of which passes just yards east of the megaliths at WKLB (Knight & Perrott 2008). The angle that WKLB is off north-south (3.5°- 4.0°) is identical to the angle that the Wessex Astrum is also off N-S.

One of the problems with landscape alignments is where to position the terminal points. For instance, Stonehenge is a very compact site on the landscape, whereas Avebury henge is very large. With *The Wessex Astrum,* the five alignments approach the henge from different directions and terminate at various locations (op. cit. p. 130 – and map above). So too with the Astrum lines as they converge on Glastonbury (op. cit. p. 74). It is satisfying, however, that as these lines converge on terminal points, they 'take in' the main sites in that area. For instance, at Avebury the various lines include Silbury Hill, Windmill Hill, the summit of Waden Hill, Tan Hill, Milk Hill, the Cove, the Obelisk, and WKLB. This would suggest that more than mere coincidence is involved here. Whilst not drawing any conclusions, I would like to point out that between 1998-2008 a total of seven crop formations appeared between WKLB and Avebury that were *precisely* on the Stonehenge–Avebury line.

In *The Measure of Albion,* John Michell and Robin Heath have very accurately surveyed the Stonehenge to Avebury alignment to an accuracy of feet (Heath

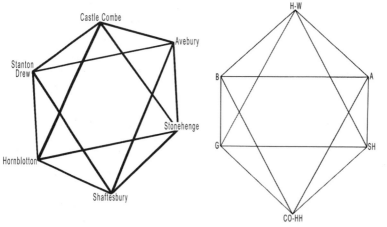

Left: The *Wessex Star* (after Robert Coon). Above: The *Wessex Astrum* (after Knight & Perrott). Both of these hexagrams involve WKLB on their Stonehenge-Avebury lines. Right: Details of the Stonehenge-Avebury line of the Wessex Astrum.
(Diagrams not to same scale.)
G = Glastonbury, B = Brockley, CO-HH = Child Okeford/Hambledon Hill, H-W = Holywell/ Wotton, A = Avebury, SH = Stonehenge.

Avebury
Waden Hill
West Kennet Long Barrow
Earthworks/Wain's Dyke
Milk Hill/White Horse
Ridgeway
Alton Priors
Woodborough
Hilcott Hall
Charlton
Goddard's Cleeve/Rushall Hill
Casterley Camp
Hilltop trig point
Aligned tumuli
Cursus
Stonehenge

and Michell 2004). Their results would suggest that the statistics and proportions of site alignments equate to the three radii (the mean, polar and equatorial) of the Earth (op. cit. p. 103-104). They measure the Stonehenge-Avebury line as 17.3192 miles, which they point out is almost exactly the square root of 300. They measure the distance along the line between the Cove at Avebury to blocking stone 45 at WKLB as '7,464.96 ft, or 864 x 8.64 ft... This is 27 times the radius of Silbury Hill and one part in 2,800 of the Earth's mean radius' (op. cit. p. 105). They see stone 45 as an important 'markstone', the only one surviving along the Avebury-Stonehenge line, and they also mention how the track up to the site runs along the alignment. Heath and Michell convincingly demonstrate that our British prehistoric ancestors were, '... an archaic culture with an elaborate code of science, based on the magic of number... capable of such great achievements in science and ritual magic that we are only just beginning to recognise them' (op. cit. p. 120).

Silbury Hill, WKLB and the Ancient Surveyors
In his seminal book, *The Keys to the Temple*, David Furlong advocates that as well as straight lines, more complex geometric figures are laid out in the Wiltshire landscape (Furlong 1997). He maps out two overlapping circles, a vesica pisces, and that the line joining the two centres runs parallel with the axis of the St Michael Line. He further sees connections between the geometry and proportions of this landscape vesica and that of the Great Pyramid at Giza (op. cit. p. 61-65). He accurately measures how a line drawn from the centre of the west vesica to WKLB is exactly 90° to a line from WKLB to Silbury Hill. He sees both these sites as being 'main surveying points' for laying out monuments in the area, and how the 90° angle is crucial in surveying: 'Once WKLB had been chosen and the orientation set then another key surveying point would need to have been established, as all surveying needs two points of reference... Herein lies the genius of the relationship between Silbury Hill and West Kennet long barrow' (Furlong, op. cit. p. 240). Of interest is the fact that Furlong's right-angled triangle is taken from the extended western end of WKLB, which Paul Devereux had found to produce the line-of-sight effect between WKLB, Silbury Hill and Windmill Hill.

John Michell and Robin Heath have also put on record the importance of Silbury Hill as a surveying point: 'This great artificial mound, built of chalk blocks, is a monumental relic of the prehistoric surveyors who located the sacred places of Britain and unified them by their mysterious science of number, music and geometry' (Heath & Michell 2004, p. iv).

Graham Tucker has recently advocated another vesica pisces formation involving WKLB (Tucker 2006). He expands this (image below) into a full-blown 'Flower of Life', a symbol found in ancient cultures. I am sometimes sceptical of claims for such forms on the landscape but this one is very precise and only covers about two miles from north to south, and includes several key sites. I have elaborated on his original find, and have added sites he may not have been aware of, or did not think relevant, such as G55, 'Silbaby'/Waden Mound, the Palisades, the Beckhampton Penning stones, and further Bronze Age

175

tumuli. The centre of the Flower is north of the Palisades, on Waden Hill (grid ref: approx. 109684).

Gary Biltcliffe has discovered a vesica pisces, similar to those of Furlong and Tucker, on the Isle of Portland (Biltcliffe 2009, p. 45). Biltcliffe considers alignments to have mathematical, geometrical, and spiritual elements, and that some were, '… part of a divine geometrical plan devised by ancient and modern geomancers to link their holy places' (Biltcliffe 2009, p. 71).

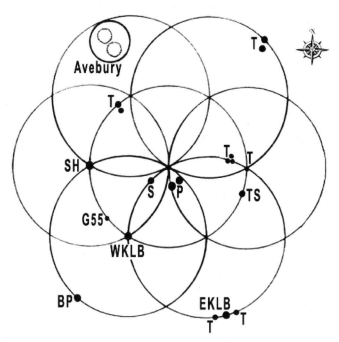

The 'Flower of Life' involving key sites in the Avebury area, including WKLB.
(Redrawn after Tucker, with additions by the author.)
S = 'Silbaby', BP = Beckhampton Penning stones, TS = The Sanctuary,
SH = Silbury Hill, P = Palisades, T = tumuli.

Also in the Avebury area, Tony Peart has described a six-petalled landscape star and triangle within a circle at Temple Rockley, just east of Avebury, which has the henge at one of the points (Knight & Perrott 2008, p. 27). Roma Harding has recently uncovered a vesica pisces associated with the Wessex Astrum hexagram (pers. comm.).

Of the many other landscape 'figures' proposed over recent years, some are 'questionable' to say the least. I am not invalidating these, just merely digesting them with a pinch of salt!

Archaeologists A B and P J Woodward have recently stated the possibility that barrows were more than randomly placed on the landscape: '… barrows were sited at set distances from the monuments and the monuments were placed such that many barrow sites were clearly visible from them… barrow distributions reflect far more than the even spacing of settlements' (Woodward 1996). Another penny drops.

I do not pretend to have included all the alignments for this area that have been proposed down the years. I have included those that are important to the general debate, and some others that 'floated my boat'. Landscape alignments give us further proof that our Neolithic and Bronze Age ancestors were more skilled and accomplished than we have given them credit for. This links rather nicely to the next chapter, where Neolithic precision and observational proficiency reaches dizzy heights, so to speak, as we look at the astronomical alignments of WKLB.

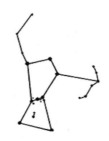

Chapter 15.
Sun, Moon and Stars –
Neolithic Astronomy

Twinkle twinkle little star,
How I wonder what you are.
(Trad.)

Ancient star-gazers were looking up at the skies long before the time of West Kennet Long Barrow. Neanderthal Man was arranging burials to align east-west. Mesopotamian, Greek, Egyptian and Babylonian cultures all recorded their close observations of the movements of the Sun, Moon and stars throughout the turning year. British archaeology, until recently, was slow on the uptake regarding Neolithic astronomical alignments in Britain. This is somewhat strange, considering the famous Stonehenge mid-summer sunrise alignment has been acknowledged and accepted by academia for many decades. Many considered Stonehenge to be unique, a 'quirky' exception, even though the writing had been on the wall for some time. In 1720, John Toland noted how Callanish was astronomically aligned to the Sun, confirmed in 1808 by Thomas Headrick.

In 1846, Rev E Duke wrote *Druidical Temples of Wiltshire,* suggesting that a model of the Solar System was laid out in Wiltshire, with sacred sites marking the planetary orbits, all centred on Silbury Hill as the Sun. Perhaps, as a result of such implausible claims, astro-archaeology as a discipline has taken a long time to get off the ground, so to speak: '… archaeologists are often unwilling to look up out of the ground' (Service & Bradbery 1979, p. 25).

So when Alexander Thom accurately surveyed hundreds of British prehistoric sites and found precise alignments with the Sun, Moon and the stars he received a cold and cynical academic reception. So too with Gerald Hawkins' initial work on the alignments of Stonehenge. The academic argument went something like this: 'Primitive Neolithic farmers, eking out an existence during such brutal and savage times would not have had the time or capability of plotting the motions of the heavenly bodies with such accuracy'. Oh really?

Recent work by Martin Brennan in Ireland (Brennan 1994), and Nicholas Mann and Philippa Glasson at Glastonbury (Mann & Glasson 2007), convincingly argued the case for astronomical alignments involving Neolithic sites. My work on the megalithic sites of Dorset revealed more astronomical alignments than the sum total previously known for the county (Knight 1996).

It has taken many decades for astro-archaeology to be well established, and one of its champions was, ironically but crucially, 'one of their own' - an academic. Prof John North (1934 - 2008) was primarily a historian, but one who had an interest in the history of astronomy, which led him into the subject ever deeper, resulting in his 653-page classic, *Stonehenge: Neolithic Man and the Cosmos* (North 1996). In it he meticulously reinterprets the early history of science and astronomy, establishing that the midwinter sunset at Stonehenge was at least as important as the famous midsummer sunrise.

But his chief motivation, as far as I am concerned, was his demonstration of how Neolithic farming communities throughout Wessex were following the journeys of the Sun, Moon and the stars and were aligning, even designing, their long barrows to mark such movements. Astronomically, Stonehenge was not an exception; it was built using knowledge that was, by that time, 'standard issue'.

I pay tribute to John North, and I lean heavily on his findings, and wish it to go on record that his work was the main inspiration for me to look at WKLB through the eyes of the Neolithic star-gazing shaman. This resulted in the discovery of several unrecorded alignments, as well as personally experiencing some sunrises and sunsets that will live with me forever.

So the penny is at last dropping, as archaeologists acknowledge that our Neolithic brothers and sisters were capable of accurately observing and mapping the heavens: 'The shaman knew, and could interpret, the cycles of nature, the workings of the heavens – the cycles of the Moon, the progress of the Sun…' (Moore & Gillette 1993, p. 70). Archaeologists, '… are recognising that orientation is as important as architecture and artefacts to anyone examining the ritual centres of prehistory' (Burl 1983, p. 5).

There are more than sixty long barrows on Salisbury Plain, and most are on high ground with open views of distant skylines, making them ideal for astronomical observation. John North detailed long barrows that were *self-aligned* with astronomical events (North 1996, p. 28-178). These include some near WKLB, such as Horslip, Beckhampton Road, and South Street. Postholes found at several long barrow sites may indicate that wooden posts were erected as sightlines. Piggott found several outside the mound at Wayland's Smithy, and posts are also indicated at other Wiltshire barrows, such as Fussell's Lodge. John North thought both these examples had astronomical associations (North 1996, p. 29-37 and p. 40-47). Some of the anomalies found at WKLB during the 2001 geophysical survey (see p. 80) may indicate pits that once held wooden posts.

I had previously uncovered unrecorded astronomical alignments involving *Neolithic sites* in Dorset, such as at the Grey Mare and Her Colts, the Hellstone and at Knowlton (Knight 1996). But what of WKLB? Was I to be disappointed in my quest to find ancient astronomical alignments here? Far from it. Would I even be able to witness solar, lunar, and stellar astronomical events at WKLB today? You bet ya!

WKLB - Looking for A Direction

In an astronomical survey of any ancient site, an accurate plan is required. An exact east-west alignment had been proposed for WKLB by William Stukeley as long ago as the 18th Century. John North found otherwise. He accurately obtained an axis orientation of 267° - 87° that is to say, 3° north of due east. He noted that, 'One much-copied plan - by one of archaeology's most expert draftsman – displaces the WKLB by 15°' (North 1996, p 23). He may have been referring to some of the diagrams in Piggott's reports, where the axis appears to be almost 15° off the true direction, if the compass on the diagrams is to be believed. Plans of the site have appeared in numerous works, and nearly all show the axis of the barrow as exactly east-west. In his plan of the site, Roger Joussaume gets the alignment correct (Joussaume 1988, p. 61). North does not see this 87° orientation as bad workmanship, but rather it enables more accurate alignments with the stars, whilst not affecting potential equinox sunrise observations from the west chamber. Incidentally, this 3° means that a line drawn at 90° from this is 3° west of due north, which is also the axis of the *Wessex Astrum* landscape hexagram (centre image p. 174).

Although seemingly devoid of direct sunlight, the chambers and passage at WKLB are also about light! Over the past two years I have observed amazing sunrises and moonrises and have been witness to the rays from these two celestial orbs penetrating corners and crevices where, at first glance, it would seem impossible. This is the brilliance of the monument: it is dark, yet allows in the light, it is claustrophobic, yet from certain points inside one can see the outside world.

Sue Wallace and myself did some site visits in 2010 to check the plans of the monument, to determine the axis for ourselves. We also established what views of the outside world could be obtained from different points in the interior of the barrow; this also involved sending laser beams into the chambers and obtaining compass readings for sightlines.

Notes on Co-ordinates, Skylines and Intentionality

For astronomical purposes, I have used the following co-ordinates for the east end of WKLB: Latitude: 51° 24' 30" N, Longitude: 1° 50' 56" W (based on Heath and Michell, 2004, p. 135). I have taken the height above sea level as 177m (580ft), this being the result obtained for the *forecourt* by Piggott at the 1955-56 excavations.

The computer programme used in my work was *Skymap Lite*, 2005 edition, programmed by Chris Marriott. This has enabled me to look at the skies above WKLB, in any direction, on any day, for any hour and minute, going back to 4000 BC. The star maps reproduced here are done so under licence, with graphics by the author.

Where the Sun, Moon, or a star rises and sets depends very much on latitude and longitude, but also on the height of the horizon. The higher the skyline above the observer, the later the object will appear to rise, because it has to clear the skyline first whilst it moves upwards and south (to the right). So too with setting objects, which will set earlier and further to the left if the skyline is above the observer. Fortunately (and not by chance, I believe) WKLB is positioned on a ridge where most of the skylines are either very similar in height, or just slightly above or below it. Even when there is a slight elevation of the skyline compared to the barrow, like to the south and west, it is minimal. The Neolithic people chose the site with great skill, a high place that afforded distant views with minimal obstruction by any woodland in the valleys.

At a recent conference, I was told that *intentionality* is the 'big thing' in archaeology at the moment. This asks us to consider whether just because there is an alignment with an interesting astronomical event, does this automatically mean the orientation was deliberate: John North pointed this out with great honestly: 'Deciding between deliberate and accidental alignments is one of the central problems... ' (North 1996, p. 6). I cannot speak for John North, but for my part I am simply putting on record what I have found, and leave it to the reader to decide. However, the sheer number of alignments marking 'key events' leaves me in no doubt that something was going on at WKLB thousands of years ago that cannot have been co-incidence. This also applies to the design of the monument. John North again: 'That the plan has a definite geometrical rationale can hardly be denied... and we are certainly not short of independent evidence that Neolithic geometry and stellar astronomy were closely allied'. The ancients were, after all, mirroring in their monuments the principles they saw operating in the cosmos around them.

Archaeologist Aubrey Burl has recently acknowledged the connections between the Neolithic burial sites and astronomical observations: 'Death and the heavens were major concerns of the living as they farmed their isolated settlements' (Burl 2002, p. 85). This implies that a 'burial' monument may also double as an astronomical 'observatory'. Life and death, Earth and sky, were elements of one Universe, where all was interlinked and co-existed.

Having obtained the *Skymap* computer software, I set out to see what secrets the barrow was hiding. What I was to find has left me even more in awe of what our Neolithic ancestors were capable of, and the depth of their relationship with the cosmos.

The Sun

The Sun determined the lives of prehistoric people, just as it determines our activities today. The Sun was at the heart of many ancient cultures all around the world, most famously with the ancient Egyptians, the Mayans, and the Aztecs.

It would appear that it was also the object of attention by the designers and users of sites across North Wiltshire in the Neolithic; Terence Meaden found solar alignments associated with the Cove and the Obelisk at Avebury; Michael Dames sees the monuments of the landscape around Avebury as being key elements in the veneration of the Goddess, each representing aspects of the solar year (Dames 1996). Maria Wheatley informs me that she thinks that burials at WKLB would have only taken place at certain times of the year, a further link with the turning solar year.

The Sun rises and sets at different places on the skyline depending on the time of year. It rises approximately SE at midwinter, gradually moving northwards along the horizon until it rises due east at the spring equinox. It then continues northwards until the summer solstice, when it rises approximately NE. The whole process then reverses, until midwinter is reached again. So too with the sunsets, which move from roughly SW in midwinter to NW at midsummer. The solstices and equinoxes, however, do not divide the year equally, due to the Earth's elliptical orbit.

Exactly where the Sun rises and sets depends on latitude, longitude, and the height of the skyline relative to the observer. We speak of azimuth when referring to where celestial objects rise and set: 0° is due north, 90° due east,

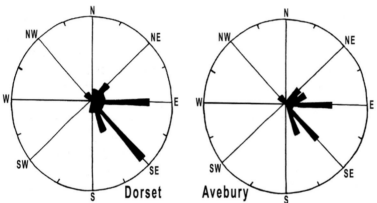

Comparison of the orientations of long barrows. In each chart the outer circle represents 18 barrows. Left: based on 47 Dorset long barrows (after Knight, 1996, p. 7); Right: based on 31 long barrows around Avebury (after Burl, 2002, p. 101).

180° is south, and 270° due west. Due to the wobble in the earth's rotational axis, the Sun does not rise and set in exactly the same position as it did in the Neolithic, although it is not far off. For instance, sunrise from the latitude of Glastonbury, Avebury and WKLB occurred around 48° in 3000 BC, whereas today it is around 49°. The midwinter sunset in 3000 BC was around 129° but today is slightly left of that, at about 128°. The movements of the Moon and the stars are far more complicated, as we shall see.

North sees WKLB as a site primarily of stellar alignments, which we shall look at shortly. To my surprise, he hardly comments on the near-equinox alignment, which I think is key to the west chamber. This is also surprising, when one considers that 80% of megalithic tombs in the Avebury area had entrances between the east and southeast. I have previously shown how the 47 long barrows in Dorset also show a bias in direction, with 18 orientated towards the southeast and 14 to the east (Knight 1996, p.7). This is reflected by Burl's orientations of 31 long barrows in the Avebury area, where the two most favoured directions are again east and southeast (Burl 2002, p. 101). I have compared these results in the diagram above. Burl suggests that as it is autumn/winter when the Sun rises in these preferred directions, they coincide with a time when farming activities were more relaxed than in spring and summer. He also considered that long barrows in the Avebury area were more inclined to be solar orientated, whereas around Stonehenge were aligned more with the Moon (op. cit. p. 100).

Perhaps the directions of sunrises and sunsets showed the routes to ancestral worlds – to the Afterlife. WKLB is very nearly east-west; in some aboriginal traditions, such as the Native Americans, west is associated with Grandmothers and the east with Grandfathers. The alignment of WKLB would seem fitting then for this 'ancestral' site.

My only regret in this section is that the images are in black and white. Those attending my PowerPoint presentations based on my work will see them in their full and often glorious, breathtaking colour. They can also be viewed in colour online on my FaceBook pages.

Equinox

Equinox sunrise the favoured alignment in the Avebury area, narrowly pushing the midwinter sunrise into second place. Twice a year, around March 20 - 22 and September 19 - 22, the Sun rises exactly east, providing there is a level horizon. Terence Meaden found the alignment of WKLB to be noteworthy, regarding stones 21 and 22 and the equinox sunrise. Don't forget that the blocking stone (45) was not part of the original barrow. Meaden incisively observed that when the Sun is heading north along the skyline at the spring equinox, the rays of the Sun illuminated the 'Skull Stone' first, and days later shone on the 'Living Head' stone. The Sun is passing from the winter ('dead') half of the year, to the summer ('living') half. It was to celebrate, '…an early version of the Rites of Spring' (Meaden 1999, p. 103). Six months later, as the

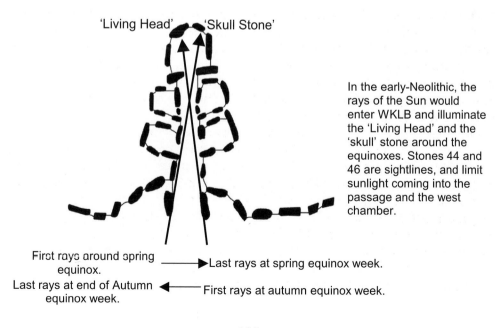

'Living Head'   'Skull Stone'

In the early-Neolithic, the rays of the Sun would enter WKLB and illuminate the 'Living Head' and the 'skull' stone around the equinoxes. Stones 44 and 46 are sightlines, and limit sunlight coming into the passage and the west chamber.

First rays around spring equinox. ———▶ Last rays at spring equinox week.

Last rays at end of Autumn equinox week. ◀——— First rays at autumn equinox week.

Sun progresses south along the skyline, it shines on the 'Living Head' *before* the 'Skull Stone', heralding the onset of winter. I have produced my version of these events above. Perhaps WKLB was indeed at the heart of equinox celebrations twice yearly (see Service & Bradbury 1979, p. 241-2).

I have calculated that if stone 45 were absent, the point of true sunrise (rising out the skyline) would be observed from the west chamber between March 10 and April 6 in the spring, and between Sept 7 and Oct 4 in the autumn (I have demonstrated how at Knowlton, Dorset, the Sun rises out of the Great Barrow a week either side of Equinox, as viewed from the central Neolithic henge (Knight 1996 and 1998). So although the axis of the barrow is not exactly east-west, the equinox sunrises were easily accommodated and observed from the west chamber. Today, the Sun rises in line with the axis around March 24-26 (just after equinox) and Sept 17-20 (just before equinox).

It will be observed that stones 44 and 46 are key to limiting the Sun's light into the passage. North shows these stones in his plans of WKLB, that they were present prior to any 'blocking', and I agree with him; they were part of the original design. The south face of stone 46 is skilfully aligned with the direction of the first and last rays of the Sun. Stone 44 is slightly off that alignment now, as the stone was moved slightly by Piggott, who found it sloping at quite an angle (in the diagram above, it is shown in its original position).

It has been said that because of the shortness and narrowness of the megalithic passages of long barrows they were far too imprecise to be used for astronomical purposes (Burl 2002, p. 101). John North held the opposite to be true, as do I. If anything, this narrowness and restriction refines any potential

Above: Virtual impression of the Sun rising around equinox in the Early Neolithic, seen from the west chamber. Right: Autumn equinox sunrise on Sept 22, 2010. Stone 45 is in the foreground. The two barns in the middle distance are a good guide to where the Sun rises at this time of year. (Image: Sue Wallace.)

184

sightlines, fine-tuning them. North considers that stones 44 and 46, the two flanking stones, '… should not be dismissed as merely helping to seal the entrance, for they have another important function' (North 1996, p 76). Two stones at the entrance of Wayland's Smithy perform a similar purpose (North 1996, Fig. 16). Other examples of twinned stones projecting beyond entrances can be found across Neolithic Europe, such as at Alsberg (Denmark), Bois Cotousier (France), Capilla dos Mouros (Spain), and the temple of Ggantija in Gozo (Malta).

It must have been an inspiring and uplifting experience thousands of years ago, as the Sun rose and light flooded the passage and west chamber. I have tried to recreate the scene above (and on cover) by removing stone 45.

We can of course observe equinox sunrises from outside WKLB today, and Sue and I were at the equinoxes of 2010. The September 22 sunrise was magnificent, and minutes afterwards the blocking stones turned golden (see cover). But the sunrise experience had not finished. As a result of the work of John North and Martin Brennan, and my own visits to Malta, I was impelled to stay around for a while to see what happened **after** the Sun had risen and climbed higher into the sky; for it is not necessarily just the *axis* of a site that is meaningful astronomically.

Incredibly, not long after the Equinox Sun rose, it cleared the south edge of stone 45 and a thin arc of sunlight penetrated the passage; then, for several minutes, it even illuminated the 'Skull Stone' This was unexpected considering the presence and bulk of the blocking stone. Soon afterwards, the stones on the north side of the passage also received

Not long after sunrise, the rays of the equinox Sun penetrate the passage and shine on the 'Skull Stone'. The interior seemed to come alive - see also back cover. (Image: Sue Wallace.)

sunlight, which even penetrated part of the NW chamber! Photographer Marina Graham was also inside with us, photographing the unfolding wonder, which she had observed on previous occasions. The scene is captured above and on the back cover. It was a magical moment that brought the interior to life.

Later that day we also observed the equinox sunset. It set well to the right of the masts on Morgan's Hill, to the right of the axis of the mound, confirming that the mound is not exactly orientated east-west. A site visit on October 4 revealed the Sun setting in line with the mound, as it disappeared from view into the partially obscured Morgan's Hill (see images p. 56).

The power of light itself should not be underrated. 'Might it be a mistake to focus on the Sun as an *individual*? Might it not have been the *light* of the Sun that mattered' (North 1996, p. 528). (This may also hold true for the Moon.) Paul Devereux has painted a scene of shamans waiting within the dark depths of Neolithic tombs, '… waiting to receive the ecstatic golden blast of soul-searing solar light…' (Devereux 1997, p. 187). Marina thinks that stone 45 has always been in place, defining what light can access the interior. I am not so sure. The archaeology would suggest it was erected centuries after the barrow was constructed. However, we should not rule out that its shape and position was completely detached from later astronomical observation. One thing is sure; the stone certainly has a big influence on what happens today.

Archaeologist Catherine Tuck links Neolithic chambers and the Sun with rebirth: 'Inside the Goddess, the bones lay in their chambers, covered by her rounded, pregnant belly awaiting the penetrating, life-bringing rays of the Sun – and rebirth' (Tuck 2003, p. 52). Wyvern Dowser Shaun Ogbourne informed me that: 'The rising of the Sun and the Moon has a profound effect on earth energies, and on anyone using the barrow – even if the Sun was not visible in sky'. Although many more people today celebrate the midsummer than the midwinter, Shaun told me that the most powerful experiences he had had at WKLB were at the latter.

Summer Solstice

The midsummer sunrise, which is today around June 20-22, is famously associated with Stonehenge, and is honoured every year as thousands make a pilgrimage to the monument to witness the event (weather permitting!). I have previously described summer solstice alignments with Neolithic sites in Dorset, such as at Grey Mare and Her Colts (sunset), the Hellstone (sunset), Litton Cheney (sunset), as well as sunrise at the Nine Stones (Knight 1996). Many more have been found across Britain. Locally, the Cove stones at Avebury face the midsummer sunrise (Meaden 1999, p. 67). But what of WKLB?

Preliminary calculations showed me that the SE chamber was all-important around this date. Site visits confirmed that within the chamber one would have originally been able to see the skyline (before stone 45 was erected) between azimuths 40°-55°, which is well within that needed to observe the midsummer sunrise in the Neolithic – or today for that matter.

So on June 19, 2010, we went up to WKLB for the sunrise. Three deer crossed our path on the way up, but it clouded just before sunrise. The following morning we tried again. We arrived at the lay-by around 4.15am (BST), to find a carpet of mist around Silbury – a truly magical sight. Jupiter was pure white and brilliant in the south, and on the way up the path a hare ran across the fields. Two nesting swifts sat on the blocking stones, as if to herald the Sun's appearance. Anticipation grew as sunrise approached until, suddenly, it appeared, at around 4.56am (BST), a golden orange orb ascending out of Overton Hill. As I had suspected, it shone through trees on a group of barrows (grid ref: 661686) as viewed from the west end of the mound, and rose just to

Mid-summer sunrise, June 2010. Left: The Sun rises out of the right barrow on Overton Hill, when viewed from the west end of WKLB mound; Right: the Sun rises to the right of the barrows, viewed from above the chambers (stone 45 at bottom of image). The Sun is moving to the right all the time as it rises. In prehistoric times it rose left of the present sunrise point, right out of the site of the barrows. (Images: Sue Wallace, using zoom.)

the right of them from the forecourt, on a heading of about 49° (the skyline is only slightly higher than WKLB); the Sun's disc cleared the hill at 5.01am. The sunrise was visible from just inside the SE chamber, and illuminated the walls a few minutes later (see next page for image) and shadows were cast by us onto the stones. I stood in the chamber, bathed in golden sunshine wondering if someone else had been standing here, watching the same scene, thousands of years ago. The power of the Sun's light was palpable. Surely the rising of the solstice sun, as seen from the SE chamber, could not have gone unnoticed and may have been an *intentional* design feature. Martin Brennan concludes that, in the final analysis, '… light itself emerges as the primary symbol of the mound builders' (Brennan 1994, p. 204). Life on this planet owes its very existence to our Sun, a realisation that would not have been lost to Neolithic shamans.

The Sun shone into the SE chamber for around 15 minutes, until it moved too far south to be seen. Our magical sunrise was completed by the appearance of a deer, which ran away from us across the wheat fields.

The Sun rises in the same position for over a week around this time. But were the *later* Bronze Age barrows constructed to mark out the summer solstice alignments when viewed from WKLB? The Sun now rises slightly to the right to

187

the barrow group, but in the Neolithic and Bronze Age would have risen further to the left (north). WKLB had been sealed before their construction, but the alignment may still have been honoured. The barrows are not on the distant skyline, as they would have been too small to really stand out. I have shown

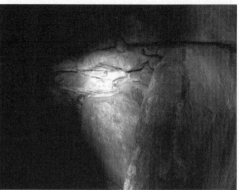

Left: Summer solstice sunrise as seen from inside the SE chamber. Above: The light from the rising Sun illuminates the SE chamber with a golden glow.

previously how several Dorset Bronze Age tumuli were positioned to be viewed, in an astronomical context, from Neolithic sites, such as at Mount Pleasant and Knowlton (Knight 1996). Regarding WKLB, John North concluded that, 'Long after the tomb ceased to be used for burial, it must have continued to function as a focal point' (North 1996, p. 77-78).

We also observed the summer solstice sunset in 2010, on two evenings in a row. The first was on one of our drumming/meditation group evenings. The second was from East Kennet long barrow; I had worked out that it should be possible to see the Sun set into or close to WKLB. On the first occasion, we also saw the Sun perched over Silbury Hill as we crossed the valley of the Kennet. From WKLB, the Sun then set in the NW, over Beckhampton. I noticed how the last glint was to the left of where the skyline hill (wooded) sloped down and met the nearer hill, the one that hides Beckhampton. It has been noted

Convergence
of hills

WKLB
megaliths

The midsummer sunset seen from East Kennet long barrow. The convergence of hill lines may also be relevant to ancient sunsets. (Telephoto view.)

elsewhere how sightlines can coincide with the convergence of hills.

The second sunset was from half way along East Kennet long barrow (image above). The Sun first contacted the skyline directly above the megaliths of WKLB, but we lost it to cloud soon afterwards, before it set (around 310°). We could see, however, that this would be where two hills converge at the solstice point, described above. Of course the Sun would have set slightly to the right of this point in the Neolithic (azimuth 311°), so at that time this convergence may have marked the point of *first* contact of the solar disc's *bottom* edge. Marina Graham has informed me that the exact alignment between WKLB and the solstice sunset is at the *southern end* of East Kennet long barrow. Nevertheless, the scene of an orange Sun setting with WKLB below it and Silbury Hill to the right, midst the background of a sleepy landscape, will live with me forever. We could almost feel the presence of our distant ancestors standing beside us, observing the same scene. (To visit the site, seek consent from the landowner at 'Fox Twitchen', Church Lane, East Kennet.)

Samhain, Imbolc, and Other Events
On Nov 1, 2010 we went to WKLB again to observe the sunset on this Samhain date. Although it was obscured by low cloud at the last moment, I estimated that the Sun's first contact was around 247°, just south of a clump of trees know as the Beckhampton Penning plantation. This is in fact the site of a former long barrow. In 3500 BC, Samhain sunset was in this direction, and it may be that the long barrow was close to the upper edge of the solar disc, marking the last moment before it disappeared.

We saw the 2011 Imbolc sunrise on a frosty morning with Venus and a thin crescent moon hanging low in the dawn sky, and a temperature that hung around -8.5°C! The NE chamber is open to receive the rays of the rising sun at Imbolc, in early February. Nowadays the sun enters this chamber a few days later, due to a stone cemented in place by Piggott, on top of stone 35, which juts out to ruin the view. Sunrise, at 7.58am, was nevertheless superb, framed by stones 44 and 45; soon after it cleared the top of stones 43 and 44.

It is surprising how the Sun can penetrate the passage and the NE, NW and W chambers at various times *after* sunrise, when the Sun climbs away from the horizon. The angled gap between stones 43 and 45 allows this, as well as when the Sun clears the top of stone 44 (to shine into the NE chamber). Penetration of the Sun's rays into the NE and NW chambers can potentially occur between the autumn equinox and the winter solstice, and then again back through to the spring equinox, often sometime *after* the actual sunrise. Prior to the erection of stone 45, the Sun's rays were much less restricted.

Winter Solstice
The midwinter sunrise is the second most favoured orientation for long barrows in the Avebury area, with eight aligned monuments. The nearby Beckhampton Road Long Barrow was *self-aligned* with the mid-winter sunset, according to John North. The Horslip, Beckhampton and South St long barrows left no evidence that they were ever intended for burial, and observance of sunrises on key dates may been one of their functions.

189

Above: Sunrise near midwinter from WKLB, taken on December 17, 2010. The Sun has just risen out of the southern end of East Kennet long barrow, marked by the dark trees in the foreground.
(Image: © Marina Graham, used with permission.)

Right: Midwinter sunrise, Dec 23, 2010, from the centre of the forecourt, where the sun is framed by stones 44, 45, and the top of 43, all of which are dusted with snow.

In 2009 we observed the midwinter sunset from WKLB, and in 2010 we observed both the sunrise and sunset. This sunrise was one I had been looking forward to, due to its proximity to East Kennet long barrow.

The sunsets of 2009 and 2010 were blessed with thin clouds overhead, which turned stunning hues either side of sunset. The Sun's first contact with the distant skyline west of Tan Hill was around 3.45pm. In 2010, I noticed that when standing a few yards east of blocking stone (45) just before sunset, the disc of the Sun shines between stones 43 and 45, due to a narrow gap and the angles of the stones. It may or may not be coincidence, but it certainly makes

Midwinter solstice sunset observed from the barrows on Overton Hill seen on December 2010, with WKLB below it. (Telephoto view.) The Sun was not a clear disc, but shone through a nebulous veil of thin cloud.

for a fine spectacle today. The best place for the sunset, however, is to capture it setting between stones 2 and 43. The sunset is beautifully framed by the stones, as shown below.

Days before the winter solstice of 2010, we also observed the sunset from the prominent group of barrows on Overton Hill, which had previously been involved with WKLB at the mid-summer solstice sunrise. As I suspected, the alignment also works looking the other way at midwinter. From the barrows the Sun sets on the distant skyline directly above WKLB (image above). It now occurs above the western end of the mound, but would have set above the east end, above the megaliths, in the late Neolithic and the Bronze Age. Sunset here was around five minutes later than at WKLB, due to the higher elevation of the barrows, and the more distant and lower skyline.

Regarding the midwinter sunrise, the event of 2010 coincided with heavy snowfall and thick cloud during solstice week. I am indebted to Marina Graham, who observed the sunrise on the morning of December 17, and whose image is reproduced here (top left image, p. 190). The Sun reaches a standstill for several days so the image here is still valid regarding the view around the solstice. Nowadays the first glint of the Sun appears at the skyline immediately above East Kennet long barrow. The angle along which the Sun rises is about 30°, and in Neolithic times the first glint of the Sun would have been just to the right of where it rises today, above an area just south of the mound. This is still very close if we are talking about a coincidence concerning any sightlines. I feel that perhaps feasts and fires were going on in the forecourt of East Kennet, or in the area immediately south of it. It could be that large fires in this area would have been seen as 'rebirthing' the fire of the Sun immediately above it. It may have been realised that just before sunrise, although out of sight, the Sun was passing behind and 'through' East Kennet

Midwinter solstice sunset 2010 at WKLB. Left: the Sun glints through a narrow gap between stones 43 and 45. Right: the full glory of the midwinter sunset framed between stones 2 and 43.

long barrow. Perhaps the Sun was symbolic of the interred ancestors also being reborn with the Sun: '… the way to the afterlife may have been guided by the rising Sun… illuminating the chamber itself' (Williams 2010, p. 112).

The morning of the actual 2010 solstice was overcast, so we unfortunately missed out on the sunrise, as well as the total eclipse of the Moon (we'll get it next time on the solstice in 400 years time!). We eventually got up to WKLB for the sunrise on December 23. It was a crisp −3.5° when we arrived at the lay-by, and the Moon shone bright in the west. Snow crunched under our feet as we walked up the hill, as we endured a biting north wind, which gnawed at our faces. WKLB was blanketed in snow, which even dusted the mighty megaliths (see image p. 218). Unfortunately, thin cloud came over shortly before sunrise, but we briefly caught a hazy Sun soon after it had risen, although not as clear as in Marina's shot. I stood in the forecourt, behind stone 45, with the sun and East Kennet long barrow perfectly framed by snow-dusted megaliths (image, top-right p. 190). The frozen landscape was laid out before us, white and seemingly asleep, and nearby sheep paid us little heed. Someone had been up there before us and etched spirals into the frozen snow (see p. 221). Soon afterwards, we made hot drinks from a flask, thawing chilled faces and fingers, breaking open a festive chocolate cake! We expressed our gratitude to the ancestors and said a 'Happy Solstice Ernie' to my Dad.

At the same event, it struck me how the Sun, shortly after midwinter sunrise, would formerly have been briefly seen from inside the NE chamber, before it went too far to the right. It would have appeared over the highest part of stone 44, which has its apex at that point, at around azimuth of 134-135°. This is now not possible due to the later erection and height of stone 43. This alignment can still be appreciated when one stands on the capstone of the NE chamber.

The Moon
The Moon has been venerated for thousands of years and images of it were drawn on cave paintings and, much later, on Neolithic chambered monuments (Brennan 1994). In

Virtual reconstruction of the rising full Moon, seen from the west chamber, in the early Neolithic.

many cultures it is regarded as a Goddess, such as Diana and Luna, and has inspired many a poet to put pen to paper. The Moon causes the tides and has long illuminated Man's nocturnal hunting parties. The Neolithic people of WKLB may have already held knowledge of the Moon's complicated movements and cycles, as well as to why its face waxed and waned. The movements and phases of the Moon may have been of equal importance to the activities of the Sun.

Right: this painting on slate by Kerry McKenna captures the Moon's silver light entering WKLB.
© Original in colour.
(www.kerrymckennaslates.webs.com)

The rising and setting of the Moon fluctuates over an 18.61 year cycle, caused by the 5° tilt in the orbit of the Moon relative to Earth. During that time the Moon rises and sets in various directions between two extremes, the Major Standstills, which are the most northerly and southerly azimuths at which the Moon can rise and set. In between are the Minor Standstills, when the Moon rises and sets closest to east and west respectively. The last Major Standstill was in 2006 AD and the net one will be in 2024-5. In between will be a Minor Standstill in 2015.

There are, however, some annual principles concerning moonrise points, regardless of the lunar cycle. For instance, in the summer the full Moon always rises south of due east; in the winter months the full Moon always rises north of due east; around the two equinoxes the full Moon rises in the vicinity of due east, and sets not far from due west. Quite often in summer months the full Moon will rise close to East Kennet long barrow and, at times, directly above it (image p. 194).

It has long been proven that many Neolithic monuments have intentional lunar alignments, most famously seen at Callanish and Ballochroy (Thom 1967), Stonehenge (Hawkins 1963) and the Boyne Valley (Brennan 1994). I have described Neolithic lunar standstill alignments found at the Dorset Cursus and Maiden Castle (Knight 1998, p. 143 & 158). The fact that so many ancient sites seem to align with lunar standstills verifies that people followed the Moon's movements with great care and accuracy over many years: '… the complicated pattern of risings and settings might have been appreciated through tenacious observation over long periods of time' (North 1996, p. 224).

Kathy Jones comments that the bias of long barrows towards east and southeast could be lunar-related: 'The entrances to long barrows often face towards the east or south east, so that the rays of the rising Moon could flood the chamber. In ancient times the Moon was often associated with death, its waxing form being filled by the souls of the dead. Ancestors visited the earth from their lunar home travelling along the full Moon beams into the long barrows, where they could be contacted' (Jones 1991, p. 86-87).

So is there any evidence that WKLB had lunar alignments in the Neolithic or Bronze Age? It is my belief that there is.

The Moon and WKLB

Aubrey Burl considered that on Salisbury Plain the long barrows were aligned on the rising Moon (Burl 2002, p. 85). The axis of WKLB does not seem to be aligned with a lunar event, but the monument does involve lunar risings. A most striking one is that at the Major Standstill, which in Neolithic and Bronze Ages times rose at around an azimuth of 40°. Incredibly, like midsummer, this is also marked by tumuli on Overton Hill (marked by a tree clump) at 40.5° (see

The full Moon rising from the skyline above East Kennet long barrow (marked by tree clump), at midsummer solstice 2005. Stone 45 is in the foreground.

image p. 53). Although the actual moonrise would only have been visible from the forecourt, not long after, the rays of the moon would have entered the SE chamber, just like the midsummer sunrise. This should be quite a spectacle at the 2024-5 standstill.

Every now and again during its 18.61 year cycle the Moon will rise in line with the axis, the passage and the west chamber. Back in the early Neolithic this must have been an incredible sight, the light of its brilliant full disc flooding down the passage into the west chamber, illuminating the 'Skull Stone' and the 'Living Head'. This happened, for instance, on Sept 17, 3500 BC, March 26, 3473 BC, March 26, 3465 BC, and again on October 26, 3547 BC, to mention but four. My impression of this magical event is on p. 192, as well as a painting of the moon's silver rays lighting the stones (p. 193).

John North has suggested that chalk balls/spheres found at Neolithic sites, such as at Windmill Hill and Stonehenge, link fertility with the Moon, with these objects resembling both the testes and the white disc of Moon (North 1996, p. 543). It is interesting that Thurnam found 'chalk ball-like nodules' in the west chamber, which the moon would periodically illuminate.

On August 24, 2010, we observed the full Moon rise; several minutes later it was high enough to clear blocking stone 45 and shine directly into the NE chamber (image below). On Sept 23, 2010, we also observed the light of the (Equinox) full Moon enter the interior of WKLB, just after 9.00pm (BST). This was at azimuth 110°, when it had reached an altitude of just over 20°, its light just clipping the NW and NE chambers. It would seem that, depending on where it is in the lunar cycle, the rays of the full Moon may periodically enter the NE and NW chambers between August and October, and around equinox can even reach the 'Skull Stone' of the west chamber. Likewise, the rising full Moon can *potentially* shine into the SE chamber between November and January (when it rises in the general direction of the midsummer sunrise), depending on the stage in the lunar cycle, and thus its azimuth and altitude.

Also of note is that WKLB is on a heading of 40°-41° from the former Beckhampton Penning stone circle, enabling the Northern Standstill Moon to rise directly above WKLB, when viewed from the former site.

Marina Graham has informed me that at the northernmost lunar maximum, the Moon sets into Silbury when viewed from East Kennet Long Barrow. I make this alignment 46°-47° N of E-W (316° true). John North states this alignment should be 49°-50°. Marina may be referring to the point of *first* contact with the horizon, rather than its last glint.

On June 19, 2005, I observed the full Moon rise out of the skyline immediately above East Kennet long barrow (image above), just before the lunar Major Standstill of 2006. It was a stunning sight. The actual standstill in the Early Neolithic was around azimuth 144°, which is the direction of the hill on which the Harestone stones stand. It could be that the stones are older than we think, or that they succeeded a pre-Bronze Age site.

Later in WKLB's history, the Palisades were erected in the valley below. Visible from there

The full Moon shining into the NE chamber on August 24, 2010. (Image: Sue Wallace.)

the barrow is on the skyline (see image p. 34). Every summer the ecliptic crosses WKLB during the night, when seen from Palisades, so the Moon and planets periodically set into the mound. So too around the time of the Palisades construction, when the full Moon episodically set into the very chambers of WKLB, appearing to disappear into a mound that may still have been white (image below).

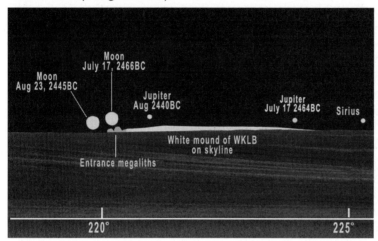

Some events visible in the later Neolithic from the Palisades Enclosures. The full Moon would have regularly set into WKLB, two examples being shown here. Jupiter was also setting into the monument for several years around this time. The height of the ridge dictates the azimuths of these events.

The Stars

Stars have long been associated with the ancestors. In Native American tradition the stars were thought to be the campfires of the ancestors, and in Guatemala and Peru, stars represent the 'souls of the righteous dead'.

Kathy Jones observed that, '… one only has to be at ancient sites under the clear night-sky to realize the significance of their positioning' (Jones 1994, p. 5). Standing, as I have done, on top of WKLB on a moonless, starlit night, with the Milky Way straddling the sky, one can appreciate how our prehistoric brothers and sisters may have been influenced by such wondrous sights. By observing the seasonal movements of the stars, the shamans of WKLB may have conceived that the *stars were revolving around them*: 'We can transcend the boundaries and move between the stones, ultimately to place ourselves at what may once have been understood as the centre of the cosmos' (Watson 2001, p. 311).

The risings and settings of the Sun and the Moon are only slightly different now than in the Neolithic, but the positions of most stars visible to the naked-eye have changed radically, particularly stars closest the solar system: 'The change in the direction of the sunrise and sunset at the solstices is one fifth of a degree every 1,000 years… whereas the Pleiades rose 10° south of due east at Stonehenge in the early 4th Century BC, but 12 centuries later they rose due east' (North 1996, p 25). John North concluded that long barrows were aligned with 2 or 3 bright stars, which can be used to accurately date them.

Until 2009-10, I had undertaken very little study of stellar alignments of sacred sites, primarily because these needed computer programs to show where stars were thousands of years ago. I did have some success in 2001, when I calculated that Sirius and the winter solstice sunrise point were at the same azimuth for a while in the early Neolithic, and how the Grey Mare and Her Colts long barrow, in Dorset, was aligned with this double event (Knight 2001, p. 22-24). I also speculated that it could explain why so many long barrows align SE, due to this 'double whammy' of solar and stellar positioning. (Below, we shall see how Venus may also have been relevant.)

Inspired by this, and the work of John North (1996) in Wessex and Nicholas Mann and Philippa Glasson (2007) at Glastonbury, I set about seeing what alignments might be involved with WKLB. With the *Skymap* program I was able to magically 'transport' myself back to 4000 BC, and any date since then, to see what the shamans of WKLB were looking at all those eons ago. What I found still leaves me spellbound, in awe of the abilities of the Neolithic sky watchers of the Avebury area.

When undertaking this work, the height above the horizon at which stars become visible has to be taken into account, as this varies considerably. The brighter the magnitude of a star, the earlier and lower it will be visible after rising and, conversely, the lower and longer they will be visible at setting. By way of an example, here are the heights above a clear skyline when some stars become visible: Sirius 0.74°, Vega 1.4°, Spica 2.12°, Arcturus 1.43°, and Procyon 1.7°. Due to the dimming effect of the atmosphere, fainter stars may not be visible until they are several degrees above the horizon.

I had been carrying out an in-depth analysis of stellar positions throughout the early part of 2010. I then attended a talk by Nicholas Mann and Philippa Glasson in Glastonbury on August 17, 2010. During their inspiring, and to me very relevant, presentation they showed alignments they had uncovered at Avebury and the nearby Cove of the western avenue (the remnants of this being the megaliths 'Adam and Eve'). It was with great joy, and immense relief, that they confirmed several of the alignments and azimuths of stellar events I had suspected at nearby WKLB. Nicholas made available to me several of his findings, prior to the publication of his work (Mann 2011), for which I am deeply grateful.

The independent work of Mann and myself seems to re-emphasise what has been suggested elsewhere, that it was in fact the stars, not the Sun and Moon, that originally preoccupied the astronomer-shamans in the Mesolithic and early Neolithic. Referring to Stonehenge, John North concluded that, '... observation of the stars was then important, perhaps more important [than solar alignments]'. I set out my findings below, plus those of some academics who have been forward-thinking enough to also look up at the skies, and not just down into the earth.

Landscape and Inter-Monument Alignments

We have seen how some long barrows and later sites may have been positioned with solar alignments in mind. But what of the stars? Before we look at what people were observing from West Kennet long barrow, I must share some very interesting information recently obtained from Nicholas Mann. I think we will then get a feel for how monuments in the Avebury area may have been aligned with each other, and with natural landmarks, with relevance to the stars. Nicholas Mann holds great stead in what he sees as an important event that took place in the Neolithic. He advocates that the position of WKLB in the landscape was *predetermined* by astronomical alignments that existed between the barrow and Windmill Hill. The barrow was built soon after the occupation of Windmill Hill by the early Neolithic farmers. Mann incisively points out that at that time, the bright magnitude 1 star Alpha Centauri (the second brightest star, after Sirius, in Neolithic skies) and the constellation Crux, the Southern Cross, were rising directly above the site of WKLB, *when viewed from Windmill Hill*: 'When viewed from the central enclosure of Windmill Hill, Alpha Centauri (a bright and prominent double star) rose over the location of the long barrow between 3700 and 3500 BC, exactly the time of its construction, at an azimuth of 153°-155°... allowing for the extinction angle, this is the length of the barrow' (Mann 2011). Just before this, Crux rose in the same position (see images below). Mann also states that the rising of Alpha Centauri is aligned with both the Cove and the 'D' setting of stones within Avebury henge, dating them to around 3300-3000 BC.

Because of the slow precessional rotation of the Earth, both Crux and Alpha Centauri eventually ceased to be visible, the last star of the cross of Crux disappearing from view around 2500 BC, which is, interestingly, around the time WKLB was closed. 'As Alpha Centauri reappeared each year in early

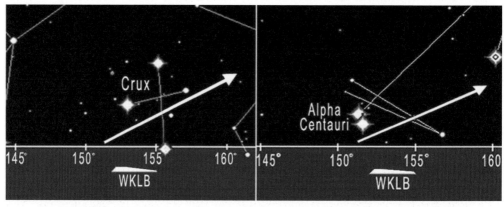

The rising of both Crux and, a little later in the evening, Alpha Centauri around 3700 BC, viewed from Windmill Hill. WKLB is aligned with the *visible* appearance of the brightest stars at this time. Arrows denote direction of movement as the stars rise.

November, at dawn, and then rose earlier and earlier before being seen for the final time at sunset in early May, the Crux-Centaurus stars would have appeared as the stars defining winter' (Mann 2011). Interestingly, John North found that three stones of the SW and SE chambers align with the setting of Alpha Centauri at this time. He also notes an alignment with that star at the North Stoke Cursus, in Oxfordshire, with long barrows near the Dorset Cursus (North 1996, p. 76), and it's setting at Stonehenge (op. cit. p. 327). When Crux was disappearing from the latitude of Avebury and WKLB, Silbury Hill was built, the final major Neolithic monument of the area.

John North has shown how the rays of the two brightest stars of Crux would have been seen from the back chamber of Wayland's Smithy, '...grazing carefully shaped stones' (North 1996, p. 52). He also documented eleven instances in the Stonehenge and Avebury area of alignments between three or more long barrows which are also aligned to stars of Centaurus and Crux (North 1996, Fig 71), and another four alignments of three or more barrows with the rising and setting of Sirius.

Further to this, it may be possible to now explain why WKLB was not built on the highest part of the ridge on which it stands. By necessity, the barrow had to be slightly down from top of the ridge for the Windmill Hill – WKLB stellar alignment to be realised. The alignment continues on south to Knap Hill.

Regarding other inter-monument alignments, Orion rose over the site of WKLB as seen from Horslip long barrow around 3700 BC. And, from The Sanctuary, Aldebaren (the bright star of Taurus) set into WKLB around 2800 BC, the date of the early phase of The Sanctuary, according to archaeological evidence.

I strongly refer the reader to Nicholas Mann's book, *Avebury Cosmos,* for an in-depth study of the astronomical alignments of the Avebury area.

Now, what were the shaman star-gazers observing from WKLB itself?

Neolithic Star-gazing at WKLB

John North has put forward a good case for WKLB being aligned to several stars around the time it was built. I have been able to add more to his results, confirming that the monument was used for astronomical observation. This may have been for calendrical use, to herald special events in the year, or for divination purposes, much the same as astrologers have been interpreting the stars for thousands of years. An azimuth of 87° for the axis of WKLB would also result in some stellar alignments not possible if the barrow and the passage were exactly east-west.

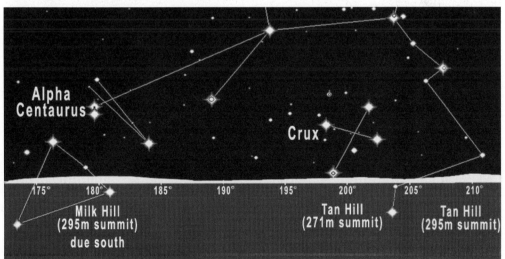

Looking south around midnight on March 25, 3650 BC, from WKLB. Alpha Centauri is south directly above Milk Hill, just as the first star of Crux, the Southern Cross, sets. Later, Crux will completely set into the west summit of Tan Hill.

199

We shall soon go into the chambers themselves, but let us begin first with the movements of the stars as seen from outside of the barrow, such as standing on the mound or in the forecourt at the east end.

The Crux-Alpha Centauri event described above also had relevance when viewed from WKLB. In the early Neolithic, Alpha Centauri was due south when over Milk Hill summit, just as Crux was beginning to set behind easterly summit of Tan Hill; later, Crux would set into the 195m (westerly) summit of the hill. Both of the highest hills in Wiltshire are involved when viewed from WKLB. The view shown above looks south at midnight towards end of March in 3650 BC, or at 10.00pm a month later in April.

Mann and Glasson found alignments with Crux at Glastonbury, such as how it rose over Chalice Hill when seen from St Edmund's Hill (Mann & Glasson 2007, p. 70 & 73).

Orion and Sirius

The next alignments involve the constellation Orion (known variously as the Hunter, Giant or Warrior) and Sirius, the Dog Star. Orion features prominently in many ancient myths and cultures, a bright winter constellation with the famous 'belt', controversially linked with the plan of the Pyramids at Giza. Orion was known as the lover of Diana, and was where the soul of Osiris rested.

The heliacal rising of Sirius (its first appearance after weeks of being too close to the sun to be visible) was important to the Egyptians, as it heralded the arrival of the life-giving Nile floods. At magnitude −1.09, Sirius is the brightest star in the sky (surpassed only by the planet Venus on occasions). Egyptians equated Sirius with the Goddess Isis, and with Anubis (Jones 1994, p. 106); a scene at Thebes showing the star is dated 3285 BC. Regarding its

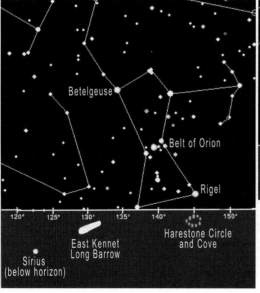

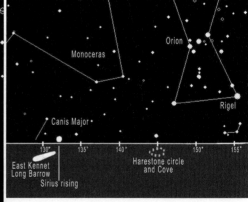

View from WKLB on the evening of Dec. 25, 3650 BC. Left: 6.00pm. The complete figure of Orion clears the horizon, with Rigel above the Harestone stones. Earlier, the stars of the Belt became visible above East Kennet long barrow. Above: 6.50pm. Sirius rises above the south end of East Kennet, and is visible soon after.

200

associations as the Dog Star, the Phoenicians called Sirius *Hannabeach,* the Barker! Hippocrates believed that the star physically effected people, and the Greeks had *Dog Days,* times when the star influenced the Earth. The Dogons of Mali believe that a race bringing great knowledge came from Sirius.

Orion precedes Sirius across the sky, its belt pointing to the Dog Star, and they both reach visual prominence in the night skies during the winter. Sirius is much higher in the sky now than in ancient times; in 3650 BC it rose at around 133° (or 43° south of due east - level horizon assumed) and had a maximum altitude of only 13° (North 1996, Fig. 32). Today it rises around 117° and reaches an altitude of about 18°. The rising of Sirius was involved with astronomical alignments at Glastonbury (Mann & Glasson 2007, p. 78-84).

I found it amazing that of all the places Sirius and Orion's Belt might rise between 3700-3500 BC, when viewed from WKLB, they **both** become visible **above** East Kennet long barrow; the alignment for the 'business end' of the barrow is 132° (or 42° south of east). Sirius appeared very soon after rising, due to its brilliance. The stars of Orion's Belt are fainter, but came into view with the naked eye directly above the barrow. The heliacal rising of the Belt is just before dawn around August 1 – the old festival of Lughnasad! As in Egypt, its appearance may have been associated with harvesting and the Grain Goddess.

Two more phenomena occur involving Orion. The first was noted by John North, and I have done my own figure of it below, based on his description. In the early Neolithic, when viewed from the north ditch of WKLB, or the fields just to the north, the mound formed an artificial skyline, and Orion appeared to rise, skim along the top of the barrow mound, (with Rigel appearing briefly) before setting. My figure below is diagrammatic, due to the length of barrow.

Orion rises out of chambers   Due south - Rigel appears over mound   Orion sets into mound

Diagrammatic view showing the movement of Orion over WKLB around 3600 – 3500 BC, seen from the north of site or from the north ditch (after John North) Limitations due to scale.

The second example is shown on the next page, in which Orion sets into the chambers of WKLB, seen from the forecourt or the open ground just to the east. Here Orion the Hunter goes down into the Underworld. In Celtic mythology he is Caomai, the 'Armed King', to the Saxons he was the giant of winter, Waendel, and he has parallels with Herne the Hunter. Odin or Woden was a powerful Northern European God who led a wild hunt, and is remembered at nearby Waden (*Wodens*) Hill. Mann and Glasson associate Orion with the Otherworldly lord Gwynn ap Nudd of Glastonbury, stating that he was an astronomer (Mann & Glasson 2007, p. 62 & 65). In Greek mythology, Orion is a giant who was described in some texts as the son of Mother Earth, often accompanied by his faithful dog, Sirius. In one myth, he is plunged into a deep sleep by Dionysos, during which his eyes are put out. Orion then has to travel to the Sun to regain his sight. Does this have parallels

Looking west during the early hours in December 3650 BC. This scene would have been repeated for centuries to follow. Orion the Hunter journeys down to the Underworld. Did Neolithic shamans follow him into the darkness of the chambers?

at WKLB, whereby the shaman would go into the Underworld to dream sleep and stay there until illuminated by the rays of the rising Sun. In another tale, Orion ventures into the realms of Hades, where he hunted wild beasts (Guirand ed, 1974), a metaphor, perhaps, for our dark inner natures. Considering these associations with the Underworld, I wonder if the shamans followed Orion into the dark depths of WKLB, journeying to these dark realms themselves. Gwynn ap Nudd is associated with the colour white, and one can perhaps see a link between this and venturing down under the white mound of WKLB. Above the entrance at the same time, the Twins of Gemini stood vertically, in line with axis - spectacular! Note also how the Milky Way seems to mirror the white mound, as the galactic axis was almost horizontal. At around the time WKLB was built, the Milky Way formed a complete ring above the horizon: 'Alpha Centauri and Crux are embedded within the low band of the Milky Way, which at that time was visible in its entirety, wrapped around the horizon. In this era, throughout the winter months, the galaxy ringed the horizon for an hour or more' (Mann 2011).

Standing on top of the mound soon afterwards, the last thing visible of Orion, his club, would have set into Morgan's Hill. These circumstances would have been repeated, with just minor star shifts, over several centuries until around 2500-2400 BC, when Orion and Gemini began to set too far north for this alignment to be realised; *this date is around the time when WKLB was closed off!*

During the life of the barrow, three other bright stars, Capella, Regulus (in Leo) and Spica (in Virgo), also shone directly due west, seen from either the mound or from just outside the entrance.

Deneb and Silbury Hill

Looking north from WKLB in the early Neolithic there would have been no Silbury Hill, but on the skyline were the enclosures on Windmill Hill, which were contemporary with the barrow. At around this time the brilliant star Vega just hugged the horizon, but Deneb, the brightest star of Cygnus the Swan, did set for around 2-3 hours. No brighter star rose and set so close to due north as Deneb.

At this time, when viewed from WKLB, Cygnus set into Windmill Hill. John North has Deneb alignments at Wayland's Smithy, Horslip long barrow, Beckhampton Rd long barrow, and South St. He puts great stead in the importance of Cygnus to Neolithic culture, just as Nicholas Mann does over a decade later at Avebury.

The Moon is associated with Cygnus the Swan in some ancient cultures. Andrew Collins sees the whole of the Avebury landscape connected with a cult concerned with the movements of Cygnus in ancient times (Collins 2008). In Inca cosmology Cygnus was the 'centre of origin' (Collins 2008, p. 78) and Collins aligns the axis of Avebury henge with the setting of Cygnus around the time of its construction. He also cites old records of migrating swans residing in the River Kennet and the water-filled ditch

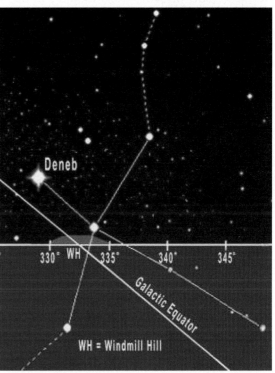

The setting of Cygnus into Windmill Hill around 3650 BC. The Galactic Centre and the Milky Way also set into the hill. Deneb was prominent over the hill shortly before setting.

around Silbury, which would leave in the Spring. Brigit has associations with springs and of swans, and has been linked with Swallowhead Spring. In many shamanic cultures birds represent out-of-body journeys. In Teutonic myths the Valkyries were female spirits who could turn themselves into swans and then change into human form. This may link with the shamanic concepts of 'shape-shifting' and 'spirit-flight'.

The constellation of Cygnus is also called the Northern Cross. John North noted that as Cygnus marked the northernmost point of sky, the star alpha cruces (the brightest star of Crux, the Southern Cross) marked the southern most point in the sky, until the latter ceased to be visible around 2,800BC.

So, in the early Neolithic, observers standing on WKLB saw Deneb 'poised' over Windmill Hill briefly before setting just to the east of it, whilst the actual Galactic Equator, marked by the stars of the Milky Way, set into the hill itself (image above). In many cultures the Milky Way is seen as a path to the ancestors, accessed when its misty realms touched the earth. The Dogons called the Milky Way the 'Path of the Blood', and the Inca called it the *Mayu,* or 'Celestial River' (Collins 2008). The Aztecs regarded the Milk Way as *Mixcoatl*, the 'cloud-serpent', who was the god of the Pole Star and of the hunt.

As described above, when looking south from Windmill Hill, Crux was visible over WKLB, whilst when looking from WKLB in the opposite direction, Cygnus, the Northern Cross, was over Windmill Hill. And while all this was going on, the Milky Way was completely encircling the sky just above the horizon: 'With the two crosses embedded in the Milky Way north and south, this must have been a magnificent spectacle… ' (Mann 2011).

Looking north from WKLB in the *later Neolithic* the landscape was dominated by the newly erected mound of Silbury Hill. I suspect that another two events around this time were also noted by late-Neolithic star-gazers. Around the time Silbury was built, both the 'W' of Cassiopeia *and* Deneb were positioned directly over Silbury. Again, the chalky course of the Milky Way was involved,

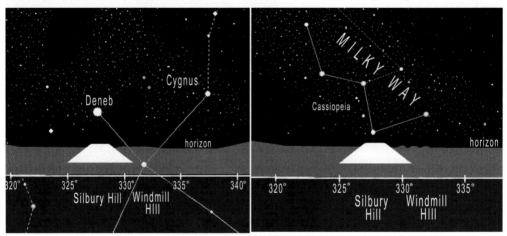

When Silbury Hill was completed, both Deneb and the 'W' of Cassiopeia hung over the mound just before setting, as these views from WKLB show. The Milky Way was also setting into Silbury, appearing to 'flow' into it.

as it descended into Silbury Hill, like the flow of a cloudy river into the newly erected white mound. The whiteness of the new 'wonder monument' was mirroring the whiteness of the Milky Way. Again, Deneb hovered over Silbury just prior to setting, as Cassiopeia did later in the night. The views above are that of around 2500 BC. Deneb then went below the horizon for around two hours, between azimuths 342° and 18°. The 'W' of Cassiopeia became circumpolar (never setting) by 1200 BC, and Deneb from around 500 BC.

Early Neolithic articulated burials favour an east-west orientation (head in west). Was this mirroring the general phenomena of risings and settings of celestial objects? Later on, in Beaker times, north-south orientations were favoured (with the head in the north). John North asks whether this change was due to the shift in position of Cygnus in the sky (North 1996, p. 21).

It may also be relevant that the only time the centre of the cross of Cygnus and the brilliant star Vega are vertically aligned in the sky is when they are in the east - in line with the axis of WKLB!

The Ditches

Before venturing into the interior of WKLB, I must mention that John North considered that the *ditches* of long barrows were more than holes in the ground left by the removal of material for mound construction. He sees them as having much astronomical merit. By accurately computing the shape and directions of several long barrow ditches, he concluded that significant observations of stars could be made by standing or sitting at suitable points, including some at WKLB.

Seen from the ditches, the adjacent mound provides an artificial horizon. Viewed from the southern ditch of WKLB, for instance, the brilliant magnitude +1 star Arcturus, which was then circumpolar (never setting) would have 'set' into the mound and then 'rise' less than an hour later! Vega would also appear to 'set' into the mound when viewed from the south ditch. Both Sirius and Rigel, the lowest bright star in Orion, behaved in a similar manner (see diagram p. 201) when viewed from the north ditch.

North also speculated that observing platforms may have been erected in the ditches, and that all these four 'spectacularly chosen' bright stars were involved: 'It would be hard to imagine a simpler monumental design showing more intellectual brilliance than this' (North 1996, p. 84).

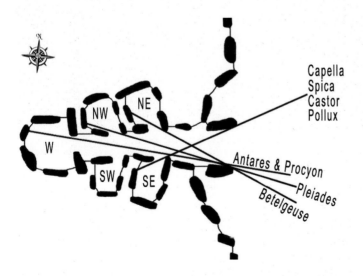

Capella
Spica
Castor
Pollux

Antares & Procyon

Betelgeuse
Pleiades

Stellar alignments inside WKLB during the early Neolithic. The alignments do not point to where the stars rose, but to the direction they either became visible to the naked eye, or else appear from behind aligned stones. It is assumed that stones 44 and 46 (the symbolic 'horns') were in situ at that time. (After John North, with additions by the author.)

The 'Star Chambers'

John North referred to, 'West Kennet and its Star Chambers', which is ample testament to North's belief that stellar alignments were key to understanding the design of the monument (North 1996, p. 72-81). He saw the upright stones (44 and 46) as important, being accurately positioned and, '… carefully worked' and noted how some of them have flat surfaces which define where celestial bodies may or may not be seen from the inside. I have already commented on these. North makes a good observation that the alignments he advocates may have been visible by *adults standing* in the chambers, so were not merely symbolic; they were not visible from a ground position in the side chambers, where the *deceased* were lying, but were being viewed by the living.

Even before we enter the interior there were once sights to be seen near the entrance. When standing in the centre of the forecourt, the east edge of stone 44 is aligned to 133°, or 43° south of due east. It may be remembered that this was the direction Sirius rose in the early Neolithic.

You may also recall that from the SE chamber the skyline on Overton Hill can seen between azimuths 40° - 63°, some views being over the top surfaces of stones 36, 37 and 46. Within these parameters some bright stars would have been seen to rise in the early Neolithic from inside this chamber. These include the magnitude 1 star Regulus (in Leo), and the 'W' of Cassiopeia, which was fully visible in this direction after its brief dip below the northern horizon.

The bright stars Capella, Castor, Pollux and Spica all appeared from behind the east end of stone 46 soon after they rose, as they moved south (see diagram p. 205). North gives this azimuth as 63.7°. All these stars are prominent and relatively close together in the evening skies of summer and

Virtual reconstructions of two stellar events at WKLB in the early Neolithic. Left: the Pleiades star cluster seen from inside the NW chamber. Above: The bright star of Orion, Betelgeuse, soon after rising, as seen from the NE chamber.

autumn. Spica, in Virgo, is also involved in an alignment at Fussell's Lodge, Wiltshire. These stars then moved south during the night, but by the time they were in line with the axis of WKLB, they would have been too high to have been visible from anywhere other than near the entrance, due to their altitude.

From inside the SE chamber it was periodically possible to witness the rising, in the NE, of the brightest planets, Venus, Jupiter and Saturn, when the ecliptic was in that direction.

John North found that from the NE chamber, one of the bright stars of Orion, Betelgeuse, was bright enough to be visible at an azimuth of 110º. Aldebaren, the brightest star in Taurus, the Bull, would have also been seen from the chamber entrance soon after it rose. Interestingly, a deer antler was found at this spot (see image p. 108). Both the bull and the deer have horns. It makes me wonder if the shaman of WKLB may have associated the stars we call Taurus not with a bull, but a stag. We shall return to this chamber soon, regarding the Pleiades.

The rising of Antares, the brightest star in Scorpio, and of Procyon (the 'Little Dog Star' of Canis Minor) align closest with the axis of the passage. In the early Neolithic they were rising around 89º-90º but would not have been visible until somewhat later, when they were seen from the 'Skull Stone'. Around 3650 BC, Antares was rising almost exactly east, first becoming visible around 93º (image below, left). By 96º it was obscured by stone 44, when that stone was in its original position. Soon after this they both became too high and too far south to be visible from the back of the west chamber. In the early Neolithic, the heliacal rising of Procyon, as it moved away from the Sun, was in the dawn sky around August 1, Lughnasad! Both Procyon and Antares set almost due west at this time (image below, right), being last seen above Morgan's Hill. Nicholas Mann and Philippa Glasson found alignments involving Antares at Glastonbury (Mann & Glasson 2007, p. 66)

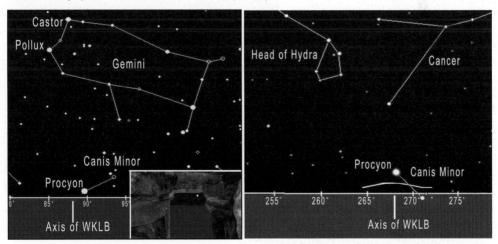

Looking east and west from WKLB on Dec 22, 3650 BC. Left and inset: Procyon rises soon after sunset and is visible from the back of the west chamber (inset). The scene was the same at 2.02am on August 3, 3675BC, as Procyon made its heliacal appearance.
Right: The setting of Procyon before dawn. The wavy white line is the skyline of Morgan's Hill. The star was too faint to be visible soon after, due to the atmosphere.

The Pleiades

The Pleiades (or 'Seven Sisters'), is a well-known cluster of magnitude +2 and +3 stars, said by the Greeks to predict harvest time. Ancient knowledge was given to Native Americans by *Star Women* who came down from the Pleiades. This star cluster has been extensively described by many other ancient cultures, such as the Romans, the ancient Chinese (c. 2350 BC), and the Hindus (c. 1730 BC). In fact, these Indian texts speak of, *The Great Year of the Pleiades,* their term for the 25,900 year cycle of precession. The heliacal rising of the Pleiades in May was marked at Cuzco, Peru, where the cluster was known as the *Storehouse,* because of its connection with agriculture. We can also recall the plan of WKLB, which may be seen as a bull with horns (image p. 92). This is a further connection with Taurus, the Bull, for the Pleiades are in that constellation. It has been suggested that bull/oxen hides may have been hung, possibly to form a 'door', across the entrance.

Although rising around an azimuth of 96° in the Neolithic, because of their dimness, the Pleiades would have been too low to be visible from the west chamber. However, the cluster would have been seen about 20-25 minutes later from the NW chamber (see image p. 206).

It is worth recording that the SW chamber was, and remains, the only chamber from which it was impossible to view the outside world, due to stones 12 and 13 blocking the view; this may have been intentional when the interior was designed. This was where three female skulls were placed in a row at the back of the chamber, one of which was elongated. John North notes, however, some of the stones of the chamber point to the setting of Alpha Centauri. This event would never have been observed following the installation of the capstone, but may nevertheless have been a *symbolic* alignment.

Venus

Like the stars, the bright planets (Mercury, Venus, Mars, Saturn and Jupiter) also change their positions, but these are very complicated and much more rapid. Prehistoric alignments are difficult to prove, as these 'moving stars' are very erratic. The calculation of their risings and settings were regarded by him as, '… correspondingly burden-

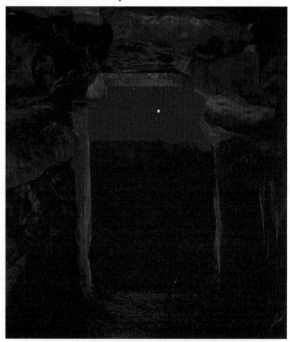

Looking out from the west chamber, at 3.50am, November 21, 3495 BC. Venus is seen as a brilliant star in the east before dawn. This event occurred several times during the Neolithic.

some' (North 1996, p. 130). The one exception to this may be Venus. It is the brightest 'star' in the sky, at times bright enough to cast shadows. It is never far from the Sun, but its rapid movement and brilliance did ignite the interest and imagination of ancient people, especially in the astral myths of Mediterranean and Middle Eastern cultures, and of the Mayans. Babylonian tablets telling of Venus' movements in the skies date back to the 6th Century BC. Venus, of course, has frequently been regarded as the Goddess of Love.

Being inside the orbit of the Earth, Venus is bound by the Sun, and can never stray more than 45° from it. Every 8 years the direction of the winter solstice sunrise coincides with the rising of Venus, when the planet is at its brightest. It has been suggested that this double phenomena may have been a contributing factor in the alignment of many passage graves, such as the alignment of Newgrange (Knight & Lomas 1999, p. 282), and that the planet played a pivotal role in the theology and science of the ancient world (op. cit. p. 392). John North calculated that in Wiltshire, between 3600-2000 BC, the extremes of Venus's settings were: '44° north of west [314°] and 44.5° south of west [225.5°]', the differences being close to right-angled. Regarding observing these extreme risings and settings, North concluded that, '… anyone focusing on Venus's extreme positions, and doing the job with care, might have found the horizon positions [of the extremes] since both were in principle observable' (North 1996, p. 576-577).

At some of the extreme rising points of Venus in the 3rd millennium BC, the position was also very close to the rising point of Sirius at that time, imbuing that direction with potential magic. John North considered that the alignment of Horslip long barrow might be a contender for a Venus alignment.

Inevitably, Venus would at times have risen in line with the axis of WKLB. Being the brightest 'star' in the sky, this spectacular event must surely have been noticed, and perhaps expected. One of many examples was just before 4 am on Nov 21, 3495 BC, just before dawn, when Venus appeared above its extinction angle in line with the passage, its brilliant light of magnitude -4.0 (much brighter than Sirius) being observed by anyone within the west chamber (see image above). This view continued for around a week. The darkness was pierced by the light of Venus – perhaps signalling a resurrection of sorts. Venus is a strong candidate for the Star of Bethlehem, with all the implied connotations of birth and rebirth, on both an individual level and for all Mankind. In Mexican folklore, Venus is often depicted with a bow and arrow, wearing a skull mask. This offers tempting links between Venus, Orion the Hunter, and the skulls of the ancestors.

I would suggest that Venus was held with great awe and wonder in the Neolithic. The appearance of this bright 'star' drastically alters the appearance of constellations it hurriedly races through, and perhaps would have been seen to *interact* with the 'fixed stars', animating them, adding new dimensions to existing myths. We will encounter the planet again later as we look to 2012, when Venus will bring forth its message of love once more.

Chapter 16.
Interaction Today –
Care and Use of the Monument

'We can *all* do it if we work together with love,
care and concern for the earth and all its manifestations.'
(Hamish Miller)

West Kennet Long Barrow is one of Britain's prehistoric wonders. It has come a long way in the last five and a half thousand years – having witnessed over twenty two thousand seasons. Up on a ridge, deep in the Wiltshire landscape, it has witnessed the coming of metal tools, plagues, the Norman Conquest, two world wars, the rise of technology, and the first man on the Moon. Left to its own devices, it may have outlived Mankind.

However, people started taking an interest in the sacred barrow once more, and this time it was not for spiritual, ancestral, or astronomical reasons. The monument bore the brunt of farmers taking away chunks of its mound and stones; it also survived, somehow retaining its dignity, invasive excavations and a somewhat insensitive restoration; and it has endured thousands of people who have ventured into its interior, most wearing their 'tourist hat'.

It is ironic, therefore, that the greatest threat to the monument today comes from the very people who come to honour and revere the site, the ancestors, and the Earth. Damage to the stones from soot and deposits of wax are now woefully common, as I can attest from my regular 'tidy ups'. People who no doubt come with good intentions do not always think about the repercussions of their activities, and of the effect of what they leave behind.

Let me point out at the outset, that I am not banging a drum for authorities such as the National Trust or English Heritage – I myself embrace Pagan beliefs. The information below is principally aimed at fellow-Pagans. A few examples of what I am referring to may not go amiss.

Ritual Litter and Damage to the Stones

At the summer solstice of 1996 serious scorch marks were left on some of the interior stones at WKLB. At the mid-summer of 2001, scratch marks, unreadable though they were, were made on stones inside the chambers. Robert Wallis reported that, 'There is the problem of fire damage at West Kennet, caused by mainly the lighting and thoughtless positioning of candles…. One forecourt stone has been so damaged that a fractured piece of it had to be repaired with a gluing agent' (Wallis 2003, p. 169).

Over the years, items such as cigarette butts, condoms, tampons, and beer cans have been left behind in the chambers. But, fortunately, this type of rubbish is not the most common. That category is what has become know as

Left: soot deposits and burning of megaliths, October 2010. Right: This large pile of 'ritual litter', which filled a rucksack, was collected on **one** visit to WKLB in the summer of 2010.

'ritual litter', left behind following ceremonies, rituals, and meditations, etc. Items include metal tea-light holders, candles, candle wax, fruit, coins, feathers, crystals, small stones, and various effigies from clay models to corn dollies. Chalk graffiti is also daubed on stones, which, if not removed by someone who really cares about the site, may take years to wear away. David Taylor points out, "… it isn't just tourists and road builders who damage ancient sites, recent "pagan" activity at WKLB is caused by a mindless minority… " (Taylor 1997). A votive offering may be left behind, with all good intention, by Pagan, Druid, or New-Ager, but it is 'litter', none the less.

It is a little sickening for me to have to point out that most of this refuse is left by Pagans and 'Earth Healers', which is the great irony of it all. *I* am a Pagan, not an archaeologist or other 'straight' preaching from an academic soapbox. It saddens me that the people who do this are letting down fellow Pagans.

At sunset at Samhain 2010, Sue and I went up to the barrow, only to find intentional damage to one of the skylights, and also lots of candle wax, which had been allowed to drip down the sides of several megaliths. As well as numerous metal nightlight holders, there was even a casino chip for $1, and sherds of glass in the west chamber from the smashed skylight.

211

On a weekly basis, Sue and I retrieve all sorts of rubbish from inside WKLB. Although we are thankfully not alone in this practice, I would like to 'recruit' others to the cause – including you!

Before we look at how we can best accommodate the various requirements of people who visit WKLB today, I would respectfully request everyone who visits WKLB to please follow this proposed *Code of Practice*.

Some Do's and Don'ts

1) NO OPEN FIRES, even outside; the archaeology of the site extends beyond what is immediately obvious.

2) Please do not light candles or nightlights next to or on top of the stones, or under their overhangs (where the undersides will become sooted), or in holes or crevices. If the light is fading, use fully-enclosed lanterns, or else battery-powered or eco torches.

3) Should you need to light a nightlight, place it only in the **centre** of the chambers. There is no evidence that the original ancestors burnt or sooted the stones – they were very careful, and so should we. Afterwards, remove any spilt or dripped wax.

4) Do not leave **anything** behind you when you leave, be it general rubbish or 'ritual litter'. The ancestors are interested in your intentions and what is in your heart, not what you leave for others to clear away.

5) During the daytime, please do not 'totally occupy' the west chamber - there are four other chambers which can also be used for ritual and meditation, and which are less intrusive to other visitors. If you wish to use the west chamber for ritual and healing work, please be aware of others wishing to enter, and make your stay there as brief as possible.

6) Do not mark the stones in any way whatsoever, even with chalk. Our ancestors do not seem to have, so what gives you the right to!

7) Be aware of who may already be in WKLB when you arrive, or who may arrive whilst you are there, respecting other people's rights to also be in the chambers. It's all about respect. Arriving at WKLB and bashing a drum whilst others are meditating is very disrespectful. Wait your turn. The monument has been there for 5,500 years – it's not going anywhere.

8) Please take away any candle fragments, empty nightlight holders and other such items you may find inside. It may not be your litter, but I believe that clearing items will help those who follow you to enjoy a more enhanced experience of this magical sacred site. And, perhaps, the Ancestors may be pleased with your efforts too. As a Pagan myself, I am conscious that people may have left items inside with great intent and love. When clearing the inside

of such items, I do so carefully and mindfully, and often re-deposit items such as corn dollies, flowers, fruit and other **biodegradable** items on the mound outside. The objects therefore stay on the barrow, but Mother Nature is now able to take them naturally back into her body.

9) As you enter, the first chambers on the left and right (the SE and NE chambers) often house nesting swallows during the summer. Please respect their presence, and that of their newly hatched young. Please do not drum or chant in these two chambers when nests are occupied.

The Balance
There is a delicate balance between sacred sites remaining open for ritual and ceremonial use, and the preservation of the archaeology. The National Trust Plan Strategy Statement affirms that the organisation is obliged to, '... *Continue to attempt to accommodate 'new religious' and other visitors drawn to Avebury… the National Trust does not discriminate on the basis of why people come but is concerned with how they respect the sites and other users'*. Discussions have taken place in recent years between Pagans, Druids, farmers, local government, archaeologists, English Heritage and the National Trust, most notably regarding issues surrounding Stonehenge. High profile Druid Arthur Pendragon has been a thorn in the side of officialdom for many years, as he has fought to re-open sites for ritual purpose, and to have skeletons reinstated into burial mounds. All sides are rarely in agreement on every issue, of course, but dialogue is always a good thing, and hopefully all issues will eventually be resolved to everyone's satisfaction.
In the past I have arrived at WKLB to find English Heritage staff moving around the interior armed with gloves, brushes and bin-bags, cleaning-up after a festival, especially the summer solstice. I believe that my fellow Pagans and I should ourselves be custodians of WKLB, to clean it up on a regular basis. I do not expect anyone to clear up after me – do you?
At the end of the day, English Heritage have the power to close, and even back-fill, the monument, as they have had to do elsewhere. I am sure they do not want to do this, but their prime responsibility is for the care of the monument. If things got so bad that damage to the monument threatened its preservation, I would be the first with a shovel in my hands to help them fill it in. A love and reverence for this monument resides deep inside me; one could say I have been consumed with adoration for it. So closing it off would be a very bitter pill indeed for me to swallow, but one I would accept.
I would suggest that if everyone who visits WKLB, for whatever purpose, follows my guidelines, then this hallowed place may stay open forever.

Respectful Use of the Monument
I am not being a killjoy, or discouraging people from doing ceremony and ritual inside WKLB. Far from it – I regularly lead groups into the interior to do that very thing. But after our activities, anyone coming in would not even know we had been there – not from physical evidence anyway.

For instance, at Samhain 2010 we had gone to WKLB to pay our respects and give thanks to the ancestors. The atmosphere inside was cool and damp, and we could see our breath, even though it was not particularly cold outside. Placing a hollowed-out pumpkin (with a carved smiley face) in the west chamber, we duly paid our respects. Afterwards, we packed the pumpkin back into our rucksack and, after clearing up other people's litter, left the chambers cleaner than when we arrived.

Honouring the ancestors inside the west chamber with a drum and a pumpkin, Samhain 2010.

However, all is not doom and gloom. The situation may have improved somewhat in recent years, but the problem has not gone away. Every week I go up to WKLB and almost always have to tidy up something. People like Clare Slaney and Greywolf have shown how to use such sites responsibly and they belong to a growing collection of responsible fellow-Pagans, who, like us, want to ensure the chambers stay open for use by **everyone**. (For a discussion on these issues see Wallis 2003, p. 168-194.)

Full Moon gathering at WKLB, with drums and a didge being played as we watched the setting Sun, before going into the chambers below. After such events there are no physical signs that we have even been there!

214

Respect for others and a tolerance of other people's beliefs is surely one of the wonderful tenets upon which modern Paganism is based. On one summer afternoon I went up to WKLB with a group of Americans, some of whom were on a spiritual quest, but we could not access the west chamber because two men had 'occupied' the whole chamber, having even laid out rugs, and were chanting, playing a sitar, and recording a CD! The music, I must admit, was beautiful as it echoed around the chambers. But they were not showing respect to the many others who were visiting on that busy summer solstice weekend. Why did they not occupy one of the side chambers? Why did they think they had priority over other visitors?

People come to honour and pay their respects to the ancestors, which is a noble thing that I often do myself, but how about respect for the living also? I hold regular daytime field trips to the site, but always respect other visitors, and never 'occupy' the site to the exclusion of others. My full Moon drumming/chanting events are held around and after sunset, by which time the site is usually devoid of other people. If others do roll up, they are invited into the gathering. In any case, I encourage those present to use *all* the chambers, as well as the mound and forecourt outside.

Peace ceremonies can be held at WKLB if carried out with respect. Here, we gather around a crystal skull in August 2010. (Image: Alex Smith.)

On one occasion, whilst we were inside drumming, a woman came to the site to sleep there for the night. She did not want to bother us, but on finding her patiently waiting outside, I invited her in from the cold. She moved into the SE chamber, out of the wind. I had no right whatsoever to exclude her from the site whilst we were holding our ceremony, regardless of our 'earth-healing' ideals. I hope the ancestors were pleased. WKLB belongs to no person, to no spirituality, to no sect, nor does it exclusively belong to Pagans, archaeologists, English Heritage, or any one else. WKLB is for the whole of society, for everyone. In Neolithic times, WKLB represented the whole community, and belonged to that community, to the people. In my opinion, nothing has changed. This is the magic of WKLB; it belongs to the past, the present, and the future.

Prevention is always better than cure. We should respect this wonderful legacy of times when the ancestors were central to people's spirituality. After all, one day we will all be ancestors. What goes around comes around, so we should *take* nothing but photographs and, with the exception of a few footprints in the snow, *leave* nothing behind except our love.

'Don't change the site, let the site change you.'
(From the ASLaN Charter.)

Chapter 17.
2012 and the Way Forward

'Learn well… and we will see if your insanity can be cured.'
(From the movie *Avatar.*)

'The change from night to day is really only hours.'
(Jeff Lynne, ELO).

We live in interesting times, in an age of great challenges and flux. We are being confronted as a species to see if we have the ability, indeed the right, to survive on this planet. We are being challenged by issues such as global warming, escalating human population, third world poverty, and depletion of the Earth's natural resources.

It has been suggested by many academics that severe challenges also faced the builders and users of WKLB thousands of years ago. Contrary to popular 'New Age' belief, the Neolithic was not some 'Golden Age' when everyone was into mysticism, love, and tree-hugging! Far from it. It was a time of significant change, when rising populations and farming methods were radically altering the landscape: 'New ideas caused profound shifts in ideology and human social organisation… [with] deforestation and agriculture' (Russell 2002, p. 176). One could in fact argue that the Neolithic was when it all started to go downhill!

But I see a distinct difference between then and today. Neolithic people had a closer connection with the land, the skies, and with the other life forms around them; and the clans of WKLB only **took what they needed**. No more - no less. To take too much of what they depended upon would have been a concept totally alien to them. We cannot say that of today. Now, we are, quite literally, biting off the hand that feeds us.

Lucy Wyatt, in her excellent *Approaching Chaos,* has given indications that living densely packed in cities is not Mankind's natural way of living. Yet despite this, she shows there was a time when civilisations, indeed entire cities, did manage to live in harmony with the landscape, and that we now need to, '… stop wasting time and resources, and re-examine the ancient past with more respect… we can then face the future with a clearer mind' (Wyatt 2010, p. 316). And, I would suggest, with a clearer conscience.

So what has all this to do with West Kennet Long Barrow, its archaeological record, and interacting with the site today? Well I believe it is this: What is the point of scientific studies of the past if they do not serve the present and the future. In the Neolithic, the people of WKLB were using all *their* available science, technology, and knowledge to serve *their* clan, seeking to leave healthier legacies for those who were to follow. One of the aims of the *'Landscape and Perception Project'*, spearheaded by Paul Devereux, is to get participants to, '… take away modern filters and look at the landscape in a primary way… and listen with Stone Age ears' (Devereux 2010). I see looking back with 'new eyes' as actually being of vital importance to our future. We need to look at what worked and what did not all those years ago, and how aboriginal cultures today uphold many traditions that were around in the Neolithic, and why certain practices and beliefs have survived. As lightworker Frann Haykin told me, 'It's all about where we are heading, and understanding the past as a means to this'.

Spiritually, we are children who have separated ourselves from our Mother, roaming aimlessly, without direction or purpose. This loss of connection is numbingly perpetuated by consumerism, stimulants, and political power games. But I believe that our Mother never abandoned us, and that we can begin today to extend our hands to her, and with them our heart. In going out into the landscape we can find a little more about what makes *us* tick – for going out is ultimately going within. Ancient people saw themselves as part of the land, not separate from it. ***We and the Land are one.***

Midwinter solstice at a beautiful, snow-covered WKLB. This time
of year was particularly sacred to our ancestors, and is a
wonderful time to visit the monument, when it is relatively quiet.

In my novel, *Thirteen Moons – Conversations with the Goddess*, the Earth Goddess leads the hero out into the living landscape to connect with it, to **see** it for the first time. In doing so he finds himself. This reminds me of Jake Sully, the hero in the movie *Avatar*. By deeply connecting with the planet Pandora and the interconnectedness of all things, Jake found what made *him* tick, gaining new values and ideals that changed his life – and saved the planet!

By visiting sacred sites and walking the old tracks, I believe humankind may yet come to see the Land as our ancestors once did, and regard the Earth as sacred as they did. For when we regard an object as sacred, such as a crucifix, rosary beads, or holy book, we cannot possibly destroy it. Holding the Earth as sacred may be Man's only way of surviving the present global chaos. We all share a responsibility for the state of the planet, and we all share a responsibility for healing sick Albion – this holy island of Britain.

If this book leads just a few people to regard our Planet as sacred, then it will all have been worthwhile. To appreciate and admire WKLB is to appreciate and admire those who built it, and the generations who used it. They were all Pagan by definition, with a close personal connection to their landscape. I do not see any downsides to regarding our lands and Planet Earth as sacred. Do you?

We all have ancestors, or else we would not be here. Our very identities, to a certain extent, owe much to where we have come from. How many people, however, still have their great great grandparents alive today? The line of our immediate living ancestors may go back four generations if we are lucky, but then what? This may have been relevant to the users of WKLB too, many decades after the initial burials. They valued the collective wisdom of many generations of ancestors, most of whom they had not known personally: 'We have fewer and fewer concrete links with our own identifiable ancestors, so we look for generic ancestors in the distant past' (Whitley 2002, p. 125). I believe that we can still connect with our ancestors, no matter how long ago they lived, to the betterment of our lives today. They may yet be listening.

I have already described statements from many people who had profound experiences, some of which changed their lives. They connected with 'something' or 'someone' who gave them knowledge from the **past** that could be of use to them **today** and in the **future.** This was the basis of the shamanic practices at WKLB in the Neolithic – and people carried out such practices over many centuries **because they worked!** The shamans were not obsessed with death, quite the contrary - they were embracing life! Kahlil Gibran put it excellently in *The Prophet*: 'You would know the secret of death? But how shall you find it unless you seek it in the heart of Life'. Life and death have always gone hand-in-hand.

Today, I believe it is not more knowledge we need to acquire, but more wisdom. The two are not necessarily the same thing. Aspects of science and technology, after all, have been misused to wreak environmental disaster on the planet.

We have reached a crossroads, and it is no coincidence that 2012 is upon us.

2012 AD

I have set out below the star chart for the midwinter sunrise 2012, when the rising Sun, at the junction of Sagittarius and Scorpio, will coincide with the very centre of our galaxy. This only happens every 26,000 years, signalling the end of one cosmic cycle and the genesis of another. A brilliant Venus will rise before the Sun, as if heralding a new age of love and compassion. I may well be up at WKLB, as I do at every midwinter: I cannot think of anywhere better to be for this auspicious sunrise, at a place of the ancestors, to connect with the old as the new begins, and to be with my father.

Much wisdom, and a good deal of nonsense, has been written about 2012 as this 'monumental' year has approached; I guess the subject sells books. I believe that 2012 does indeed herald a new cycle, which goes deeper than a galactic alignment and the completion of a calendar carved on a block of stone by the Mayans. Despite many negative forecasts, I suspect the Sun will still

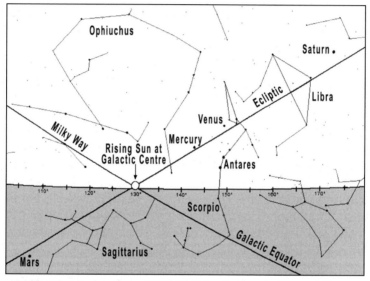

2012 midwinter sunrise at WKLB. This alignment of the solstice sunrise and the centre of our galaxy only happens about every 26,000 years. Venus, the Goddess of Love, precedes the Sun.

rise on December 23. What 2012 *is* doing is creating a focus for those wanting to heal the world, and with it, Mankind. It is a focus that is creating an energy, a gathering snowball that has been set rolling and continues to grow. The old ways are gradually falling away, as the recent global banking crisis has shown. It is the natural order of things – evolution in action. The outmoded ways of how we treat our fellow humans and the Earth have not worked, and continue to degenerate as both the population and greed of Man grow hand in hand.

I am not one of the 'doom and gloom merchants' who foresee cosmic disasters crashing out of the skies, as in the Book of Revelations. I see 2012 to be a stepping-stone for the long road back to getting this Planet balanced again. Some see this event as a 'wake-up call': '... an opportunity to transform ourselves in the light of our developing knowledge of the cosmos' (Mann & Glasson 2007, p. 112).

Moreover, make no mistake: we are not fighting for the survival of the Earth. She can take care of herself! I believe she has been a very patient Mother up to now. I repeat, **up until now.** Planet Earth will do whatever she has to do to restore a balance for **all** life, not just us. She will do whatever is needed. Just like the planet Pandora did at the end of the movie *Avatar;* the planet was not taking sides by kicking out the humans, but this was the only way to restore the balance. Food for thought. Our place on this planet has to be earned. The Neolithic shamans sitting inside WKLB knew this, thousands of years ago. We have forgotten the basic concept for respecting all life. It is time now to embrace it again. I do not see that we have any choice.

Mother is waiting and watching. How long must we continue to test her patience? Every mother has to chastise her children at some time or another.

Midwinter Spiral Heart (Photo: Sue Wallace).

And although it may not seem like it at the time, from the child's point of view, the bottom line is actually the Mother's love for her child. Mother Earth owes us nothing. We owe her everything. It is about time we started showing some appreciation. I cannot begin to imagine what the alternatives are. I am 100% positive about the survival of life on this beautiful planet, and that it will continue to evolve. Killing the planet is not the issue, is it? Planet Earth is on a magical mystery tour, and I hope we are going to be along for the rest of the ride. Can we be? 100% yes to that one. In the long run, will we be? Sorry, but I am not yet sure.

WKLB was built by individuals who were able to say to the world, 'We are part of a community – our survival depends on us belonging to the community'. This is as true today as it was 5,500 years ago. Nothing has changed. We are now part of a global community, all sharing the same challenges. And West Kennet long barrow still stands there, on that ridge south of Avebury, watching over the landscape, continuing to age with grace and dignity. I believe it wants to be utilised again, it yearns to be a focus for the high spiritual ideals it once was. People come and go, religions come and go. But WKLB remains…

I believe West Kennet Long Barrow is here today because it may yet turn out to be as vital to us as it was over 5,000 years ago.

'You must be the change you wish to see in the world.'
(Mahatma Gandhi.)

Acknowledgements

I would like to thank all those people, known and unknown to me, who assisted me on my Quest. If I have left anyone out by not mentioning you by name, I am nevertheless still extremely grateful.

In particular, thanks go out to:

Busty Taylor and Maria Wheatley, for their site visit and info;

Heather Heaton and her gifted ladies for their site visit.

Members of the Wyvern Dowsers, who undertook the earth energies survey;

Gunther Schneck for his dowsing and energy insights;

Antiquarians and archaeologists whose expertise and assessments of WKLB were invaluable;

All the authors whose information and wisdom I have repeated here;

Devizes Museum, whose staff and collections of books and displays were truly priceless.

The following artists, who gave permission to use their work: Rick Kemp, Ann Menzies-Blythe and Kerry McKenna.

The owners at 'Fox Twitchen', East Kennet, for permission to visit Harestone Down and East Kennet long barrow.

English Heritage, for permission to reproduce two images;

Kent's Cave, for the mannequins used in the 're-enactment' scenes.

Thanks to the following, who kindly gave permission to use their images: Diane Gall, Chris Murray, Sandy Walker, Alex Smith, Steve and Karen Alexander, Marina Graham.

My thanks also go out to the following, for information received: Susan Hale, Dave Shorten, Corwen Broch, Jackie Queally, David Griffiths, Cheryl Travers, John Grigsby, Brenda Wallace, Julie Umpleby, Ann Menzies-Blythe, Frann Haykin, Karen James, Claire Marshall, Les Miles, Pauline Smith, Marina Graham, Rick Kemp, and all the participants of our drumming and meditation events at WKLB.

♥ Last, but certainly not least, I would like to thank, with all my heart, my partner Sue Wallace, who mercilessly proof-read the manuscript, took several of the images reproduced here, and accompanied me on countless site visits, giving me the benefit of her observational skills and acute attention to detail. She encouraged and reassured me throughout, with patience and, when needed, humour.

About the Author

Peter Knight is well known for his inspirational PowerPoint presentations, workshops, and field trips on topics relating to sacred sites, ancient wisdom and dowsing. He has been leading tours to sacred sites since 1995 and has spoken at several international conventions in the USA, Malta, and across the UK. He is co-founder of the Dorset Earth Mysteries Group and has been awarded honorary member status of both the Dorset Dowsers and the Antiquarian Society. He is also a member of the Wyvern Dowsers and the British Society of Dowsers.

Peter has had six books published previously, and has contributed to several magazines. He has appeared on BBC local radio, and on TV, such as on Channel 4's *Don Roamin'* with Monty Don. Peter is the founder and organiser of the Convention of Alternative Archaeology and Earth Mysteries, held annually in Dorset and Wiltshire, which gives a platform to both new and leading researchers. In 2004 he established Stone Seeker Publishing, and in 2006 founded Stone Seeker Tours, which promotes holistic tours of sacred sites across the UK and Europe. He also conceived and hosts the *Ancient Ambient Chill-Out*, combining funky world music with large-screen images of sacred sites, planet Earth, and tribal cultures.

His PowerPoint presentations are informative and inspiring. The subjects he speaks on include, West Kennet, Avebury, Stonehenge, Ireland, Malta, Dorset, Glastonbury, dowsing, stone circles, the symbolism of Church architecture, sacred geometry, and several other subjects (see website).

Peter lives near Avebury and his interests include walking, drumming, world music, dowsing, prehistoric art, astronomy, shamanism, and photographing Nature. He is a father, a vegetarian and follows a Goddess-orientated spirituality, whilst honouring all spiritualities and religions.

His 'mission' is to help people connect with sacred sites and sacred landscapes, as a means of enhancing the lives of individuals, and to actively help, and promote, planetary healing.

Peter is available to do an inspiring and informative full-colour PowerPoint presentation about this book to local groups and societies, as well as to lead field trips to West Kennet Long Barrow, and the surrounding sites.

Contact Peter by e-mail at: stoneseeker@waitrose.com
Web site: www.stoneseeker.net
Peter also has pages on MySpace and Facebook

Other Books by Peter Knight

Ancient Stones of Dorset
Published in 1996 by Power Publications. 208 pp (gloss finish). Still the most comprehensive work on Dorset's megalithic sites. 147 photographs and 132 drawings. Maps of alignments, site plans, and grid references, earth energies, astronomy, newly discovered stones. Recently reprinted: thousands now sold!

Sacred Dorset ~ On the Path of the Dragon
Published in 1998 by Capall Bann. 292 pp, 119 photographs and 82 line drawings. A thorough work on Dorset's ancient spiritual heritage, which includes hillforts, wells and springs, the Cerne Giant, Sun and Moon, the green man, fairy and giant folklore, dragons, trees, and much more.

Dorset Pilgrimages ~ A Millennium Handbook
(with Mike Power)
Published in 2000 by Power Publications. 144 pp (gloss finish), over 100 photographs and line drawings. Day-long pilgrimages across Dorset, visiting churches, stone circles, megaliths, wells, etc. en route.

Earth Mysteries ~ An Illustrated Encyclopaedia of Britain (CD-ROM)
Published in 2003 by Stone Seeker Publishing. Over 350MB of information – the biggest overview of British earth mysteries ever published. Compatible with Windows Word (Windows 98, XP, etc). Over 250 colour and b&w illustrations, maps and line drawings. A-Z format, plus resources and fully cross-referenced - like a giant website, with over 1000 hyperlinks.

Thirteen Moons ~ Conversations with the Goddess
Published in 2007 (new ed. 2010) by Stone Seeker Publishing. Peter's novel has been receiving rave reviews. The book's hero is contacted by the Earth Spirit on 13 full moons at sacred sites across Europe (such as Roslyn, Stonehenge, Avebury, Glastonbury, Ireland and Brittany). The Goddess gives him lessons on how to connect with the Earth Spirit, and divulges what the human experience is all about and how we can live fulfilling lives in harmony with the Planet – before it's too late! The culmination is the gift of *13 Insights*.

The Wessex Astrum – Sacred Geometry in a Mystical Landscape
(with Toni Perrott).
Published by Stone Seeker Publishing in 2008. The story and details of the groundbreaking discovery of the huge landscape hexagram, involving Stonehenge, Avebury, Glastonbury, and the St Michael Line. New megaliths, forgotten wells and springs, Knights Templar sites, a secret cave and much more are described in this fully illustrated work.

Signed and dedicated copies are available from the author.

Stone Seeker Tours

Peter Knight founded Stone Seeker tours, which is dedicated to holding profound and holistic experiences at sacred sites and in the landscape.

Are you planning to bring a group to visit sacred sites in the UK? Are you looking for spiritually inclined outings? Do you have seekers wishing to truly experience places like Stonehenge, Avebury, Glastonbury, Dartmoor, Jersey, Ireland, or Dorset?

Stone Seeker Tours specialises in tailor-made excursions. You bring the pilgrims and we will provide the expert guides, and unforgettable experiences. The following subjects will be expertly covered, and individual topics can be included or excluded, depending on your focus and requirements:

~ Archaeology ~ Landscape alignments ~
~ Symbolism of Megaliths ~ Shamanism ~
~Astronomical alignments and observations ~
~ Sacred geometry ~ Earth energies and dowsing ~
~ Crop circles ~ Church symbolism ~ Myth and folklore ~
~ Drumming, meditations and healing circles ~

Peter is the main guide for Stone Seeker Tours. He has been taking groups around sacred sites for many years, including a wide variety of 'alternative' groups, such as dowsers, healing circles, and personal development groups. He has a good sense of humour and is very enthusiastic, which makes for entertaining and informative tours. His trips are a spiritual experience, as pilgrims interact with the Goddess landscape.

Sue Wallace, our other guide, is an accomplished dowser and healer.

List of localities:

Stonehenge (can also include the Cursus and Woodhenge) – Avebury (including West Kennet Long Barrow and Silbury Hill) – Ancient Dartmoor – Glastonbury (Tor, Abbey, Chalice Well, etc) – Dorset stone circles and leys – Neolithic Jersey – Winchester – Megalithic Brittany – Knowlton and Cranborne Chase - Sacred Cornwall – Dorchester and Cerne Abbas – Malta - Knights Templar sites - Prehistoric Ireland – Shamanic drumming at sacred sites.

Peter also has in-depth knowledge of other areas too, so please enquire! Retirement and disabled parties can be catered for, with special wheelchair-friendly itineraries.

www.stoneseeker.net

Bibliography/References

Aubrey, John (1665-97). *Monumenta Britannica.*

Barratt, J (1994). *Fragments from Antiquity: An Archaeology of Social Life in Britain 2900-1200 BC.* Blackwell.

Bayliss, A, Whittle, A, and Wysocki, M (2007). *Talking About my Generation: the Date of the West Kennet Long Barrow.* Cambridge Archaeological Journal, 17: p. 85-101.

Biltcliffe, Gary (2009). *The Spirit of Portland – Revelations of a Sacred Isle.* Roving Press.

Brennan, Martin (1994). *The Stones of Time: Calendars, Sundials and Stone Chambers of Ancient Ireland.* Inner Traditions International.

Burl, Aubrey (1983). *Prehistoric Astronomy and Ritual.* Shire Publications.

Burl, Aubrey (1989). *The Stonehenge People.* Barrie and Jenkins.

Burl, Aubrey (2002 ed.). *Prehistoric Avebury.* Yale University Press.

Case, H (1995). *Some Wiltshire Beakers and Their Contexts.* Wiltshire Archaeological Magazine, Vol. 88, p. 1-17.

Collins, Andrew (2008). *The Cygnus Mystery.* Watkins Publishing.

Cook, Ian A, et al (2008). *Ancient Architectural Acoustic Resonance Patterns and Regional Brain Activity.* Time and Mind, Vol. 1:1, p. 95-104.

Coon, Robert (1993). *Spheres of Destiny – The Shaftesbury Prophecy.* Glastonbury Circle.

Cope, Julian (1998). *The Modern Antiquarian.* Thorsons.

Cunnington, Maul (1927). *The Pottery From the Long Barrow at West Kennet.* Devizes.

Currivan, Jude (2007). *The 13th Step – A Global Journey in Search of our Cosmic Destiny.* Hay House.

Cyriax, T (1921). *Archaeological Journal,* Vol. 28.

Dames, Michael (1976). *The Silbury Treasure.* Thames and Hudson.

Dames, Michael (1996 ed.). *The Avebury Cycle.* Thames and Hudson.

Dames, Michael (2010). *Silbury – Resolving the Enigma.* The History Press.

Devereux, Paul (1989). *Earth Lights Revelation.* Blandford.

Devereux, Paul (1992). *Symbolic Landscapes.* Gothic Image.

Devereux, Paul (1997). *The Long Trip – A Prehistory of Psychedelia.* Arkana.

Devereux, Paul (2001). *Stone Age Soundtracks – The Acoustic Properties of Ancient Sites.* Vega.

Devereux, Paul (2010). Lecture on Nov. 12 at *Stars and Stones Winter Forum*, Suffolk.

Devereux, Paul (2011). Lecture on Jan. 17 at meeting of the Wyvern Dowsers.

Devereux, Paul & Jahn, Robert G (1999). *Preliminary Investigations and Cognitive Considerations of the Acoustical Resonances of Selected Archaeological Sites.* Antiquity 70, p. 665-666.

Dowd, Marion A (2008). *The Use of Caves for Funerary and Ritual Practices in Neolithic Ireland.* Antiquity, Vol. 82, p. 305-317.

Edmunds, M (1999). *Ancestral Geographies of the Neolithic: Landscape, Monuments and Memory.* Routledge.

Furlong, David (1997). *The Keys to the Temple.* Piatkus.

Furst, Peter T (1976). *Hallucinogens and Culture.* Chandler and Sharp.

Gimbutas, M (1974). *The Gods and Goddesses of Old Europe.* University of California.

Graves, Tom, and Poraj-Wilczynska, Liz (2008). *The Disciplines of Dowsing.* Tetradian
     Books.
Greywolf (2008). *The World Drum*: www.druidry.co.uk/theworlddrum.html
Guirand, Felix, editor (1974 ed.). *New Larousse Encyclopedia of Mythology.* Hamlyn.
Hale, Susan Elizabeth (2007). *Sacred Place – Sacred Sound: The Acoustic Mysteries
     of Holy Places.* Quest Books.
Hawkins, Gerald (1963). *Stonehenge Decoded.* Nature, Vol. 200.
Heath, Robin, and Michell, John (2004). *The Measure of Albion.* Bluestone Press.
Johnson, Anthony (2008). *Solving Stonehenge.* Thames and Hudson.
Jones, Kathy (1991). *The Ancient British Goddess.* Ariadne.
Jones, Kathy (1994). *The Spinning Wheel of Ana.* Ariadne.
Joussaume, Roger (1988). *Dolmens of the Dead.* Cornell University Press.
Keiller, A, and Piggott, S (1936). Antiquity, Vol. 10, p. 420.
Khan, Hazrat Inayat (1996). *The Mysticism of Sound and Music.* Shambhala.
Knight, Christopher, and Lomas, Robert (1999). *Uriel's Machine.* Century.
Knight, Peter (1996). *Ancient Stones of Dorset.* Power Publications.
Knight, Peter (1998). *Sacred Dorset – on the Path of the Dragon.* Capall Bann.
Knight, Peter, and Power, Mike (2000). *Dorset Pilgrimages: A Millennium Handbook.*
     Power Publications.
Knight, Peter (2001). *The Grey Mare and Her Colts – The Goddess, the Sun God and
     Sirius.* Journal No. 2, Dorset Earth Mysteries Group.
Knight, Peter (2007 and 2010). *Thirteen Moons – Conversations with the Goddess.*
     Stone Seeker.
Knight, Peter, and Perrott, Toni (2008). *The Wessex Astrum – Sacred Geometry in a
     Mystical Landscape.* Stone Seeker.
Lewis-Williams, J D, and Dowson, T A (1993). *On Vision and Power in the Neolithic.* In
     Current Anthropology, Vol 34, Issue 1.
Lewis-Williams, David, and Pearce, David (2005). *Inside the Neolithic Mind.* Thames
     and Hudson.
Lévy-Bruhl, Lucien (1983 ed.). *Primitive Mythology.* University of Queensland Press.
Lonegren, Sig (1986). *Spiritual Dowsing.* Gothic Image.
Mann, Nicholas R, and Glasson, Philippa (2007). *The Star Temple of Avalon.* The
     Temple Publications.
Mann, Nicholas R (2011). *Avebury Cosmos.* O Books.
Manwaring, Kevan (2004). *The Long Woman.* Awen.
Marshall, S, Currie, G, and Glastonbury, P (2010). *Investigation of a "Sun Roll" Effect
     in Relation to Silbury Hill.* Time and Mind, Vol. 3, p. 291-302.
Meaden, Terence (1991). *The Goddess of the Stones.* Souvenir Press.
Meaden, Terence (1999). *The Secrets of the Avebury Stones.* Souvenir Press.
Megaw, J V S (1960). *Penny Whistles and Prehistory.* Antiquity, Vol 34, p. 6-14.
Michell, John (1983). *The New View Over Atlantis.* Thames and Hudson.
Middleton, Andrew, Young, Jeremy R, and Ambers, Janet (2004). *Folkton Wold Chalk
     Drums.* Antiquity, Vol 78, March 2004.
Miller, Hamish, and Broadhurst, Paul (1989). *The Sun and the Serpent.* Pendragon
     Press.
Moore, Robert, and Gillette, Douglas (1993). *The Magician Within – Accessing the
     Shaman in the Male Psyche.* Morrow.
Mortimer, Neil (2003). *Stukeley Illustrated: William Stukeley's Rediscovery of Britain's
     Ancient Sites.* Green Magic.
Needham, Rodney (1967). *Percussion and Transition.* In *Man*, New Series, Vol. 2, #4,
     p. 606-614.

North, John (1996). *Stonehenge – Neolithic Man and the Cosmos.* Harper Collins.

Parker Pearson, Michael (1993). *Bronze Age Britain.* English Heritage.

Parker Pearson, Michael, and Ramilisonina (1998). *Stonehenge for the Ancestors.* Antiquity, Vol 72, p.308-26.

Parsons, Julien (2002). *Great Sites: Belas Knap.* In *British Archaeology,* Issue 63, Feb 2002.

Piggott, Stuart (1958). *The Excavation of the West Kennet Long Barrow: 1955-6.* Antiquity, Vol 32, p. 235-243.

Piggott, Stuart (1962). *The West Kennet Long Barrow Excavations 1955-56.* HMSO.

Piggott, Stuart (1985). *William Stukeley: An Eighteenth-Century Antiquary.* Thames and Hudson.

Pitts, Mike (2000). *Hengeworld.* Century.

Pollard, Joshua (1997). *Neolithic Britain.* Shire.

Pollard, Joshua, and Reynolds, Andrew (2002). *Avebury – The Biography of a Landscape.* Tempus.

Pryor, Francis (2003). *Britain B.C.* Harper Collins.

Queally, Jackie (2009). *Arks Within Grail Lands – Rosslyn and Glastonbury in a New Light.* Self-Published.

Richardson, Alan (2001). *Spirits of the Stones.* Virgin Publishing.

Russell, Miles (2002). *Monuments of the British Neolithic.* Tempus.

Service, Alastair, and Bradbery, Jean (1979). *The Standing Stones of Europe.* Weidenfield and Nicolson.

Sherratt, Andrew (1995). In *Consuming Habits,* ed. Goodman et al. Routledge.

Smith, A C (1885). *Guide to the British and Roman Antiquities of the North Wiltshire Down.* Devizes.

Smith, Isobel (1965a). *Excavation of a Bell Barrow, Avebury, G.55.* Wiltshire Archaeological Magazine, Vol 60, p. 24-46.

Smith, Isobel, (1965b). *Windmill Hill and Avebury.* Oxford.

Smith, Martin, and Brickley, Megan (2009). *People of the Long Barrows.* The History Press.

Stukeley, William (1722). *Itinerarium Curiosum.* Centuria.

Stukeley, William (1743). *Abury.* London.

Taylor, David (1997). *The Undreamed Region – Barrows in Folklore and Archaeology.*

Thom, Alexander (1967). *Megalithic Sites in Britain.* Oxford.

Thomas, J (1991). *Rethinking the Neolithic.* Cambridge University Press.

Thomas, Julian, and Whittle, Alasdair (1986). *Anatomy of a Tomb – West Kennet Revisited.* Oxford Journal of Archaeology, Vol. 5, p. 129-156.

Thomas, Nicholas (1976). *Guide to Prehistoric England.* Book Club Associates.

Thurnam, John (1860). *On the Examination of a Chambered Long Barrow at West Kennet, Wiltshire.* Archaeologica, vol. 38, p. 405-21.

Thurnam, John (1867). *Examination of a Long Chambered Barrow, at West Kennet, Wiltshire.* Wiltshire Archaeological Magazine, Vol 10, p. 130-135.

Tilley, Chris (1994). *A Phenomenology of Landscape: Places, Paths and Monuments.* Berg.

Tilley, Chris (2007). *The Neolithic Sensory Revolution: Monumentality and the Experience of Landscape.* Proceedings of the British Academy, Vol. 144, p. 329-345.

Trubshaw, Bob (2005). *Sacred Places – Prehistory and Popular Imagination.* Heart of Albion Press.

Tuck, Catherine (2003). *Landscapes and Desire.* Sutton.

Tucker, Graham (2006). Medway Crop Circle Group website.

Underwood, Guy (1972 ed.). *The Pattern of the Past.* Abacus.

Wakefield, I D (1999). *Legendary Landscapes.* Nod Press.

Wallis, Robert J (2003). *Shamans/Neo-Shamans.* Routledge.

Watkins, Alfred (1927 and 1983 ed.). *The Ley Hunter's Manual.* Turnstone Press.

Watson, Aaron (1996). From *Listening to the Stones.* Lecture given to T.A.G. Conference.

Watson, Aaron & Keating, David (1999). *Architecture and Sound: an Acoustic Analysis of Megalithic Monuments in Prehistoric Britain.* Antiquity, Vol. 73, p. 325-36.

Watson, Aaron (2001). *Composing Avebury.* In *World Archaeology,* 33:2, p. 296 – 314.

Wheatley, Dennis and Maria (2002). *Leylines & Earth Energies of Avebury Henge.* Celestial Songs Press.

Wheatley, Maria, and Taylor, Busty (2008). *Avebury – Sun, Moon and Earth.* Wessex Books.

Whitley, James (2002). *Too Many Ancestors.* Antiquity Vol. 76, p. 119-126.

Whittle, A (1991). *A Late Neolithic Complex at West Kennet, Wiltshire.* Antiquity, Vol. 65.

Whittle, A (1996). *Europe in the Neolithic: the Creation of New Worlds.* Cambridge University Press.

Whittle, A (1997). *Sacred Mound, Holy Rings.* Oxford: Oxbow Monograph.

Williams, Mike (2010). *Prehistoric Belief: Shamans, Trance and the Afterlife.* The History Press.

Woodward, A B and P J (1996). In *Proceedings of the Prehistoric Society: 1996.*

Woodward, A (2001). *British Barrows - A Matter of Life and Death.* Tempus.

Wyatt, Lucy (2010). *Approaching Chaos.* O Books.

INDEX

233